ORP Orzeł

The Spirit of Poland

An Historical Thriller, based on a True Story

By Bernard Woźny

If you must fight, do not fight for yourself.
Fight for your family, your friends, your lovers, your people.
Only then, will your battle be honorable.

For all those on eternal patrol

Acknowledgments

If there is anyone that I must thank for helping me write this book, it will be The History Guy.

www.youtube.com/c/TheHistoryGuyChannel

I always admired his channel on 'History that deserves to be remembered'. He led me to the story of the ORP Orzeł which raised my ancestral patriotism. This inspired me to reveal this extraordinary adventure to the wider world.

Many others have assisted:

Catherine McGreevy, who likened my writing to 'All Quiet on the Western Front'. Jerry Matlan, who advised me on naval questions. Michael Brandt, who advised me on everything else.

And a whole bunch of Polish people who all said, "Of course we know this story!"

Editing: Jordan Kantey, he was the first to correct me on Polish spellings.

Special thanks to:

British National Archives: www.nationalarchives.gov.uk

Narodowe Muzeum Morskie w Gdańsku:
https://en.nmm.pl

Prologue

The Second Polish Republic may be just over a hundred years old, but Poland has been a sovereign nation for more than a thousand. It has spawned kings, built and – as the frequent marching ground of invading armies – rebuilt empires. Throughout its history, cultural influences from across Europe and the near east have enriched it, while its own riches have been pillaged repeatedly as the tides of ceaseless European conflicts have swept across its borders.

During this volatile history of glory and turmoil, Poland has maintained its culture as a unified people. It's nationhood always seems to rebound as if it is impervious to any defeat.

On September 1, 1939, Nazi Germany invaded Poland, materializing the geopolitical concept of Lebensraum (German for "living space"), which was effectively a colonization of Eastern Europe. This date marked the start of World War Two in the European theater.

At that time, Poland deployed a mixture of military equipment, some outdated such as cavalry, which fought alongside modern technology of the day. What they lacked was a full understanding of new military concepts such as *blitzkrieg* (or 'lightning war'), an all-out onslaught central to Nazi Germany's tactics. By the end of September 1939,

Poland surrendered, hoping to save the Polish population from further suffering.

Until the liberation in July 1944 by the Soviet Union, the Polish people continued to suffer terribly. Many argue that Poland suffered after 1944, but that is not a topic for this book.

What follows is the story of a Polish submarine, the ORP Orzeł (or Republic of Poland Ship Eagle). She was one of the most modern submarines of her day. Although submarines are usually considered offensive weapons, she was commanded to defend the small Polish coastline against seaborne invasion.

Chased and hounded by the enemy. Seemingly abandoned by her captain. Under threat of internment in a neutral port, her remaining officers and crew rebounded to escape. Unable to continue their patrol in the tightly controlled Baltic Sea, with nowhere to go, not even home, they decided to continue their fight with the Royal British Navy. Sailing to Britain lead them to even more danger

This is the story of the ORP Orzeł, as recounted by an imaginary crewmember, Leo Wrona.

More importantly, **this is the Spirit of Poland!**

1 Outbreak of War

Ship's Log entered by: Lieutenant Jan Grudziński
Date: September 1, 1939
Location: Port of Gdynia, Poland
Entry: We received orders to activate the Worek Plan to defend the Polish coast and Polish ports from possible German invasion. Orders are effective immediately. Preparing to leave port. We cannot leave without the full complement of officers and crew. I am waiting for the captain to arrive back from shore leave.

In my dream, I didn't remember what she said, but my Mama was very upset.

"Get up!" The voice roared.

"But Mama, I don't want to."

Is that an alarm clock I can hear?

"Get up Blackie, and I am NOT your Mama! We're preparing to leave port!"

It was Lieutenant Piasecki who was shouting. He was going through all compartments rousing the crew. There was lots of shouting echoing throughout the boat. Something was happening and the crew were beginning to run to their posts.

Damn it! I thought to myself, *I'm not at home in bed, I'm on my ship and hell has come to wake me!*

I stumbled out of my bunk and quickly straightened my tunic. It was normal for a submarine's crew to sleep in their clothes. I stowed away my bedsheet, blanket, and pillow, making the bunk ready for the next man. There are sixty crew and only twenty bunks, so we all had to share a bunk with two other men. Only the officers had their own quarters. All the ranks like me had to sleep and work in shifts.

Looking at my watch, I saw it was 04:30. *The change in the watch isn't until 06:00, so something must be happening. Maybe another stupid drill?*

Lieutenant Marian Mokrski poked his head around the watertight door. "Hey Blackie, Grudziński wants you on the bridge on the double."

"Aye, sir, I'm on my way." I never did like waking up from a dream.

My submarine, the ORP Orzeł, the pride of the Polish Navy, was brand new. Only commissioned seven months before, the previous February. Like her sister ships, she was paid for with money raised by the public, like war bonds. That makes her the 'People's Submarine'. I called her mine because I was the second engineer. Poland had four other submarines, one of them, called the Wilk, was our sister ship. But I must tell you that the Orzeł was the best. I knew that because she was my submarine.

In addition to being the second engineer, I was Petty Officer onboard the ORP Orzeł. My name is 'Blackie', or at least that is my nickname. My real name is Leo Wrona, but *wrona* means 'crow', and they are always black. Because I was always working with the engines, I often had oil and grease on my hands and clothes. I sometimes wished they would call me 'Lion' (because that is what Leo means).

Mornings were not usually this exciting when we are still docked. I could tell we were not moving because I couldn't hear my engines.

Rubbing the sleep from my eyes, I headed out through the watertight door and made my way through the sub.

"Coming on deck," I announced as I entered the control room.

"OK, Blackie," Lieutenant Andrey Piasecki replied. "Get yourself up top, 'Panienka' wants to see you, and he's up the conning tower, on the bridge."

"Aye, sir," I replied as I started climbing the ladder to the tower.

'Panienka' was the nickname for our second-in-command. His real name was Lieutenant Commander Jan

Grudziński. They called him *panienka* or 'damsel' as you might say, because of his light, feminine appearance. He'd only been with us a few months and a lot of the crew already thought he was a bit of a softie with no fight in him. I thought he was ok. He studied at some bigwig navy school, but the most important thing was that he knew a lot and saw things for what they were.

I quickly climbed the ladder into the conning tower. Halfway up was a 40mm anti-aircraft gun. It was stored upright but could quickly be winched to the upper platform when needed. I squeezed around it onto the observation platform. Standing outside in the fresh air, I could see the sun wasn't up yet. There was a pleasant orange glow in the eastern sky telling me it soon would be. Saluting, I said, "Wrona reporting, Sir."

Lieutenant Grudziński returned the salute and said: "At ease, Wrona."

Grudziński stood alone in the observation platform. Normally he would be in the bridge, which was the forward command room in the conning tower. He was a short and lean man but very upright, and he always seemed to be stiff and straight. He often liked to smile. Putting all this together is probably why we nicknamed him 'the damsel'. However, this morning his usual smile turned into a grimace. He raised his binoculars back to his eyes and scanned the dockyards. "Where the hell's the captain?" he muttered to himself.

Lowering his binoculars again, he turned towards me. "OK Wrona, we've received orders and are preparing to make way. I'm short-handed on loading the provisions. Get down there on the dock and help Bosun Kamecki and Seamen Uliczny loading those crates."

"Are we at war, Sir?"

"We have orders to activate the Worek Plan immediately. Now get down there and start loading on the double."

Some of the crew thought that Grudziński was a bit bitchy in the way he talked. I don't think he ever meant anything nasty, he was always direct and to the point. He didn't say we were at war, but something was going on if we were taking up our position according to the Worek Plan. I climbed down the conning tower and out the hatch onto the deck. I ran along to the aft gangplank to where Alex Kamecki and Stanley Uliczny were running back and forth, loading crates onto our sub.

Alex seemed annoyed with the orders, especially because they'd been given by Grudziński. He shouted to me as he headed up the gangplank with a box. "Grab any of those boxes on the dock, pass them down the aft hatch. These are food and supplies. There's a couple of guys down below who are storing them."

Stanley scampered past. "Has the war started?" I asked.

"How the hell should I know? I just work here," Stanley said with a shrug.

Stanley was very amenable to labor. In fact, he thrived on it. He was the original working-class hero. He would say, "My mother always told me the devil makes work for idle hands."

As I grabbed a box, there was a brief flash of light in the southern sky, shortly followed by a second. I didn't think much of it as it could have been a ship's searchlight. But a few moments later I heard the distinct boom, followed by a thud – it sounded like a bomb or heavy gunfire.

"What the hell was that?" Stanley asked.

I looked at my watch – 04:48. "No idea, it could be anything," I replied. "Let's get working."

As we both grabbed a box and headed up the gangplank, another double flash was in the southern sky. One bright flash followed by a shorter dull flash. Moments later, the same boom followed by a dull thud. Looking up at the conning tower I could see Grudziński looking towards the south with his binoculars.

Alex had passed his box below and was running back to the dock. "Come on lads, let's finish this quickly," he said in passing.

Stanley and I were passing our boxes down the hatch when 'Freckles' shouted up from below. "Hey, what's going on up there?"

Freckles was our nickname for Victor Piegza, the Quartermaster in charge of all our food and supplies. He was also our head chef and we always joked that his talent was to make good food into a pile of flatulence. But in all honesty, I have never seen a man produce such wonderful meals from an almost empty cupboard.

"Oh, nothing," Stanley replied. "It's just all hell is rising with the dawn, but you're safe down there. Be a good chap and rustle up a nice breakfast for us?"

Freckles climbed the ladder and looked out the hatch. Just then there was another double flash followed by the booming thud.

"Jeez!" he said, ducking his head back down in the hatch. "What was that?"

"Oh don't look at that!" I shouted, "You'll turn into a pillar of salt, just like Lot's wife in the Bible. It's the wrath you'll get if you don't make a nice breakfast!" I then ran down the gangway to fetch another box.

As we worked like ants carrying things to their anthill, the distant flashes and booms continued. I could see Grudziński in the dim morning light, waving orders from his conning tower to keep men by the hawsers, ready to cast off. Mostly he kept his binoculars focused on the south, but he also scanned the skies searching for aircraft. His final scan would be along the dockyards, where I knew he was searching for our captain.

When we were done, since the dock wasn't in a blackout, all three of us stood at the bottom of the gangplank and lit a cigarette. As a submariner, you have to make the most of your smoking opportunities whenever you can. Smoking was strictly forbidden in any part of the sub at any time. While at sea we sometimes had a chance to smoke on the conning tower, or on deck. This only happened if conditions were good while running on the surface and if the captain allowed. We huffed and puffed on our cigarettes as hard as we could.

"So what do you think?" asked Alex.

"I reckon there's some nasty trouble happening down at Gdańsk," said Stanley.

"Do you think it's that Nazi battleship doing their supposed 'friendly' visit?" asked Alex.

"Maybe," Stanley replied.

"It's either we're blasting that dreaded Nazi battleship or they are blasting us," I added. "Grudziński told me the Worek Plan has been activated."

"Oh shit," Alex moaned, "That means only one thing, Germany has invaded! Those stupid fuckers have actually done it!"

"Don't worry mate," Stanley kindly added, "We're a big nation, and if war has started, they'll take forever to penetrate our country. Anyway, they can't take us because our army will fight back with a vengeance. What's more, France and England are on our side and that crazy Mr. Hitler will have to turn his armies around when they start attacking him in the west."

"Oh, you think so? The stupid English let Hitler walk into Czechoslovakia – what did they call it? Appeasement? I bet they'll sell us down the river too."

"Well, who knows," Stanley interjected. "I still think we're pretty big."

"All deckhands, report!" Lieutenant Grudziński shouted from the conning tower.

"I guess that includes us," I said. And we all moved up the gangplank as slowly as possible to allow us to smoke the maximum amount of cigarette before flicking the stubs into the water.

When we reported back to Grudziński, he stated our orders:

"Seaman Uliczny, remain on deck, I may need extra hands to cast off.

"Boson Wrona, report back to the engine room and stand by to start engines.

"Bosun Kamecki, remain on watch here in the tower, I need extra eyes."

"Aye, sir," we all replied, and assumed our duties.

Going down the conning tower ladders and into the main control room, I saw all men were at their posts, awaiting instructions. In the engine room, I met with my boss, Warrant officer Wacław Foterek. He was the King of the engine room.

"Hey what news do you have, Blackie?"

"We have to wait for orders to start engines."

"So I don't already know that? I want news, something I don't know yet."

"We have orders to activate the Worek Plan."

"I also know that, now give me something useful."

"There's a steady series of explosions in the south around the mouth of the Vistula River. No one is sure what it is, though."

"Hm, I heard some of them. It could be our fortress at Westerplatte. The German light battleship, Schleswig-Holstein was at anchor in the estuary, just off Westerplatte. I can't imagine them firing at that close range so it could be something in the city."

Foterek took a rag from his back pocket and fiddled and polished some random levers and dials. He would do this whenever he was bored or troubled – at that moment I thought he was troubled. Foterek was a busybody and we all knew it. He wanted to know everything, and he wasn't ashamed of it. The reason he gave was simple: 'If I don't know what's going on, then I don't know what to fix first,' he would say.

"What exactly did you hear?" he asked while he looked for smudges. "What did it sound like? Did you see any aircraft?"

"I didn't see or hear any aircraft. What I saw was a bright glow followed by a smaller glow, then a few seconds later I heard a cracking boom, followed by a thud. This repeated several times while we were on the dock. I counted the seconds, and the delay was about fifty seconds."

"The time delay suggests the port at Gdańsk, but the sound suggests the battleship has opened fire on something. Germans are living in the city so they won't be shooting at Gdańsk. The only other target would be Westerplatte, but that would be at point-blank range. What was the time delay between the boom and thud?"

"It was very quick, a second or two."

"Oh my God, that sounds like they're firing point-blank into Westerplatte. If that's what they're doing, then that's insane! Those poor fellows on Westerplatte, they must be going through hell!" He continued polishing random items more frantically than ever. "And you said no aircraft?"

"That's right, sir, nothing."

"Hm, that is strange."

"What do we do sir?"

"What do we do?" Foterek retorted. "We wait for the order to start engines! As you said, we must take up our positions for the Worek Plan. But, in the meantime, I want you to go to the control room and check on the instruments. Check batteries, fuel, depth gauges, and report back." Then he added, "Check on everything. That's an order."

"Aye, sir." And off I went through the ship, leaving Foterek to polish his precious engines.

As I said, Foterek was a busybody, but with good reason. I was his eyes and ears and he always sent me on reconnaissance missions to find out information or any gossip I could gather. So there I went, off to the control room under the ruse of calibrating the instruments.

———

As I went through the narrow corridors of the sub, there were blank, silent faces throughout the ship. Whether they were at their posts or sitting on the edges of their bunks, the men's faces wore the same stunned and numb expression. They were waiting for confirmation that war had begun.

"Coming on deck sir," I announced as I entered the control room.

"What do you want Blackie?" Lieutenant Piasecki asked. "You should be at your post in the engine room."

"Yes sir, but Warrant Officer Wacław told me to check and calibrate the instruments here."

"OK, carry on."

I took out my notebook and pencil and started making notes of all the mechanical information. Battery charge, fuel levels, oil capacity, etc. As I did so, I was waiting for people to discuss the situation. I wanted them to say something about what was happening, but nothing was happening, nobody had much to say.

"Sir, permission to go up to the bridge and conning tower to check instruments there?"

Lieutenant Piasecki seemed to look right through me and know what I was up to. He stared at me for some moments, then eventually said, "Sure, off you go, but be quick about it."

I climbed the ladder and was almost at the first level when I heard the radio operator below me. Chief Petty Officer Kotecki handed a message to Lieutenant Piasecki saying, "This is just in from Westerplatte, they say they are under bombardment."

"Hold on, Blackie," Piasecki said.

Piasecki read it, folding it in half as he passed it up to me, saying, "Hey Blackie, give this to Grudziński and ask him where the captain is."

Grabbing the note, I flew up the ladder to the top of the conning tower where I knew Lieutenant Grudziński was. The sun was now beginning to rise above the horizon, its bright orange glare glistening across the bay. Alex was still on watch with Grudziński and looked particularly worried.

"Message for you, sir."

Looking at it briefly, Grudziński said, "Confirmation of what I already know. You can see the smoke rising from Westerplatte. The bombardment has been non-stop for about an hour now."

We both looked at our watches. 05:55.

"Why are you not in the engine room?" Grudziński asked.

"Foterek told me to check and calibrate the instruments in preparation for departure."

In the distance to the east of us, one of our submarines was now exiting the harbor.

"Is that the submarine Wilk I see departing the harbor?" I asked. "Are they also taking their position on the Worek Plan?" watching the old Wolf steaming into the sunrise, I couldn't help but think that we would now be the last sub to leave.

Before Grudziński could answer, he turned to look to the north where we could hear the drone of several airplanes heading in an easterly direction. We couldn't identify them at first, but one by one they slowly nosed down into a steep dive. As they accelerated downwards, we could hear the unmistakable scream of the Stuka dive-bomber!

"Oh Jeez," Alex said, "here comes the blitzkrieg!"

"Looks like they're targeting the airfield just north of here," Grudziński said. "We'll be next once they smash all our planes. I don't think we can wait much longer. Get back to the engine room on the double and tell Piasecki to get up here!"

As I dropped down through the tower, I could hear the distant, muffled explosions of the Stuka's bombs and Alex urging, "Where the hell is the captain!?"

"Sir," I said to Lieutenant Piasecki. "Looks like an air attack on the airfield north of us, and Grudziński wants you up top." As he disappeared up the ladder, I said, "Still no sign of the captain!"

Running back to the engine room I said nothing, but my face and hurried manner must have told everyone about the war that was unfolding outside. I was so out of breath that I could hardly explain anything to Foterek. it wasn't the exertion, it was the adrenalin stirred up by the realization that we were at war!

After I told Foterek what was going on, we talked about the situation and what it could mean.

"They are probably only attacking Poland on the coast. Germany would want to capture Gdańsk, so they could connect Prussia with the rest of Germany," Foterek said. "So I think Gdańsk will be the center of activity. It makes no sense for Germany to attack the whole of Poland, we are too big. If France attacked Germany in the west, they couldn't fight everybody."

"Yes, you're probably right," I agreed. "They would be stupid to invade the whole of Poland. If they only take the coastal areas, then maybe they could hold off England and France in the west."

"You have a point there." We may have agreed, but none of us had enough facts to know what was happening.

Foterek continued. "Whatever is happening, aircraft are looming overhead. It is only a matter of time before the docks here in Gdynia become a target. If we stay here much longer, we would be sitting ducks. So you say you saw the Wilk leaving port?"

"Yes, we're the last sub here."

Just then the Engine Order Telegraph – the device that shows orders for changes in engine speed in the control room - rang and the leaver moved from stop to standby, then the revolutions counter was set to zero. Then the phone rang with a call from the control room.

"Foterek here," I heard as he answered. "Start engines but no revs, just be prepared to move out."

Grudziński was ordering us to start engines, but to hold steady. We checked the time, it was 06:15.

"Looks like we're finally going to leave port," I said.

We stood by our stations in the engine room for what seemed an eternity.

"Maybe we're leaving without the captain?" I suggested. "Grudziński was anxious to get moving and he did talk with Lieutenant Piasecki."

"No I don't think so," Foterek replied. "I think he's just getting ready."

It wasn't until many minutes later that we heard over the tannoy for all to hear. "This is the captain speaking, prepare the ship for leaving the dock."

We checked our watches. It was 06:30.

"Thank the saints for that," I heard Foterek say.

After maybe five minutes of waiting, the Engine Order Telegraph moved from standby to ahead 1/3, followed by a signal on the revolutions clock to move us forward slowly.

At last, we were leaving the dock!

We all checked our watches again: 06:35. We knew the bow of the Orzeł was facing towards the open sea. The deckhands would have cast off our hawsers and lines cleanly and shoved off the dock. Soon we would move swiftly into the bay.

2   Into the Sack

Ship's Log entered by: Captain Henry Kłoczkowski
Date: September 1, 1939
Location: Western reach, Bay of Gdańsk
Entry: Holding our designated station according to the Worek Plan. The water here is shallow, and we are at risk of being spotted by enemy aircraft.

If you used your imagination, you could visualize the bay of Gdańsk as a big sack, and we had to go in it and stay there. That's what the Worek Plan was – or the 'Sack Plan', as its name translates. As a submarine, we had to defend the bay against any possible enemy landings and attack any ships that were threatening our small coastline. Finally, we had to observe German shipping and advise our base of all enemy movements.

The Polish coast was very short and centered only on the bay of Gdańsk, or 'Danzig' as the Germans called it. There was Germany to the west and Prussia to the east, so Gdańsk was hemmed in on two sides. Both Foterek and I thought that Germany did not need to attack by sea. The Orzeł was not only a new submarine with all the latest equipment, but we were also an ocean-going sub with hunter-killer capabilities. I don't think our great military planners were thinking their clearest when they devised this plan, but we were just engineers driving our submarine, so we had to follow orders. We felt like hunters kept in the sack when we wanted to be destroying Nazi ships. But that was not to be – at least, not yet.

Our beloved Orzeł had been assigned the furthest western section of the bay, just outside of our home port of Gdynia. This was probably the worst station for our submarine, since this section of the bay was the shallowest.

Although we could remain submerged, any aircraft could easily spot us from above and we could not dive to a safe, undetectable depth. At least we were close to the Polish land-based anti-aircraft guns, so we could get some cover from any attacking aircraft.

Our first day of war turned out to be pretty quiet, at least in our sector of the bay. We spent most of the day submerged at periscope depth and kept watch on the drama unfolding around us. To our north was the Hel, where we had a naval command base. To our west was our port of Gdynia. East was the open bay, while to our south lay Gdańsk and Westerplatte.

The routine of a submarine is simple: Stay hidden and sneak up on the enemy. During the day we would have to stay out of sight and remain submerged. The deeper we were, the safer we would be. While underwater we were slow because we could only use our electric motors, but we would be silent – a secret, hidden force. At periscope depth, we were an eye to seek out enemy ships. The problem about being underwater for so long was that the air in the boat would become stale and hot, making us all sweat and stink. The engine fumes permeated everywhere and as the stink worsened, the oxygen levels would fall lower, so we could not hide underwater forever.

During the night we could surface. While we hid in the darkness, we could recirculate our air. We could run our diesel engines, not only giving us much faster speed, but also replenishing our batteries so we could spend the following day underwater.

One other thing we could do on the surface was operate our radios, allowing us to communicate with our Naval Base and listen to any civilian news broadcasts. While I sat in the mess room, I could hear Captain Kloczowski in the control room giving orders to our Chief Petty Officer, Henry Kotecki, nicknamed 'the Kat'.

"Kotecki, raise naval command and get updates on the situation." The captain came into the mess, then moved into the mess room. "Blackie," He called, "switch the radio onto the Warsaw station, find out what's going on."

I jumped up and did as I was ordered. The good news we heard was that Westerplatte, despite being heavily bombarded, was holding out against all odds. She had repulsed an assault of German marines and she seemed impervious to point-blank shots from the German battleship.

"Some good news, sir," I said. "It looks like we're holding them off pretty well. Maybe we can go home soon?"

The bad news was Poland was being attacked on all fronts by Germany, even from the south. The Luftwaffe had bombed Warsaw. It seemed that no part of Poland was safe.

The captain just looked at me and went back to the control room.

Freckles was carrying dishes back to the galley, "I don't think we'll be going home in a hurry," he said.

Smoking was prohibited at all times inside the ship, as this would only add to the already stale air we breathed. The captain allowed the crew to rotate onto deck, which allowed us to smoke. There were four men aft of the conning tower and four men forward at any one time. He gave each group a 10-minute rotation, so within about two hours the whole crew could have a turn on deck. I had my turn on the aft deck with Jan Olejnik, Vlad Narkiewicz (nicknamed 'The Fisherman') and Lieutenant Marian Mokrski, our navigator.

"Hey, Fisherman!" Marian called, "Where's your tackle? Aren't you going to catch us something?"

"He should catch us some Germans!" Jan chimed in.

"I left my stuff down below, I can't smoke and fish. Anyway, those damn Germans are making too much noise and scaring all the fish."

We could see the port of Gdynia to the east and there was a flotilla of Polish ships heading into the bay.

"Where are they going?" I asked.

"They're heading out to lay mines to disrupt the Germans," said Marian. "See that big fellow upfront? She's the destroyer Wicher, she's our flagship. There's also the minelayer Griffin in that flotilla, she can lay up to 300 mines. The other 3 destroyers we have were evacuated to England a few days ago."

"There we go," said Vlad. "As the Germans run away from us, they can sink themselves on those minefields!"

"Well, it should be a short war!" laughed Mokrski.

When Grudziński blew the signal on his whistle to rotate, it didn't seem like 10 minutes had passed.

"Come on lads, let's get back to work," Vlad said.

That night there were air raids on Gdynia. I was glad we got the Orzeł out safely, but I felt sorry for all those poor souls trapped beneath the Nazis' bombs.

All day on Saturday we sat at the bottom of the western bay of Gdańsk. We were confined to our stations in the Orzeł, so we had to stay in the engine room. Foterek joked, "We're not staying on station, we're staying on the bottom."

Captain Kłoczkowski entered the control room. The Orzeł was slightly tilted as it was resting on the muddy bottom of the bay.

'Sir," Lieutenant Grudziński saluted, "we are awaiting your orders."

"Very good, what's our status?"

"Nothing to report, sir. Sonar reported some distant traffic to the east. Three hours we received reports of several explosions to the east, possibly torpedoes or mines," Grudziński said.

"Sonar, is there any traffic nearby?" The captain asked.

"Nothing sir."

"OK, Grudziński, bring her to the surface."

"Aye, sir."

That evening at 21:00, we surfaced again in the darkness and began cruising around the western side of the bay.

"Lieutenant Piasecki, accompany me to the bridge," Captain Kłoczkowski ordered. "Grudziński, you remain in the control room."

On the surface, the dull light of a half-moon revealed a motorboat about two kilometers away.

"Who the hell is that?" Kłoczkowski demanded, peering through his binoculars.

"They're flying a Polish flag," Lieutenant Piasecki said.

The motorboat changed course, heading directly towards the Orzeł.

"Why didn't sonar warn us about this boat? It could have been a German!" Kłoczkowski demanded.

"I guess the shallow water here distorted the sound," Piasecki said. "They're heading our way, let's see what they want."

After we'd exchanged recognition signals, it wasn't long before the Polish motorboat M9 pulled alongside the Orzeł. The commander of M9 shouted, "Hey! Is that you Kłoczkowski?"

"Who else?" Captain Kłoczkowski replied. "What news do you have?"

"I'm ferrying some wounded back to Gdynia. There was a skirmish in the Eastern Bay. Two German destroyers, the Leberecht Maass and Max Schultz, were damaged in the day's battle. If you had joined that battle, we may have been able to sink both of them."

"We are assigned to the western sector," Kłoczkowski shouted back.

"All the fun is in the eastern sector, tell naval command that you will patrol there. You are wasted here."

The M9 slowly pulled away from the Orzeł. "We have wounded sailors and have to take them to Gdynia."

On Sunday morning I reported to the control room at 5 am as it was time for the change of watch. Grudziński ordered me up to the conning tower. "It's your turn up top Blackie, you can relieve Stanley."

"Sir? It must be well into the dawn by now, are we not preparing to dive?"

"We're awaiting orders," Piasecki replied.

Tom Prządka who was operating the dive planes looked at me and shrugged, shaking his head.

The crew were becoming anxious in case enemy aircraft would spot us.

At the top of the tower, the dawn's light was already upon us. Stanley handed me his binoculars as I relieved him and I took position on watch. It was a quiet morning and the captain remained quiet as if in a daydream. The sun was just above the horizon in the east.

I heard them before I could see them. A flight of twelve bombers well to the south beyond Gdańsk flying east and escorted by three fighters. They were probably heading to targets on land and not a threat to us. But then more planes appeared in the west over Gdynia, heading east out over the bay, directly towards us.

"Captain! Aircraft bearing 270," I exclaimed.

"I see them," he replied. "They are still quite distant and flying into the sun so they probably don't see us yet." After looking at the aircraft for some time, he eventually ordered, "Lookouts, get below." We hurried down into the control room. "Prepare to dive," the captain said. Turning to the helmsman, he ordered Bosun Victor Dabrowski to go below. "That includes you, Blackie, get below," he told me.

The captain was last and came down very slowly, closing the watertight hatches behind him.

Stepping down into the control room, the captain asked, "Piasecki, report our status."

I thought to myself, '*Why did he ask Piasecki? Shouldn't he ask Grudziński who is his second-in-command?*'

"Currently heading zero, six, zero degrees. All hatches and watertight doors are closed and secure. Batteries at 98%, current sea depth is sixty meters. All stations report they are ready to dive."

"OK Piasecki, take her down thirty meters."

"Sir, shouldn't Grudziński receive the orders?" Piasecki asked.

"I gave the order to you, Piasecki."

"Aye sir, blow ballast tanks three and four. Dive planes 20 degrees."

The water flooding the ballast tanks could be heard throughout the ship. These were the central ballast tanks so the weight kept us level and balanced. If it were only this weight added to the center of the ship, we would have gone down horizontally, like an elevator. With our forward motion, and our dive planes now angled downwards, the ship nosed lower like an airplane. The ship tilted forward as she went underwater, and although we were not moving fast, the forward tilt made us feel as if we were going downhill. We all held onto something as we descended.

The dive planes acted like a fish's fins, guiding the ship into the waters below. We all kept our eyes on the depth gauge as we slowly descended into the bay. When we passed the 25-meter mark, Piasecki ordered, "Dive planes, level out." With that order, the depth gauge slowed and like an airplane leveling into its cruise altitude, the Orzeł slowly curved into level flight at a depth of 30 meters.

"Good work Mr. Piasecki," the captain said. Then he turned to Grudziński. "Now that's how to dive a submarine. That comes from experience, not from reading books in the academy."

It might have been a joke, but no one laughed.

The captain then called out, "Rudder, thirty degrees to port."

"Aye sir, thirty degrees to port," the helmsman confirmed.

"Half Ahead," the captain ordered.

Piasecki rang the engine telegraph to 'Half Ahead', asking "Not full speed?"

"What's our speed?" the captain asked.

"5 knots," Grudziński replied.

We waited several minutes while we continued our heading. The captain leaned against the bulkhead, gazing upward.

"Sonar, anything to report?"

"Nothing, sir."

Then, after a pause, Sonar gave an update. "Wait. I hear depth charges hitting the water, 1, 2, 3, I think 5 or 6 behind us, and about 30 to 40 degrees to starboard." He listened to the sonar with his headphones, clicking rhythmically with his stopwatch in one hand. At the same time, he scribbled down numbers on his note pad, calculating our distance from the detected objects according to his timings.

The captain didn't wait for any more information. "Helm, hard to port, bring her about 180 degrees!" he ordered, followed by "Piasecki, full speed ahead!"

The helmsman spun the rudder all the way to the left for a hard turn to the port side. Piasecki meanwhile rang the engine telegraph to 'Full Ahead'.

Moments later we could hear the electric motors rev up as we accelerated to seven knots. We weren't as fast as a surface ship, but this was our maximum speed underwater. Seven knots is an easy running speed for a man, not even a sprint, but a good jogging pace. Because we were in such a tight turn, we all felt the centrifugal force as we spun around to our left.

As we went through our turn, the first depth charge went off with a distant boom, soon followed by another and another, each one getting louder. The captain had ordered us to turn around, and we were heading straight towards them.

"Turn complete." The helmsman called out.

Just then, the sixth and final depth charge went off. We must have been close because it gave the ship a dreadful shaking. That is when the captain reached forward and rang the engine telegraph and set it to 'All Stop'. Moments later the electric motors wound down. As we drifted forwards, I wondered what Foterek was thinking as he stopped the engines. He didn't know what was happening, as he only had the orders on the telegraph to follow.

We silently drifted forward into the bombing field. Then the captain announced, "Take her to the bottom, Piasecki."

"Aye, sir. Flood all tanks," Piasecki ordered, and this time we could hear the first and fourth ballast tanks flooding with water. This slowly brought us to rest on the bottom of the bay, right in the middle of the bombing field! As we landed on the muddy bottom, the ship was still drifting forward. We could hear the grinding of mud and rocks on the belly of the boat as she slid to a rest at the bottom of the bay.

We waited a few moments in silence.

"Sir?" Piasecki asked.

The captain raised a finger to his lips, his command to remain silent immediate.

A few long moments passed.

Sonar reported an update. "I think I hear depth charges hitting the water again."

"Where?" was the captain's only question.

"Multiples splashes to our rear and … wait, wait." He clicked his stopwatch and scribbled frantically with his pencil. "There are 6 more, about 30 degrees off our port side stern. Distance is 500 meters or more."

"Good work men, I'll be in my quarters." At that, the captain turned and retired to his room.

Once again, the booms of the depth charges could be heard, but this time they were distant and muffled.

"Wait a minute, can someone tell me what just happened?" I asked.

"A simple sleight of hand," Grudziński said.

All heads turned towards him, anxious for the rest of his explanation.

"Being slow to dive, the bombers spotted us on the surface. They then moved in to drop their depth charges on us. As we dived down to 30 meters, we would have become invisible to the bombers. To add to our evasion, we turned slightly off course and to the left and that maneuver got us out of the way of the bombs."

Questions remained in everyone's eyes.

"You see," Grudziński continued, "the Luftwaffe have a standard procedure to drop a spread of bombs on the last observed position of a submarine. The bombers then have to circle and drop another spread of bombs ahead of that position. This is a standard tactic where they assume we are running in a straight line. The captain avoided the first drop, but to hide, he immediately turned the ship back into that first drop zone."

All eyes were wide in wonder.

"You see, what the Luftwaffe do next is to fly around and continue to drop in a fan-shaped area ahead of the last known position. From an altitude, they can easily see where the last set of depth charges exploded. All they need to do is think where the sub is continuing along its course."

"No shit?" the helmsman said.

"Of course, we are now hiding in the original bomb zone. So, they are looking to drop bombs in the area ahead, where they think we are running away to."

"A bonus is if the depth charges in the first drop were deep enough or the water shallow enough for the silt to be raised by the blasts – that further helps to hide us."

"What if they circle back and begin their run again?" Piasecki asked.

Sonar reported again. "More splashes, assuming depth charges on a very wide range, approximately three kilometers to our port."

"You see," Grudziński continued, "they're still dropping charges where they think we've run to. There weren't that many planes, and they have limited bombs and limited fuel. They can only circle us so many times before they must return to base. Also, our shore-based guns may take a few potshots at them, so they should piss off and go play with someone else. My only worry is they now know there is at least one Polish submarine here in the bay."

"Well with our captain we can continue to be a thorn in their side!" Piasecki said.

"Let's hope so," Grudziński added.

"Sir, permission to return to the engine room?" I asked.

"What's up Blackie?" Piasecki asked, "Did we scare you?"

"Oh no sir, I just want to make sure my buddies are OK back there."

"Granted Blackie, off you go," Grudziński said. "Tell Foterek 'good work'."

So there we sat on the bottom of the bay, manning our stations. The story of our devious maneuver to avoid the German bombs spread rapidly through the ship. The spirits of the whole crew began to rise. Broken telephone even amplified the story into an adventure that almost sank the German fleet.

We had smelled blood. Instead of being the frightened fish hiding in a tin kettle on the bottom, we now felt a fighting spirit. We became wild sharks. Our captain was now our hero, and we felt that he could spit in the Germans' faces. He would be the one to lead us into a glorious battle – if only we could stop sitting at the bottom of the bay.

For the rest of the day, we just sat quietly, in the mud and the silt at the bottom of the bay. We didn't even come up to have a peek at the surface with our periscope, which would not reach the surface from our position. Blowing our ballast tanks and rising to periscope depth would have betrayed our presence to any patrolling ships or aircraft, so the captain's orders were to stay hidden. Some of us suspected that while the captain sat in his cabin, he was carefully planning a strategy to attack the Germans. We all agreed with this. After all, what else could such a cool-headed and smart man be doing?

"Do you want to play cards?" I would often ask.

I would ask this of anyone not on shift who seemed to be doing nothing, whenever I also was doing nothing. I carried the deck of cards with me everywhere on the ship. I didn't really want to play cards. Dealing the cards seemed futile. Playing the game seemed futile. If dealing and playing were futile, then what was the point of winning? Sitting there in the silence, parked on the bottom of an expanse of ocean, anything was better than sitting on my own. So I played a futile game of cards.

That sense of futility was contributed to by the worry that at any moment we could have a depth charge dropped on our unsuspecting heads. Even at this relatively shallow depth, as we sat on the bottom of the bay, an explosive depth charge would rupture our boat. The catastrophic inrush of water would be so fast and implosive, that we would all die instantly. Instead of a blast of fire, we would be crushed by a thundering wall of water.

There would always be the unlucky few who would be protected in their section of the ship, behind a strong bulkhead of steel. If our ship were broken, crushed, and helpless, a virtual tomb on the bottom of the sea, those poor survivors would have to wait it out in any small, dark bubble of air that remained. The limited oxygen they had in that bubble would soon be depleted, and they too would eventually be visited by the angel of death.

So there was no escape from the boredom, and the threat of death constantly haunted our minds. We waited, not wanting to look at the clock, not wanting to know how slowly time was passing. We waited for our captain to finish his devious plan and lead us into a gallant battle. We did nothing but wait for orders.

Word began to circulate that the German battleship, the Schleswig-Holstein, could soon be sailing out to sea. We all thought that this was the monster our captain had been plotting against. That sinking it would be our prize as well as our revenge. But, most of all, that it would show all of Poland that we could fight and win. A plan like that would need to be thought out carefully, so the captain was left alone. We agreed that he needed to think.

When we were submerged, the only power source we had was our huge bank of batteries. While on the surface, our diesel engines could drive us at a top speed of about 20 knots, while our electric motors could only push us along at about 9 knots. Now these batteries do not last forever, and to recharge them, we needed to be on the surface so that we could run the diesel engines.

So, as I've mentioned before, it was during the dark hours of the night that we rose to the surface. We cruised as silently as we could on diesel power and recharged our batteries. This was also when we could ventilate the ship to replenish it with fresh air. Even though it was dark, we needed to maintain a careful watch for enemy patrol vessels and aircraft.

These hours were important in the engine room where my boss, Foterek and I monitored the batteries as they charged. We worked through the night accompanied by the noise of the diesel engines, taking turns to have coffee breaks. If the captain allowed it, the crew could smoke a cigarette briefly on deck before returning to the confines of the submarine. During this cyclic routine, submerged all day and surfacing only at night, no man on board ever saw the light of the sun.

It was Sunday morning, the third day of the war. We were still running on the surface but dawn was only a couple of hours away. My shift was due to finish with the dawn, and it was at this time that Foterek would send me to the control room to calibrate instruments. Foterek liked to make sure all the instruments were reading correctly and, if time allowed, he would have the calibration done twice a day. News and gossip were also things that he liked, so my visits to the control room were a channel of information that he always tried to keep open.

"OK Blackie, it's about that time, you should go callibrate the instruments in the control room," he would say.

"Aye, sir," I'd reply, and off I would go.

It is important that the instruments in a control room read the same as the ones in the engine room. A submariner can't keep asking over the intercom, 'What is your reading on depth?' Such chatter would be too distracting in a time of crisis. Off I would go, armed with a notepad and pencil to write down all the readings of all instruments. I would then report back to Foterek and we would then compare these to the same instrument readings in the engine room. In all my days on that ship, I never encountered a difference greater than two percent. Small differences were usually accounted for by differences in temperature or vibrations or some other ambient effect. If there were ever a significant difference, then we would follow a prescribed routine to investigate why, and how to rectify it.

While there, I would gauge the attitude of the crew and gather information on what they knew and didn't know. This of course would be compared to whatever information Foterek had gathered during his wanderings through the ship on his breaks. If there was any difference between the information I reported and that which he had, he would work out a way to find the truth.

Warrant Officer Wacław Foterek was not only my officer in the engine room, but I always considered him to be the second-in-command of the whole ship. He knew every screw, bolt, wire, and component on that ship. What is more, he knew exactly how these components could fail and how they could be fixed. He was a true engineer, the Good King of the engine room, and I tried hard to follow in his footsteps.

During that Sunday morning, not much happened, but while I was walking back from the control room I meet with Stanley. He was coming off watch on the conning tower.

"How was it up there?" I asked.

"Cold!" Stanley responded, "The usual shit. Cruising on the surface, recharging our batteries. We kept a close lookout for enemy ships and airplanes."

I could see the fatigue in his eyes, he was tired and sleepy but something else was bothering him.

As we walked towards the aft of the ship, towards his bunk, he told me what he had heard and witnessed while on watch in the conning tower.

"Our ship cruised alongside the Wilk for a while, keeping a distance between them of about thirty meters. We were both recharging our batteries, but the captains took this opportunity to talk to each other."

"Oh? What were they saying?"

"Although the distance between them was small, shouting would have been incomprehensible. They had to talk using megaphones to hear each other."

Stanley recounted the conversation to me. At first, I thought Stanley had misunderstood what they said, but he insisted that what he had heard was the truth. I had my calibration notes in hand, but it was this discussion that I had to rush back to tell my boss. Foterek would need to know of this.

Leaving Stanley to sleep in his bunk, I made my way to the engine room. When I got there, I grabbed the bar above the bulkhead hatch and catapulted myself through feet first. This is a normal thing to do but I did it at a speed which suggested an unfolding emergency.

Foterek turned immediately to face me, knowing something was wrong.

"Sir!" I exclaimed.

"What the hell is it?"

"All readings are nominal, sir." That had to be my first report.

"What else?" he demanded.

"Sir, I learned something important from Stanley."

"Ah, what juicy gossip do you have?"

"Well sir, Stanley was on watch with the captain last night, and we rendezvoused with the Wilk."

"Ah, yes, the Wilk, the Snarling Wolf as they call her. Her captain is Bogusław Krawczyk, he's nicknamed 'The Tailor'".

"The Tailor?" I asked.

"Yeah, I suppose he's good at stitching up the enemy. Anyway, I heard they're laying mines on the outer bay, to thwart German attacks. How is she? Do you know if she completed her mission?"

"Well sir, Stanley told me that we cruised alongside each other for a while, as we charged our batteries in the darkness. He overheard the captains' conversation."

"Interesting. So what did they talk about?"

"Well from what Stanley told me, she has completed her mission."

"Well good for her, the wily old Wolf! She always was a sneaky one. The old Tailor probably laid them down right under the noses of the Germans. I expect we'll hear a few German ships sinking soon enough. So what else do you have to tell me, my boy?"

"Sir, there is also some news of a battle from the Tailor."

"Ah, so The Wolf tasted some blood?"

"Yes, the Tailor told our captain that he fought with two German destroyers. He engaged them in combat and tried to torpedo one of them."

"Well good for that old sea dog, what ship did he sink?"

"It was the 'Erich Steinbrinck', but all his torpedoes missed, so he didn't sink anything."

"Well, that's not good, but you can't win them all. The Tailor is a mean hunter with a killer instinct, but these destroyers can be slippery customers!"

"Did the Wilk sustain any damage?" Foterek asked.

"No sir, or at least he didn't report anything to us. But that's not all, there is something else."

"So? What else?"

"Bear in mind that what I say is second-hand news."

"Get on with it, Blackie."

"Well, Stanley says that the Tailor was telling our captain that if he had had support during that battle, he could have sunk both ships. So he proposed that we work together and hunt as a pack. That way we could be more effective in seeking out and destroying German ships. The Tailor seems to think that even our standard tactics would be effective against the Germans."

"Yeah, good for the Tailor, Commander Krawczyk has always been a hunter. So what's the plan? Are we going to work together to sink the Germans?"

"Well this is what bothers me, you see, Stanley says that our captain did not want to work with him."

"So what is the captain's plan? He must have a plan. Are we going to get that German battleship on our own?"

"I don't know! But according to Stanley, he does not want to work in a pack with the Tailor but wants to sail on his own."

"Well," said Foterek, "Our captain must have a plan of his own, wouldn't you say?"

"I don't know, Stanley seems to be telling me that our captain doesn't want to engage with any German ships at all. He wants to stay away from trouble."

"Bullshit! I don't believe that! Look at what he did the other day, he is smart and he is cunning. Above all, he is our commander! He can spit in the face of any German ship and bring it to the bottom with a blast."

"Sir, I do not disagree, all I am saying is what I heard from Stanley."

"Well the hell with Stanley, because he is a fool for saying that!" Foterek almost spat as he stamped back and forth trying to figure out the logic behind this. Eventually, he spoke. "I don't think you heard Stanley right. Or perhaps Stanley didn't understand what our captain was saying to the Tailor."

"All I am saying is what I heard from Stanley."

"Do you know what could happen if you started speaking badly of the captain? If I hear you repeat this to anyone onboard, I swear I will feed you to my diesels!"

"Sorry, sir" was all I could muster to defuse the situation.

Foterek was not happy, he was angry with Stanley for giving me bad information and he was angry with me for communicating the bad information. My good Foterek grabbed his rag and began to clean all his brass handles and levers with a furious force. He even told me to *'Fuck off*, and then he told his diesels that Stanley could *'go and fuck himself'*! To avoid his venom, I retreated through the bulkhead into the next forward section.

"What was all that about?" someone asked, sitting on their bunk.

Eavesdroppers, sitting at the door listening for tidbits of information. After my scolding from Foterek, I had no patience with anyone. I had no intention to share any more information. So I pulled my deck of cards from my pocket and presented the deck to my questioner's face. I stared into his wide eyes and asked, with a stern voice, "Do you want to play cards?!"

He recoiled and declined gracefully and I strode off.

3 Out of the Sack

Ship's Log entered by: Captain Henry Kłoczkowski
Date: September 3, 1939
Location: South of Hel Peninsula, Bay of Gdańsk
Entry: Air patrols are keeping us submerged, the shallow water in this sector offers poor concealment.

I had just woken up and was still lying on my bunk. I decided to use my Swiss Army knife to scratch markings on the painted wall to count the days we'd been at sea. I was making the scratches below the mattress level, so the other guys who slept here wouldn't easily see them. As I scratched, I thought of my father who gave the knife to me when I was younger. The black oak handle was tarnished and scratched but my Tata always told me he used this knife when he was young and that it would serve me well in times to come. It was serving me now to count the days. I was making my fourth and final scratch when Stanley walked past.

"Hey, Blackie, you can't tunnel out of here, you'll only make us all wet," he said.

I turned to look at him with a mocking eye.

"What are you doing there?" he asked.

"I'm counting."

"Counting what?"

"The days."

"What days? Is it your birthday soon?"

"No, I'm counting how many days since I've seen the sun."

"Oh, that makes sense."

"Don't you count the days?" I asked.

"Sure I do."

"So how do you count them?"

Stanley thought for a moment then he said, "I count how many cigarettes I smoke."

"So how many cigarettes have you smoked?"

"I don't know, I've lost count," he winked. "I'd love to stand here and chat, but I have to use the head. Remember, don't make any holes in our boat, or I'll tell the captain." With that Stanley sauntered off as if walking in the park on a sunny day.

The morning continued with the same routine. After breakfast, I was allowed on deck before my shift began, for an early morning smoke. It was pre-dawn, but at about 04:30 our lookouts spotted some German aircraft to the south. "All crew, get below!" The captain's order made us dispose of our cigarettes and quickly scuttle down the hatches. As the lookouts followed us down, the dive alarm sounded, followed by the captain's order through the voice pipe to dive.

"Prepare to dive," Grudziński echoed.

As the officers on the bridge descended into the control room, everyone was manning their stations, ready for the dive. The lights on the Christmas tree went from red to green one by one. The 'Christmas tree' is a nickname for the array of lights that indicate all the hatches and openings to the outside world. Red means open, green means closed. When all the lights were green, that meant we could dive.

"Pressurize the boat," Grudziński ordered.

This meant that compressed air was released into the submarine. If the air pressure remained steady, that meant there were no leaks. I think you will understand why a submarine must never have any leaks. I could feel my ears pop slightly as the air pressure increased.

I heard the midshipman call out, "Barometer steady sir." This meant all hatches were secure and there were no external leaks.

The captain was the last one down. When he saw me, he said, "Ah, Blackie, wait here."

"Aye, sir."

The captain looked around the control room.

"Where's Piasecki?"

"Sir, he's aft, checking the sonar with Foterek," Grudziński replied.

"Very well then, what's our sea depth, Grudziński?"

"Thirty meters."

"Take her down to twenty meters."

Grudziński issued orders to blow ballast tanks, instructing the helmsman to angle the bow planes.

"When level, steer a course one, three, zero degrees, speed three knots," the captain said.

"Aye, sir. One, three, zero degrees, and three knots," confirmed Grudziński.

As we went down, the captain turned to me.

"Blackie, get your tools. I want these floor panels tightened." He stamped on one to demonstrate how it rattled.

"Must be some loose bolts, sir," I said.

"Make sure they are tightly fixed. During the last depth charges, there were a lot of panels loose and banging. I can even hear things when the crew walk around."

"Aye, sir, I'll get on it. She's still a new boat, and with all that shaking she's telling us what needs tightening."

"I know what needs tightening, Blackie. When you're finished here, check the whole ship, I want a quiet ship when we are running evasive maneuvers."

"Aye, sir."

With that, he turned to Grudziński and said, "When we get level to the peninsular point, let me know. I'll be in my quarters."

What set me thinking was what the captain said about silent running. I began to think he was preparing for some daring mission. So I fetched my tools and set to work tightening not just the floor panels but anything else I could find loose, too.

By 07:00, I had finished everything from the control room to the aft torpedo room and engine room. I was heading toward the forward sections when, as I was passing through the control room, the captain appeared. He held up his hand to stop me. Both Grudziński and Piasecki, who were also on deck, saluted the captain.

"Piasecki, report on the sonar."

"Foterek checked the sonar stack and I can report there is no damage. It is fully functional."

"Very good. Grudziński, what's our position?

"We are about two kilometers off the point you requested, sir. I was about to summon you from your quarters."

"OK, now take her up to periscope depth. Let's have a look outside. Maintain slow speed, I don't want any feathers giving us away."

"Aye, sir!"

Every submariner knows what feathers are. The periscope is a small stick poking above the water allowing us to see what is going on. If we move too fast, then that periscope makes waves, like a speed boat, called 'feathers'. These feathers can be seen much more easily than a slow-moving periscope.

Grudziński issued orders to the helmsman to angle the bow planes up. He didn't have to blow the tanks as we already had neutral buoyancy. We just needed to glide up closer to the surface so we could raise the periscope. All eyes were on the depth gauges. A moment later Grudziński announced, "Periscope depth sir."

"Very good, up periscope."

The midshipmen raised the periscope and the captain positioned himself to catch the handles as they came up. He placed his eyes on the periscope and did a quick 360-degree scan. He then repeated that scan but slower, checking for details. I could see him checking at certain angles, changing the magnification as he looked at different targets.

"Down periscope," he ordered. "Looks like a bombing raid to the north on the peninsula, otherwise all clear, at least for the time being."

"Orders, sir?" Grudziński asked.

"Yes, Piasecki, I want you to take the boat on a wide, southerly turn, and head back 270 degrees. Maintain speed at three knots and check the periscope every five minutes. I want you to hold position ten kilometers off Gdynia."

"Aye, sir."

"Blackie, how's your work coming along?"

"Sir, I've completed everything from here to the stern, I'm now working my way forward to the bow."

"Very good, carry-on Blackie." Turning to Grudziński, he said, "Follow me to the wardroom, I want to have a word in private."

"Aye, sir."

I headed off with my tools towards the forward compartments with my tools, checking for lose panels along the way.

Freckles was clearing some dishes away in the officer's wardroom. "You still doing repairs Blackie?"

"Just a few more to do," I said, "I'll be finished soon." I continued forward towards the officer's cabins, these were little more than closets, but compared to our bunks, they were luxurious. I found a floor panel near the far bulkhead, kneeling I placed my tools by my side. That's when I heard the captain enter the wardroom behind me.

"Leave us," the captain ordered.

Freckles gathered his dishes and scuttled aft to the mess room. I didn't think the order was for me, so I stayed kneeling by the bulkhead and kept quiet.

I could hear the captain seated himself at a table. "Sit there Grudziński." I heard him say.

"Grudziński, I've decided to change our patrol area as there are too many aircraft here in the bay."

"Sir? Where do you plan to take us?"

"North into the Baltic."

"Sir, have we been given any intelligence on what targets to seek, or what shipping lanes to patrol?"

"We need to get away from this infernal German air cover. We cannot operate here without being spotted. They are already beginning to coordinate their attacks with surface ships. It's only a matter of time before they become effective."

"Is that what naval command is instructing us?"

"No, that's what I'm instructing us. Those are my orders."

"Ah, I see sir." Grudziński looked puzzled. "Shall I radio command and inform them of our change?"

"No, that is not what I have ordered, we will inform them when we arrive at our new position."

"But sir?"

"See to it that Mokrski plots us a course to Gotland and we can start to make our way tonight. Inform me when the course has been set. You are now dismissed."

"Aye, sir."

With that Grudziński returned to the control room, while the captain locked himself in his cabin.

I better be quick to finish these forward panels, Foterek will have to know about our change in patrol. I thought.

When Grudziński returned to the control room, Piasecki raised the periscope to make his periodic observation. This time he spotted something.

"Sir, German aircraft at two, two, zero degrees, heading about fifty degrees northeast. Range is five or six kilometers. I advise that we head for deep water and dive."

Grudziński alerted the captain, who was quickly on deck. "Let me have a look," the captain said as he nudged Piasecki aside. "What's our heading, Piasecki?"

"Two, seven, zero degrees," Grudziński replied.

"I asked Piasecki."

"Sir, I concur it's two, seven, zero degrees," Piasecki responded.

"What's our speed?"

Everyone looked at Piasecki for the answer.

"Three knots, sir."

"Sea depth?"

Again, heads turned towards Piasecki.

"Sixty meters, sir."

"OK, down periscope and take her down to forty-five meters," the captain ordered. "See what I mean about those German planes?"

"Helm, turn to starboard," the captain ordered, "heading, three, six, zero."

We were still diving down and leaning into the turn at the same time, a little like a funfair ride. As we completed the turn we leveled off with the announcement of, "Forty-five meters sir," followed by "turn completed."

"Sonar, anything to report?" the captain asked.

"No splashes, sir."

"Propellers?"

"Only very distant, sir."

Those moments waiting for sonar to announce the splashes of depth charges entering the water could seem like an eternity. All eyes looked upwards as if we could see the aircraft through the steel hull. Everyone held their breath but nothing came.

"Maybe they didn't see us," Grudziński said. "They were more than five kilometers from us."

"And they weren't changing course," Piasecki added.

"We wait down here, slow and steady for five minutes," the captain said, "then we'll go have a look."

I was in the gangway just forward of the control room. I could almost hear the clock ticking as those five minutes passed.

Eventually, the captain made the decision. "Piasecki, take her up to periscope depth."

"Aye, sir."

"Keep her slow at three knots, right rudder, steer course ninety degrees. I want you and Grudziński to keep a constant watch for enemy sightings."

When we raised the periscope, Grudziński had a good look around. "Nothing to report sir, nothing in view."

"Good," the captain acknowledged. "Keep me informed, I'll be in my cabin."

After the captain had left, Piasecki said, "Well, at least we're active on station instead of sitting on the bottom."

Grudziński leaned in close and whispered to Piasecki, "Lieutenant, can I have a word with you in the radio room?"

Kotecki was in the radio room when they got there.

"Kotecki, will you excuse us for a moment?" Grudziński instructed.

"Er, aye sir. I'm going off duty anyway, I've filed my reports."

"OK, Kotecki."

There wasn't a door to close but this was the most private they could get.

"Piasecki, the captain has just ordered me to ask Mokrski to plot a course to a new patrol area."

"So?"

"So he wants me to plot a course north to Gotland."

"Well, if those are the orders then that's what we must do."

"Yes, but those are the captain's orders; they are NOT Naval Command orders."

"Are you sure?"

"The captain was very clear about that."

"Well, we should then radio Naval Command and request permission or at least inform them of our change."

"The captain was very clear about that; he forbade me to send a signal to Naval Command."

"What? That's not like the captain, are you sure about this?"

"I'm very sure because the captain was very specific. He says it's too dangerous to remain here."

"Well that's certainly true, we're getting squeezed out of here. Those damn aircraft are nothing but trouble."

"But what should we do?" Grudziński asked in despair.

"Well, I don't know. You're second-in-command so it's your decision. But what other information do we have? Why is the captain doing this?"

"Well, from what I've heard, the Wilk and the Rys are already patrolling up north. I guess that the captain wishes to join them but I think we will be in conflict with their operational area."

"Our captain and Captain Krawczyk of the Wilk were talking yesterday. Maybe they agreed to coordinate their efforts?"

"There's no evidence of that. In fact, from what was heard between them, our captain was dismissive of Krawczyk's willingness to fight. Also, now he wants to head for Gotland. That's too far north to be effective."

"Gotland?"

"Yes, pretty much all we can do up there is go fishing!"

"Hm, well, all we can do at the moment is follow his orders."

"Well I wanted your opinion, because I thought you'd have some idea what was in his mind, but it looks like we're both confused. So I'll get 'the Kid' to plot a course for us because the captain wants to start tonight under cover of darkness."

"OK, number two – we're in your hands," Piasecki said, with a nod.

4   Gotland

Ship's Log entered by: Captain Henry Kłoczkowski
Date: September 8, 1939
Location: South of Hel Peninsula, bay of Gdańsk
Entry: We continue to hide in the shallow western reaches of the bay of Gdańsk. This is a dangerous location for a submarine. I am considering alternative locations for patrol. I am experiencing increased discomfort in my stomach. We don't have a ship's doctor or any real medication on board. I am considering alternatives for my health.

All was quiet and uneventful that afternoon. We were sitting on the bottom of the bay, as we had done many times before. The boat was tilted slightly to port as we sat on the uneven seabed. I had finished all the lose panels but Warrant Officer Joseph Stelmaszyk told me to help Torpedo man Stanley Uliczny with some routine maintenance in the forward torpedo room.

"What's wrong with you?" Stanley asked, "You seem nervous."

"I just need to get back to my engines." I said.

When we finished, Stelmaszyk, ordered me back to the engine room. I couldn't gather my tools quick enough and head aft to tell Foterek about the patrol changes.

I was getting used to all this walking around on a tilting floor. I no longer felt like a drunkard. Even when I carried my tools I was now able to move swiftly through the boat.

As I passed through the control room, 'the Kid' was busy with Grudziński at the chart table, working out some sort of course.

'The Kid', or Lieutenant Marian Mokrski, was nicknamed that because he was short, skinny, and resembled a child. He had a degree in mathematics so he was a smart cookie but most of all he thrilled in the calculations of navigation. When he was bored, he would sit for hours and just look at the charts, or any map he could get his hands on. The Kid understood the intricate details of any map and what it represented. You and I may know how to orient ourselves using a map, but this kid knew everything hidden in the details.

It seemed that Grudziński had already asked him to plot a course somewhere, so I asked, "Are we going somewhere?"

"Ah, Blackie," Grudziński said, "have you finished your maintenance?"

"Aye, sir."

"OK, good work. Now return to your station with Foterek, you may be needed there."

"Aye, sir. Will we be making way soon?"

"You're dismissed Blackie, now off you go." That was all Grudziński said before turning his attention back to the charts.

For me, that spoke volumes. Grudziński and the Kid looking at the charts told me something was being worked out. Ordering me back to the engine room said we were going to be underway very soon.

I reported back to the engine room and told Foterek what I had heard in the wardroom.

"So, we're changing location, but where? Gotland is a big island." he said.

"No, I don't know exactly where, but I did see Grudziński and Mokrski looking at a chart."

"Did you at least see what the chart was?"

"There were a few charts on the table, Gdańsk bay was on top, but then the Kid pulled out a chart of the Baltic Sea."

"Ah, maybe the Kid was trying to show you something?"

"Yes, maybe he was!" I exclaimed. "He did pull out the chart as if he was showing it to me! When he lay his hand on the chart his finger seemed to point to the southern point of Gotland."

Foterek grabbed my shoulder. "There you go, boy! I think we're going on a hunt! That southern point is probably a good place to ambush German merchant ships heading home from northern Sweden. It's about time we sunk some Nazis! Those will be rich hunting grounds!" Foterek thumped the air with his fist, "When we run out of torpedoes, we can retreat to Sweden!" Foterek then started issuing orders. "Check the pressure in the reserve air tanks, and make sure the compressor is primed and ready."

'Aye, sir," I replied.

"What is the battery charge?" Foterek shouted.

"Seventy-one percent," Petty Officer Henry Rebizant answered from the back of the engine room.

"What's the status of the electric motors?" Foterek continued.

Henry Rebizant, or Rebi, as we called him, was our electrician, so he always kept his eye on the batteries and electric motors.

"Ready to engage electric motors, whenever you are," he said.

Since we were sitting on the seabed, the compressor would be needed to blow us off the bottom. We would have to use the electric motors only, and we needed enough battery charge to at least drive us back to the surface. Once we attained neutral buoyancy, provided we were moving forward, we could use the dive planes to fly like a fish through the water.

With everything checked and double-checked we waited.

Then we waited some more.

"What was all that rush for?" I asked.

That's when the EOT or Engine Order Telegraph rang, indicating an order for the engines. The EOT was set to 'Standby', indicating a new order for the engines would be issued soon. Foterek then began issuing orders to prepare the electric motors for operation.

Soon after we heard the ballast tanks being blown. We began to sway to-and-fro as the sub freed itself from the muddy bottom and began to float to the surface. The Orzeł was once again a floating fish.

I checked the time. It was 18:45, so the sun would have set and darkness would soon be coming down.

"Looks like we're on the move for our hunt," I called across to Foterek.

"Oh, you think so? And here I am thinking we are going to the theatre."

"Well, who knows, maybe the captain wants to see the ballet?"

"No, we do the ballet every morning with those German aircraft, I think we're off to a nice restaurant for dinner. We will finish off the evening with some nice vodka and some very pretty girls to sing us some songs."

"Now you're talking Foterek, if that's your order for the day then I will do my duty."

The EOT then rang again, while the control room placed it into 'Ahead Slow'.

Foterek answered on the EOT to confirm that we would be engaging engines.

Immediately after the RPM indicator set to move us ahead at about three knots.

"Engage engines," Foterek ordered.

The electric motors were started and revved up to the requested speed. As the submarine began to move forward, Foterek turned to me and said, "Well Blackie here we go, let's hope some pretty mermaids can guide our way."

In the control room, the captain had been shown the course and was overseeing the operation. He ordered the Orzeł to slowly maneuver up to periscope depth.

"Up periscope," he ordered.

Catching the handles as the periscope was raised, the captain made a quick circular scan for any threats. He then scanned more slowly, looking around twice, before saying, "Grudziński, I need a second set of eyes on the periscope."

"Aye, sir."

Grudziński took his turn on the periscope scanning for any threats. He changed magnification and scanned the sky for aircraft.

"All clear," he eventually reported.

"Good," the captain confirmed, "now down periscope."

As the periscope was lowered, the captain winced and leaned against the chart table. The Kid had to dodge out of his way.

"Are you OK sir?" Grudziński asked.

"Do I look like I'm OK?"

Piasecki stepped forward. "Sir, what are your orders?"

"Take her to the surface, we need to charge batteries. Keep our surface speed at twelve knots and maintain the Kid's course. I'll be in my cabin, call me when we approach the Baltic Sea."

In the darkness of early evening, Grudziński brought the Orzeł up to the surface. He immediately dispatched four lookouts to the conning tower. Progress out of the bay towards the Baltic was slow but steady. Everyone in the control room kept silent as they held their attention on the course ahead.

Grudziński kept station on the bridge, while Piasecki kept watch in the control room.

Several uneventful hours passed before the radio operator, Chief Petty Officer Kotecki, came into the control room. "Sir, I've received a message from Commander Mohuczy of the Polish naval forces in Hel." He handed a message to Lieutenant Piasecki.

Piasecki read the message. "Oh crap," he muttered, "I have to pass this up to Grudziński." He began climbing up to the bridge.

Moments later, Lieutenant Grudziński climbed down from the bridge and went to the captain's quarters.

"Hey, Kotecki," the helmsman asked, "What did it say?"

"It said, we are to maintain our patrol to the west of Gdańsk."

"Oh crap," the helmsman said.

Piasecki came down the ladder from the bridge above.

"Sir?" asked the helmsman.

"Yes?"

"Are we to change course"

"Negative, we maintain current course and speed until the captain orders otherwise."

"Aye, sir."

As we waited in the control room, Piasecki asked, *"Where the hell is the captain?"*

It was some time before the captain returned to the control room with Grudziński following behind, looking frustrated.

Piasecki was the first to ask the question. "Sir, do you want any course change?"

The captain sighed, holding his hand on his stomach. "No Piasecki, we will maintain our current course and heading, as set by the Kid. What I want you to do is to take her down to periscope depth. We need to maintain stealth as we head into the Baltic."

"Aye, sir."

Sounding the dive alarm, Lieutenant Piasecki ordered the lookouts on the conning tower to come down, followed by the remaining officers on the bridge.

As everyone was manning their stations ready for the dive, Piasecki ordered to pressurize the boat. With that order, the lights on the Christmas tree went to green one by one, showing that all vents and flood valves were closed.

"Barometer steady sir," the midshipman called out.

"Blow ballast tanks three and four," Grudziński ordered. "Dive planes 20 degrees." He kept his eye on the depth gauge and just before the Orzeł reached periscope depth, he issued the order to level out. "Dive planes level." And the ship glided into level sailing.

"Keep her at 5 knots," the captain stated.

Piasecki then rang the engine order telegraph to half speed and set the RPM indicator.

"Maintaining course sir, we are at periscope depth," Piasecki said.

Grudziński just stood there with his arms folded.

The captain waited.

That's when the first noise was heard. It started at the bow and progressed the entire length of the ship along the port side. What was surprising about this noise is it wasn't a scraping, it was a beating like a hammer. It was as if someone was banging hard all along the side of our sub.

"What the hell is that?" the helmsman asked.

The captain yelled, "Helm! Hard to Port!" as he sounded the collision alarm.

———

In the engine room, when the diesel engines are running, you can't hear anyone speak. When we were running on the surface, we had to use sign language to communicate. The electric motors were much quieter, so we heard the noise as it banged alone the aft of our hull.

"Shit!" Foterek exclaimed.

"What the hell was that?" I asked

"We're in a minefield!" Foterek shouted.

We felt the Orzeł heave to port. A moment later he then set the Engine Telegraph to 'All Stop'.

"All stop! All stop!" Foterek shouted.

Silence fell as the engines came to a stop.

"What the hell was that that banging?" I demanded.

"That rattling on our port side was the anchor cable of a sea mine," Foterek answered, looking around anxiously. "There are probably sea waves above, so the anchor cable is swaying from side to side, up and down, loosening and tightening the cable – which makes that banging. We steered away from that one, but we must be careful now. Two things can happen – we either hit a mine directly head-on, or we catch a mooring cable as we move forward and drag the mine down onto our heads. Either way, we die."

"Can we reverse out?" I asked.

"No way," Foterek replied. "It's impossible to say if this is the edge of the minefield and the first one or have passed several mines and we are in the middle. Even if we went backward, the propellers are more likely to tangle in the mooring cables, and then we'd be in real trouble."

"So what do we do?"

"We pray that the captain knows what he's doing!"

"Mokrski!" the captain growled, "Is this on your charts?"

"No sir, it is probably a German minefield."

"If that is so, then it's probably here to trap us in the bay."

"Which means what sir?" Piasecki asked.

"That means it will be wide and therefore difficult to get around it. But it's probably not too deep, so we have to move forward very, very carefully," the captain replied.

So forward we went and we went very slowly. When we encountered a scrape on the port side, we steered to port which would swing us off the cable. When we encountered a scrape on the starboard side, we steered to starboard. On each turn, the captain would instruct which way to turn and this would be confirmed by the helmsman as he performed the turn. The Kid would note each change in course as we proceeded.

And so we went, zig-zagging slowly through the water, singing our song of new directions.

After a whole hour of tense crawling, the scraping seemed to stop. "I've counted nine mines that we scraped past," Grudziński said.

"Me too," the captain agreed. "That's probably the breadth of this field. Increase speed to 5 knots."

Grudziński then rang the engine telegraph but kept it at 'Ahead Slow'. He then changed the RPM dial to increase the speed. Accompanied by the increase in the distant electric hum, we continued in a straight line. If anything, the quicker pace increased the tension as nobody was sure we were clear of the minefield yet.

After about ten more minutes, the captain asked, "Mokrski, what's our current position and heading?"

"Our heading is three, three, five degrees. Given all those course changes, I calculate our position to be fifty-four degrees, thirty-three minutes north by nineteen degrees, eight minutes east. That puts us about seven kilometers off course."

"What about getting back on course?"

"I would recommend heading northwest three, six, zero degrees for five kilometers, just to make sure we clear that field. Straight north to clear the bay. We can then easily regain our original course."

"OK Grudziński, follow Mokrski's recommendation. Take her up to the surface to charge batteries. I'll be in my cabin. Keep me informed of any changes."

"Aye Captain," Grudziński confirmed. And with that, the captain was gone.

Once on the surface, the Orzeł proceeded more quickly. Instead of the five knots we were doing when submerged, we increased our speed to twelve knots. We could have done more but the captain clearly stated that we should head north in stealth. So Grudziński kept to mid-speed. This would reduce the noise of our propellers, so any German destroyers who might have been scanning the sea would have less chance to hear us.

Grudziński also ordered four lookouts onto the conning tower, so that each had a quarter of the horizon to scan. This helped to focus their attention on a narrow section of the sky and horizon. In addition, Grudziński would attend to these men on the tower every twenty minutes.

He did this for several reasons:

First, it was what an officer does – give his men confidence and reassure them that they are doing well by protecting the ship.

Secondly, to reassure himself that there was no immediate threat that his men could have missed.

Thirdly, make sure they were not just enjoying the fresh air and smoking cigarettes.

The dawn's early light was barely rising in the east, the brightest of stars were still above our heads. The North Star was still visible beyond our bow as we sailed through a calm Baltic. We began to feel safe and more secure. Perhaps the decision of Klocz, our captain, had been a wise one. If we had stayed in the bay of Gdańsk, we would be starting the ballet of avoiding planes and ships by now. We started to feel comfortable.

The last of the smokers had long since finished and gone below as we cruised north. But as in any war, peacefulness is very short-lived.

"Spotter planes south, southeast!" came a call from the conning tower.

"Distance? Heading?" Piasecki demanded.

"Approximately forty degrees off to starboard stern. Heading due west."

"They are flying from Prussia, probably patrolling the bay," Piasecki advised.

"Agreed," Grudziński said. "Sonar! Any propellers?"

"Nothing sir, at least nothing within range, only vague echoes."

"OK, some ship is out there but not close by. Something is up there in the air, but they haven't spotted us yet."

"Sir, air targets are separating." Came the call from the observers in the conning tower. "One target heading southwest, second target heading northwest."

Piasecki asked, "What do you think Grudziński?"

"Well, one is turning to patrol the bay. The other is turning to patrol the entrance to the north. That flyer will be on us in minutes."

"Full speed ahead!" Grudziński commanded while he set the EOT to 'Full Ahead'.

"We'll make as much distance as we can into the Baltic before we have to maneuver to escape that patrol. We have to be ready to dive at a moment's notice. Piasecki, go notify the captain." After that, Grudziński ordered three of the four lookouts on the conning tower back into the sub, leaving one above to track the airplane's progress. One man could get back into the sub and secure the hatches quicker than four could.

Grudziński issued orders to prepare the crew to dive. Moments later two things happened: Captain Kłoczkowski arrived in the control room followed by Piasecki, then the lookout shouts through the voice pipe reported, "Aircraft has turned and is heading our way."

Piasecki picked up the voice pipe. "What's its bearing and distance?"

"About ten degrees off to starboard stern, and about twenty kilometers and closing," came the reply.

"Captain, what are your orders?" Grudziński asked.

"Helm, what's our speed and heading?" Kłoczkowski asked.

"Twenty-nine knots, heading three, six, zero degrees."

"Good," Kłoczkowski nodded, "we'll stay on the surface for now. Piasecki, get the lookout to report when the plane is ten kilometers away."

"Sir, at this speed, we're creating a wake that is visible for them to see," Grudziński said.

"Yes, but we're charging our batteries while we run."

"Sir, I hear fast propellers," Bosun Kozowy reported.

"How many and where?" Kłoczkowski asked.

Kozowy pressed his headphones closer to his ears and adjusted knobs on his sonar console. "There are two," he said, "the first is at one, nine, five degrees, and the second is at two, five, five degrees. Both are closing fast."

"What's their range?" Kłoczkowski asked, now looking annoyed.

"I can't say exactly, there's a lot of noise at this speed, but less than eight kilometers."

"Why the hell didn't you hear them earlier?"

"They were distant and running slowly, sir. They only just increased speed and started heading towards us."

Kłoczkowski started thinking out loud. "If they are eight kilometers, and they're probably doing twenty-five knots, they should reach us in about…" he trailed off as he tried to work out the calculation in his head.

"About ten minutes, sir," Lieutenant Mokrski chimed in.

"Yes, we have ten minutes." Kłoczkowski then turned to face Grudziński. "There you see, it doesn't matter how big our wake is. That aircraft has already seen us, and called for support."

A moment later the voice pipe whistled as the lookout called down. Piasecki picked up and listened.

"Sir, the lookout reports that the aircraft range is ten kilometers."

"OK," Kłoczkowski said, "bring that lookout below. Sound the dive alarm. What's the sea depth?"

"110 meters," Kozowy reported above the alarm.

As the lookout dropped down into the control room, Grudziński asked, "All hatches sealed?"

"Aye, sir, all hatches are sealed."

The midshipman reported, "I have all green lights, the barometer is steady, the ship is sealed."

"Good work, men," Kłoczkowski said. "Take us down to sixty meters. Dive planes twenty degrees, flood tanks three, four, and five. Speed three knots, we need to run quietly."

As the Orzeł descended into the Baltic Sea, all eyes were on the depth gauge. When we reached fifty meters, Kłoczkowski said, "Helm, dive planes ten degrees, level out slowly."

At the target depth of sixty meters, Kłoczkowski then said, "Helm, steer zero, nine, zero."

"Aye, sir, steering zero, nine, zero."

"What's our sea depth?" Kłoczkowski asked.

"Too deep to hide on the bottom, sir!" Grudziński answered.

With a scouring look at Grudziński, Kłoczkowski said, "That is not what I asked! What is the sea depth?"

"110 meters, sir," Bosun Kozowy answered, looking puzzled.

Kłoczkowski kept his gaze on Lieutenant Grudziński. "In future Panienka, answer the question or remain silent."

"Aye, sir."

Kozowy looked at Grudziński questioningly.

Grudziński made a quiet, dismissive gesture towards Bosun Kozowy. The captain's second request for sea depth could be explained by noise in the control room, a simple request for clarification. The captain's public insult to his second lieutenant was a little more difficult to explain.

"Splashes, sir, one at two, nine, zero, degrees, and the second at two, four, zero," Kozowy announced.

"Distance?" Kłoczkowski demanded.

Bosun Kozowy was scribbling numbers on paper, before he said, "About two kilometers, sir."

"Shit!" Kłoczkowski swore as he wiped the sweat dripping into his eyes.

Two explosions detonated behind us, too distant to cause damage, but sounding a warning of more depth charges to come.

"They must be running faster than I calculated," Kłoczkowski mumbled to himself.

"Propellers closing fast, sir!" Kozowy announced.

"Or, we're running slower than we should," Lieutenant Mokrski said. "Either way, that changes the calculation."

Captain Kłoczkowski pointed a stern finger at Mokrski.

Grudziński became worried that his captain would reprimand the Kid. "Orders, sir?" Grudziński asked.

"What?" Kłoczkowski turned towards Grudziński with a puzzled look.

"What are your orders?"

Captain Henry Kłoczkowski looked around the control room as if searching for answers. Wagging his finger, he began to tap his head. "We need to change the calculation!" Stepping towards the Engine Telegraph, he rang it from slow ahead to full speed ahead.

Almost immediately, the humming sound of the electric motors revving up and filled the Orzeł. Accelerating to her maximum, she moved at a submerged speed of seven knots.

"Let's hold this speed for a moment or two," the captain mumbled.

The war seemed to be catching up to the Orzeł, as our German pursuers chased us from behind. The Orzeł was hemmed into a narrow chase, with both MTBs following on both flanks. Running at full speed, even the quiet electric engines of the Orzeł made it easy for the torpedo boats to use passive sonar, to triangulate onto our position. Running on the surface, these German MTBs could move fast, their intention was to get above the submarine and drop depth charges onto us.

Death would be swift.

"More plashes, sir! They're almost alongside us! Three, two, zero, degrees, and two, one, zero."

Moments later, two more explosions. This time shaking the Orzeł and its crew to the bone.

"Now! I have to change gear!" Captain Kłoczkowski shouted as he rang the Engine Telegraph to 'All Stop'. The electric motors revved down to zero.

As the engines became quiet, Kłoczkowski then shouted to the helmsman, "Hard to port! Steer, three, six, zero!"

Bosun Dabrowski confirmed the heading and the Orzeł turned north, away from its eastward path.

When the turn was completed, Captain Kłoczkowski said almost to himself, "We now run silent, dead silent."

Bosun Kozowy broke the relative silence, "Propeller approaching sir, two, eight, zero."

"Distance?"

"Very close, sir, almost on top of us."

We all froze, if this torpedo boat dropped a depth charge now, it would be right on our heads. Captain Kłoczkowski raised his eyes toward the ceiling of the control room. "Shit! God help us!" was all he could say.

Bosun Kozowy pressed his earphones tighter with his hands, listening intently to the traffic on the surface. "She's passing us, sir. Bearing one, eight, zero, but still very close."

This boat passed behind us, but too close for comfort, another one lurking further south.

"I detect a splash, two, zero, zero."

"How close?"

Captain Kłoczkowski didn't need to wait for an answer, as an explosion boomed aft of the Orzeł. The blast jolted the boat forward, knocking everyone backward. As the hole in the water closed like a clap of thunder, a second shockwave juddered the Orzeł backward. Anyone who was left standing was now pushed forwards. This double kick left everyone on the Orzeł in a daze.

Boson Kozowy, thrown from his desk, scrambled on his knees back to his sonar station.

Helmsman Dabrowski winded himself on the wheel, gasping for breath.

Lieutenant Mokrski fell across the control room floor, laid flat on his face.

Captain Kłoczkowski lay prostrate at the base of the periscope. "Holy shit!"

Lieutenant Grudziński pushed himself off the floor. "Damage? We need a damage report!"

A second explosion, this time slightly further away, detonated aft. This wasn't as powerful but if you're trying to get up off the floor, the additional shaking and feeling of concussion does not help.

"What's our speed?" Captain Kłoczkowski asked as he scrambled to his feet.

As Helmsman Dabrowski struggled to regain his breath, Lieutenant Grudziński said, "Sir, more importantly, we need to see if we sustained any damage."

Dabrowski then coughed a reply, "Two knots, sir, drifting forward."

"You're right Grudziński," the captain said, holding onto the periscope column. "Check if we have any damage."

As Grudziński busied himself, hailing the different compartments through the voice pipes, Dabrowski asked, "Sir? Do you have any orders?"

"No, we'll hold our course, until we drift to a stop," Kłoczkowski said.

Another explosion, although this time distant and muffled, was enough to rattle already frayed nerves.

"What was that?" Kłoczkowski demanded.

"That was the second torpedo boat, further south," Kozowy replied. "One. Seven zero degrees."

Seconds later a second explosion, also distant and muffled.

"Ah!" Kłoczkowski's eyes widened with glee, "You see? I fooled them!"

"Sir?" Kozowy looked puzzled.

"They didn't hear us turn!" Kozowy patted the periscope column. "They're searching our original course, dropping depth charges in pairs. The boat that went over our heads was a lucky shot, in a minute he'll drop two more charges."

Moments later another depth charge exploded nearby. This was loud but not close enough to cause damage. A second blast followed, at about the same distance.

"You see?" Captain Kłoczkowski now let go of the periscope column, standing firmly on the deck. "They'll continue to search in that eastward pattern while we slowly drift north. You see? Good old Kłoczkowski, I'm the Key to the Sea[1]!"

"Sir," Lieutenant Grudziński interrupted, "I have no reports of damage, but there are some injuries, although nothing serious."

Kłoczkowski looked gratefully at Grudziński. "Very good Lieutenant."

The torpedo boats continued east, dropping their deadly charges as they went. They did eventually come about, backtracking to where they thought their prey was hiding. As they did so, they continued dropping a spread of depth

---

[1] Kłoczkowski's nickname was Klocz, meaning "key". Translation "Klucz do morza"

charges. As they headed back west towards the drifting Orzeł, they crisscrossed their paths, dropping their charges as widely as they could.

As Bosun Kozowy called out the closing range of the boats, the crew began to cringe with fear. One of the boats would soon pass overhead and possibly drop a charge right on top of the Orzeł. Kozowy held his headphones tightly to his ear. Lieutenant Mokrski held tight with both hands on his chart table. Captain Kłoczkowski reached back to hold the periscope column. Other crewmen in the Orzeł were unaware of the impending doom and could only trust that the previous danger had safely passed.

One of the torpedo boats was once again almost above the Orzeł. It didn't matter if they detected their intended prey or not, they would now drop their charges and it would be up to chance if the Orzeł was hit.

The propellers were close and could be heard throughout the boat. Everyone looked up at the ceiling as if watching the passing torpedo boat. It didn't matter what Kozowy read from his sonar, everyone waited for the splash of depth charges.

Just then a loud PING was heard, as the hunters overhead used their active sonar to search for a target.

"Shit! They've found us!" cried Lieutenant Mokrski.

"I don't think so," Grudziński said.

"The Lieutenant's right," Kozowy said, "our echo would be almost immediate and it would sound like the original PING."

"So they can't see us?" Mokrski asked.

"Wait." Grudziński held his finger to his lips.

"That's right men, wait for them to pass," Kłoczkowski said.

Moments passed, but we heard no explosions.

"Propellers slowing, sir," Kozowy announced.

Grudziński closed his eyes, held his head back, and breathed a deep sigh.

"What does that mean?" Mokrski asked.

"It means we're safe," Kłoczkowski said. "They think we are sunk, or not worth looking for. We just have to wait for them to pass. They have throttled down to cruising speed."

The captain then leaned heavily on the periscope column, sighing deeply as he wrapped his left arm wrapped around it. He wiped his brow with his right hand before clutching his stomach. In this way, he seemed to display not only tiredness but some physical discomfort.

The helmsman was concerned and asked again, "Sir?" All eyes in the control room were now on the captain.

"I'll be fine," Kłoczkowski eventually replied. "It's probably just a little gas, breakfast was a bit heavy for my liking."

"Sir? Perhaps you should take a break?" Grudziński asked the captain. "They seem to have broken off the attack, I can continue on our course while you have a rest."

"That's a good idea, Grudziński. I'll be in my quarters, let me know if anything happens."

"Aye, sir."

As the captain headed for his room and as he passed through the watertight hatch, Grudziński could hear him break wind. All eyes were now on Grudziński who turned to face the men at their stations. Grudziński needed them to focus on the situation, so began by issuing commands. "Helmsman, what's our heading?"

"Three, six, zero, sir."

"What's our speed?"

"Drifting, sir."

"What's our depth?"

"Sixty meters sir."

"Sonar, do you hear any propellers?"

"They are getting further away, sir."

"Good. We'll hold this position for now.

A collective "Aye sir" echoed around the room.

"Sonar, keep me informed of their distance."

"Aye, sir."

"We'll continue north when they get far enough away. In the meantime, stay alert."

"Aye, sir."

"Sir?" Kozowy asked, "What's wrong with the captain?"

"This is a hard time for all of us," Grudziński said, "the captain especially. He needs to have a break, he'll be back on his feet soon enough."

———

When the sub was underway, the noise in the engine room was so great that it was impossible to talk. The only voice you could understand was a shouted '*Hey*' to get attention, or '*Aye*', to confirm. So hand signals were the only way to communicate. This was fine to get the work done; we had hand signals for everything – check oil, check the temperature, check electrics, check this, check that. The ringing of the Engine Order Telegraph could be heard, but it was a visual display that we followed. There were two voice pipes, one to the control room, and one to the bridge. A loud whistle would alert us that we needed to talk. We could easily hear what was said by cupping the cone to our ear, and then we could reply by placing the cone over our mouth. If you wanted to chat to your workmates like, '*Hey have you read any good books lately?*' forget it, all you could do in the noisy engine room was work.

Everyone onboard had a hard job to do, and we all had to do it in cramped conditions. Everyone was in the dark during an attack run or if we are evading depth charges. What set the engineers apart was they couldn't talk to each other, the only human feelings they could convey being through the eyes. When men can speak, they will make jokes like '*Ha that was a close one.*' Our eyes are the honest windows into the soul. Engineers get to know each other pretty well that way.

That is why we enjoyed our rest breaks more than anyone else on board.

As I came off duty, I saw Foterek sitting in the mess room. There were six tables, each with a two-person bench on either side. All the tables were occupied with off-duty men who were either eating or playing card games. Foterek was at a side table, using the bench as a couch, leaning with his back against the ship's hull, elbow on the table, and feet stretched forward on the bench.

Moving towards him I said, "Hey boss." He motioned for me to sit with him at the table on the adjacent bench. I stretched out like him with my back against the hull, and one leg resting on the bench. We sat in silence for a few moments as we acclimatized to the relative quiet in the mess room.

We were joined at our table by two more engineers also coming off duty, Able seaman Jan Szal and Able seaman Józef Jarmuż. Foterek and I both moved our legs obligingly, allowing them to sit with us at the table. Any time that one had, to stretch and take space, was a luxury, but it never lasted long. There is no such thing as spare space on a submarine.

Józef asked, "Does anyone know what has been happening? We've been dodging depth charges all day."

"We've been running and hiding," I said, "that's what submarines do."

"So where are we going now?" Jan asked.

"We're heading north again," Foterek said, rubbing his tired eyes.

"What is up north?" Jan continued asking, "Why are we heading there?"

"I don't know," I said, "but since the captain says, we have to follow."

Foterek then sat up straight, "I think the captain has a plan," he said. "He is going there for two reasons. First, there are fewer German aircraft to hunt us. Second, there are supply routes from northern Sweden which feed German industry. If we can stop that supply then we can hurt Germany."

"That makes sense," said Jan.

"I heard that the captain isn't feeling well," Józef said.

"He'll be fine," Foterek said. "He's our captain, and he'll see us through this."

Quartermaster Piegza, also known as Freckles, poked his head through the serving hatch and shouted, "Hey you oilskins, are you just going to sit there wasting space? Or are you going to be paying customers?"

That seemed to shake us out of our solemn glaze and back into the present.

Jozef was the first to speak up. "I think we are hungry enough to eat some slop!"

"Slop?" Freckles retorted, "The only slop I know comes out of the engine room!"

"Hey!" Foterek shouted, "before we dine, we need a bottle of your finest Champagne!"

"Phooey." Freckles retracted his head back into the galley. Moments later he appeared from around the corner with a towel draped across his arm daintily prancing like a French waiter. In one hand he carried four shot glasses and in the other a bottle of Polish Vodka.

"My dear ladies," he said, "we are so pleased you can attend our fine establishment."

As he poured out four shots of vodka he continued. "There is one question I must ask."

"Oh, what's that?" Jan asked.

"Have you washed your hands? Lord knows who or what you have been playing with today."

Guffaws rang around the mess room at the insinuation.

"For that, you can leave the bottle," Foterek said.

"Oh, I think not. Captain's orders you know, only two shots per person per day."

"What do you get Freckles? Two bottles a day?"

"Wouldn't you like to know?" he said as he bowed and pretended to stagger like a drunk back to the galley.

After the laughter in the mess room had died down we turned towards our drinks, eyeing them lovingly.

We held our glasses up, playfully sticking out our little pinkies.

"Finest Champagne," said Jan, eyeing it lovingly.

"Wonderful vintage," said Jozef, enjoying its aroma.

"The brandy of life," I said, with a wink and a grin.

"Polish Vodka!" Foterek announced proudly.

"Na zdrowie!" We all shouted as we drank the shot down in one.

Freckles passed our plates of food through the serving hatch. There was never much room to move, so Jan picked them up, placing them on our table. We ate with gusto. Breaded chicken breast with boiled cabbage and potatoes. The bread he served was getting old and slightly stale, but Freckles toasted it so it didn't matter. It may not have been the finest cuisine, but anything that could clear the pallet from the stale smell of oil and diesel fumes was welcome. As we washed it all down with mugs of hot lemon tea, we relaxed and sank into conversation.

"So how's the captain?" Jan asked. "If he is ill, what is wrong with him?"

"I hear that he spends most of his time in his cabin," I said.

"Yeah, some say he could have Cholera," Jozef added. "That could explain his sickness."

"Where would he catch Cholera from? Foterek chided. "If he has anything, it'll be syphilis."

"Syphilis? Why do you say that about our captain?" Jan asked. "Syphilis drives you crazy, and he has maneuvered us admirably to escape the German bombers."

"I heard that he maneuvered admirably with the ladies in Holland when he was there," Foterek replied.

"What?" we all asked.

"Before the war, this sub was built in Holland, and Captain Kłoczkowski was sent there to oversee the construction. The rumors I heard say that he was involved in some shenanigans with some ladies of entertainment."

"Sounds like a 'stain' on his career," I said.

"So what of it?" Jozef asked. "He is a navy man after all!"

"Yes, but the navy didn't take kindly to whatever it was he got up to. It is said that he was destined for promotion to some big commission in Warsaw, but instead, he was kept as captain of this boat."

"So what do you know Blackie?" Foterek asked. "You are my eyes and ears on this ship, what do you know?"

"Well, I don't know much more than you guys. I've heard him complain about stomach problems, but no one says what it could be. He is on the bridge or in the control room only for short periods and leaves Panienka in charge. Most of the time he spends in his cabin."

Alex Kamecki was sat at the next table with his mates. They had all finished their breakfast as they were about to head to their watch for the day. Alex had overheard what we were saying and leaned over towards us.

"I don't think there's anything wrong with our captain other than flatulence. He is complaining about something but he is full of color and doesn't look sick at all."

"That's why I think it's probably Syphilis," Foterek said.

"I also hear that he eats just fine. The officer's mess is separate and he takes his food into his cabin to eat alone," Alex continued.

Alex's mates were also on the same watch, and their silence suggested no objection to anything he had said.

A group of men from the forward torpedo room chimed into our conversation.

"Don't talk about our captain like that. If he's sick then he's sick, that's all there is to it. He's a good captain, and he's kept us safe so far."

"Yeah, safe in Gotland, where we are heading. There is no war there," Alex replied.

"What are you saying? Our captain is a coward? That's good coming from you, isn't your nickname *'chicken'*?" he raised his voice.

"Maybe Mr. Torpedo man, but being scared is a healthy way of life. When it comes to it, I'm here shoulder to shoulder with everyone."

Suddenly both groups of men were standing, staring at each other. That's when Freckles appeared with a large frying pan in one hand and a big wooden spoon in the other.

Clanging the pan like a bell he said sternly, "Round one is over! If you men wish to continue, I suggest you do it outside. Preferably a hundred meters off the starboard bow!"

Both tables apologized to Freckles. Alex and his table moved out to go on watch, nodding apologies to the torpedo men as they left. The torpedo men nodded back. Arguments could not be sustained in such a small space, every crewman knew this. If any bad words were said, the air had to be cleared quickly before any trouble brewed.

Being on watch in the conning tower did have some benefits. Fresh sea air was the main one, but this could become a disadvantage, depending on the weather. The main duty of the men on watch was to keep an eye on the horizon and the sky. The Orzeł afforded space to four men who would concentrate on a quarter of the horizon. Armed only with binoculars, they had to alert the duty officer of any ship or aircraft that came into view. That officer would then decide what action to take, given the circumstances.

It was Wednesday evening, September 6th. The Orzeł was cruising north on the surface. It was cold and breezy but relatively calm. The lookout in the conning tower was exposed to the elements.

The front of the conning tower housed the bridge. It was there that the ship could be steered while on the surface.

Jan Grudziński stood on the bridge with the helmsman where they were protected from the elements. Forward- and side-facing windows gave them visibility. At the rear of the bridge was a podium, allowing a panoramic view for anyone standing up there.

Behind the bridge was the cigarette deck. This was an open space where the watchmen stood. Boson Alex Kamecki was beginning his usual night watch with his regular lookouts. Alex leaned his arms on the deck parapet, holding his binoculars to his eyes. Alex had to observe the western sector. "Christ, it's cold," he muttered.

At the front of the deck stood Edmund Lesniak, observing the northern sector. "At least it's calm," he said.

Stanley Uliczny observed the eastern sector, while Jan Torbus kept watch behind and to the south.

"What's that?" Edmund said.

"What's what?" they all asked while keeping watch on their sectors.

"Something has appeared on the horizon, approximately thirty degrees, moving west. Looks like a ship but I don't see any lights. It just came out from against the silhouette of the island."

Stanley trained his binoculars on that angle, searching for an object. "Yup, I see it," he confirmed.

"Yes I got it too," Alex said. "That's a surface vessel, so keep tracking it. Keep your eyes on the sky, in case they have air cover."

Alex blew the whistle through the voice pipe to speak to the duty officer.

"What is it?" Grudziński replied.

"Surface ship spotted thirty degrees heading west," Alex reported.

Immediately, Jan Grudziński popped his head up above the bridge. He gazed through binoculars for a while before his head disappeared below.

Moments later Grudziński came up the ladder to the conning tower. There wasn't a direct passage between the bridge and the watch deck in the conning tower, so he had to descend the ladder into the control room and climb back to the open deck. "Has anyone been able to identify her?" he asked.

"No sir, she's too distant and we can't make out her flag," Alex replied. "She does look like a merchant ship."

"Maybe she's the Bremen? That would be a fine prize for us," Stanley said.

"No, the Bremen is an ocean-going liner doing the Atlantic routes," Grudziński countered. "At best she'll be in Hamburg for protection."

Grudziński studied her some more through binoculars. Using the voice pipe, he orders the helmsman on the bridge to alter course towards the mystery ship.

The sub then turned to head towards the unidentified vessel.

Grudziński then called for the captain. "Captain Kłoczkowski is the only one on board who can order an attack. We need to get closer to identify her first. As we approach, keep a keen eye for other ships or aircraft."

With that, all four lookouts snapped back to their posts intently observing the sea and air. Adrenalin was beginning to build in their veins with the possibility of an attack run.

Captain Kłoczkowski seemed to take a long time to come to the tower. Victor Dabrowski was at the helm, looking through the forward portals. "Where's Grudziński?" the captain asked.

"Sir, he's on the podium behind us."

The captain pulled out a cigarette and lit it before climbing onto the podium.

Grudziński lowered his binoculars and saluted. "Ah, sir, it's good you are here."

"What is it?" he asked.

"Sir, there is an unidentified ship, 340 degrees north, northwest. I have altered our course to intercept. We await further orders," Grudziński reported.

"What? Let me see." The captain took the binoculars from Grudziński and looked towards the distant vessel. After a moment, he said, "That looks to me like the Bremen. Order the helm to resume our original course."

"But, sir, the Bremen is a Norwegian ship that does coastal runs."

"Yes, I know her routes and I recognize that to be the Bremen."

"But that looks too small to be the Bremen, and she would normally stay in the neutral waters of Sweden or

Norway, she would not venture out into the open Baltic – especially at wartime."

"Are you questioning my knowledge, Grudziński?"

"No sir, but shouldn't we look her up in the merchant identification book?"

"That would be a waste of time, I'm sure that she's the Bremen."

"Sir, I think we should at least get closer to investigate, it's more likely that she is a German ship."

"I have given you my instruction, now order the helm to resume our original course."

"But sir?"

"Now, Panienka!"

Grudziński paused, as he was surprised by being called this diminutive nickname. Then he said, "Aye sir."

Grudziński stepped down from the podium and back into the bridge to order the helm to resume the original course. The captain angrily flicked his cigarette into the sea before returning down to the control room.

On the cigarette deck behind the podium, the lookouts had heard the conversation.

"What the hell just happened there?" Edmund asked.

"I don't know," Alex answered, "but it's clear that Captain Kłoczkowski doesn't like Grudziński."

"Well that's obvious, calling him Panienka," Edmund continued, "but why are we running away? Like Grudziński says, we should at least investigate."

"I don't know." Alex replied. "And people call *me* the chicken."

5   Head for Tallinn

Ship's Log entered by: Captain Henry Kłoczkowski
Date: September 12, 1939
Location: Baltic Sea, south of Gotland
Entry: I am experiencing increasing abdominal pain, unsure what the problem is. I have decided to seek medical help in a neutral port.

"Sir, we are ready to surface," Lieutenant Andrey Piasecki told Grudziński.

Grudziński checked his watch. It was 8 pm, so it should already have been dark for nearly one hour. The Orzeł had been hiding on the bottom near the port of Visby on the northwest side of Gotland.

"Any surface traffic?" Grudziński asked.

"Negative sir, sonar reports all clear."

"OK, take her up to periscope depth so we can scan for aircraft."

"Aye, sir."

Lieutenant Piasecki ordered the middle ballast tanks blown and the Orzeł rose from the bottom. He signaled on the Engine Telegraph to continue ahead with a slow RPM. The helm was given a northerly heading, and as the Orzeł eased forward, Piasecki ordered the sub's bow to be pulled up twenty degrees.

As the Orzeł approached the periscope depth of thirty meters, the dive planes leveled out and Piasecki ordered the ballast tanks to be adjusted to neutral buoyancy.

"Up periscope," Piasecki commanded.

Alex, who was standing by to go on watch, engaged the periscope to rise to the surface. When it was extended, he stood aside and announced, "Periscope ready sir."

Grudziński grabbed the handles and started scanning the environment above. This was like a little dance. First, he would pirouette in a circle to quickly scan the horizon for ships. Then he'd proceed to a slower waltz as he repeated the horizon scan but this time for details. Then he would peer skyward, searching for aircraft.

"Down periscope," he ordered.

Alex did the reverse of his previous actions, powering the periscope down.

"Alex, prepare to go up top."

At that order, Alex readied himself to climb the ladder. He zipped up his coat, pulled his cap on tight, and checked his life jacket. He looked up and kept his gaze on the hatch above. Nervously holding his binoculars which hung around his neck, he readied himself to climb up to the watch tower above. The other lookouts waited just outside the entrance to the control room. If all was clear they would be ordered to follow Alex up top and take their positions on watch. However, if Alex spotted an enemy ship or aircraft, then he would have to alert the commander to perform an emergency dive. He would then only have seconds to get himself back down the hatch into the safety of the submarine. There was the danger that he would not be fast enough to descend. If this happened, he would be swept off the watch platform and drowned at sea.

Because Alex constantly complained about the dangers of war, and the constant threat of death, he was nicknamed 'the chicken'. On every one of his watches, Alex did not act a chicken. He stood shoulder to shoulder with every one of his shipmates, ensuring their safety to his best abilities.

"Surface," came Grudziński's simple order.

"Aye, sir," the control room confirmed.

"Forward planes up twenty degrees."

"Forward planes up twenty."

"Blow all ballast tanks."

"Ballast tanks blowing."

Everyone's ears began to pop as the Orzeł rose to the surface. Grudziński checked his stopwatch as they ascended. An odd noise seemed to come from the ballast tanks.

When they reached the surface, Grudziński ordered Alex up the ladder. Alex climbed the ladder, opening the watertight hatch. When he reached the platform above, he scanned the horizon and the air above for any threats. A few moments later he called down to the control room, "All clear on the surface."

Grudziński then ordered the other lookouts to climb up.

Like any sub commander, Grudziński always carried a stopwatch. You name it and a commander needs to time it, everything from diving to surfacing. From turning circles to firing torpedoes. Everything needs to be timed. Since there is no calculating machine on board, the commander needs to use the timings to work out variables the longhand way.

On this occasion, Grudziński noticed that it took ten seconds more to surface from periscope depth than usual.

"Yes sir, before you say anything, I have noticed the discrepancy since we left the bay," Lieutenant Piasecki said.

"So why haven't you raised the issue?"

"I did raise it with the captain but he wasn't concerned."

"Why the hell not?"

"I don't know but I did get Blackie to check out the compressor. He said to check it properly he would need to work on it when we reach port."

"What? Do we need to go to the dry dock?"

"No, not dry dock but he says it will take a day to disassemble it and fix whatever is wrong and then reassemble. If we do that at sea then we cannot submerge."

"What if it fails while we are submerged?"

"I did ask him that, and he says it's unlikely. He thinks he knows what the problem is and it was probably caused while we were being depth charged. He said it was probably blowback into the compressor pipes and valves, causing some minor blockages. Warrant Officer Foterek has confirmed this."

"Well this is a concern for me and we need to keep an eye on it. Pass the message to all duty officers and log it in the duty roster. We need to track the time for blowing the tanks. If the compressor gets worse we'll have to pull into a neutral port for repairs."

"Aye, sir."

"And get Blackie to check it daily."

"Aye, sir."

The next day, Grudziński sat in the wardroom finishing his breakfast.

Lieutenant Piasecki passed through on his way to the control room. "What's up Grudziński? Today's breakfast not to your liking?"

"The food is good," Grudziński smiled, "it's just too many thinks on my mind."

Piasecki patted Grudziński's shoulder, "We all worry about the news from Poland, the Germans seem too powerful for us, but we won't stop fighting, you know that. England and France have now declared war on Germany."

"Yes, they have," Grudziński agreed, "but when will they attack Germany? If they do, that would save us, but they better hurry up. I keep hearing on England's BBC radio, the words 'Phony War', because for them it is phony. Yet for Poland, this war was anything but phony. It seemed only a matter of time before Poland would be no more."

"I believe Poland can hold out until they get mobilized," Piasecki said. He then sat down opposite Grudziński. "I don't think that's all you are worried about, what else do you have on your mind?"

Grudziński pushed his breakfast plate to one side. "The Orzeł has suffered damage during the depth charge attacks, the compressor is proof of that. If it fails while we are submerged, then we would not be able to surface easily – if at all. So far, the ship is holding together, but what if there are other problems that we are not yet aware of?"

"Foterek and his team are the best," Piasecki reassured, "they can hold this beast together for us, don't worry about that."

"You're right Piasecki, I trust them as they trust in us, but what about the captain's unusual behavior? He bravely maneuvered us safely through German bombing attacks but, on the other hand, he seems to be avoiding any conflict."

"What do you mean, avoiding any conflict?" Piasecki asked.

"We abandoned our station in the Bay of Gdańsk. Maybe this was a wise move, maybe he saw the danger we were in. He did not even confirm this with Naval Command, he simply left our station. We could have teamed up with the submarine Wilk to fight the Germans together, but he refused. Why would he not want to fight alongside a comrade?"

Piasecki looked thoughtful, "I don't know why he made those decisions, all I can say is we must follow our captain."

"I'm not saying we should not follow him, he is an experienced officer and we must stand behind him. At least, we should have investigated the surface ship we spotted the other day. He not only refused, but he ordered us to sail away from it. If he perceived a danger, why didn't he tell us?" Grudziński shook his head and shrugged his shoulders, "Or did he just run away?"

Piasecki was taken aback. "As you know, every crew member is eager to fight for our homeland, but none of us are experienced in war. Captain Kłoczkowski is the only one on board to have combat experience, he was in the Polish Bolshevik war, so he must have reasons for what he has done."

"Maybe," Grudziński dismissed with his hands, "but it doesn't stop there. He also has a strange illness that nobody seems able to identify. Our small crew does not include a doctor. We only have a medicine cabinet to fix our own wounds. It can't be contagious, otherwise, we would have contracted it by now."

Grudziński ignored Piasecki's puzzled expression, leaving silence between them.

Peter Zydroń came into the officer's mess, gathering dirty dishes. On long missions, water was reserved for cooking and drinking. Zydroń's dirty apron probably needed washing as badly as any crew member.

"Seaman Zydroń?" Lieutenant Grudziński asked.

"Yes sir?"

"Can I ask you a few questions?"

"Yes sir, of course, sir."

"You've noticed the health of our captain?"

"Yes sir, of course, sir. He doesn't seem too well, sir. He seems to have a dreadful stomach problem."

"Yes, it's a terrible thing. But has he been eating at all?"

"I don't think so, sir, at least he doesn't sit here for meals. He does drink a lot of tea though."

"Do you know if he's eating anything at all?"

"Well sir, I don't rightly know."

"Well, is he eating or not?"

"Anything's possible sir."

"What do you mean? Is someone bringing him food?"

"As I say, sir, I don't see him eat any meals, but anything's possible. Someone else could bring him food to his cabin, or he can always get his own. As you know sir, there is always food available here in the officer's wardroom. Freckles always sees to that."

"Well OK then, Peter, thanks for your help."

"My pleasure, sir. But what about the captain, is he going to be ok? With all that's happening at home, it's no wonder he's come down with something. We're all worried for him."

"Yes, everyone's worried for him and worried about what's happening at home."

Well, maybe that's the problem, Grudziński thought. *Maybe our captain doesn't want to pursue a hopeless war?*

———

In the darkness of late evening, the Orzeł broke the surface and immediately switched to diesel engines. Lookouts scrambled up to the cigarette deck and began scanning the sea and sky for threats. Helmsman Dabrowski climbed up to the bridge where he would control the Orzeł while cruising on the surface.

In the control room, Lieutenant Grudziński grabbed a rung on the ladder ready to climb up to the bridge. As he stepped up, he said, "Lieutenant Piasecki, if the captain comes back to the control room, tell him I'm up on the bridge."

"Aye, sir," Piasecki said, then checked the instruments in the control room, logging the readings for heading, speed, fuel levels, compressor gauges, and battery charge.

Kat, the radio officer, came into the control room with a folder of paper. "Sir, here are the radio communications I received since surfacing. Most of them are routine status updates, but there is one for Captain Kłoczkowski." Kat opened the folder and showed Piasecki a sheet of paper containing the decoded message.

Piasecki took the folder and read through the message, then handed the message to Kat. "You better give this to the captain right away, and wait for his answer. He is probably in his cabin."

"Aye, sir."

It was only a couple of minutes before Kat returned to his seat in the radio room, which was adjacent to the control room. Piasecki stepped over and asked, "So what did the captain say? Has he told you to respond?"

"No, sir, he kept the message and said he will respond later."

Piasecki looked surprised, "Naval command asked for our position and status update, and they said this was urgent. The captain said he will respond later?"

"That's what he said."

"Well, he's the captain, let's hope he doesn't leave it too late."

————

I had a new daily routine, to inspect all components of the ship's air system. This included the compressor, along with all the tanks, valves, and manifolds. The compressor ran the length of the Orzeł and was connected to many systems, so this took a few hours to complete. I started from the aft torpedo room, where the compressor was used to launch torpedoes, and worked my way to the forward torpedo room, checking everything in between.

I had finished my inspection and was returning to the engine room to report to Foterek. Passing through the officer's wardroom, I saw Captain Kłoczkowski hunched over a cup of hot tea. In his hand was a sheet of paper that he scrunched up and threw into the trash can. I knew the captain wasn't feeling well, so I saluted quietly as I walked by.

"Ah, Blackie," Kłoczkowski said as I passed.

"Sir," I stopped. "Is there anything I can do for you?"

"How's the compressor, is everything OK?"

"Yes, sir, I've finished my daily inspection. The pressure is good, but some valves are slow. I think the problem is partly the blowback from the depth charges, and some clogging of the ballast inlets."

"The ballast inlets?" Kłoczkowski asked.

"Yes, sir, if they have any blockage, then that will explain the slower speed to flood and blow the tanks. This can be caused by sitting on the seabed, where mud and rocks can gather in the vents."

"Hm, so you can't fix that, can you?"

"No sir, we either need a diver or we have to be in dry dock."

"OK, well good work, Blackie. Thank you for the report. One last thing, ask Lieutenant Grudziński to come and see me."

"Aye, sir, will do."

I passed through the mess room and galley where Freckles was serving breakfast to the next shift. When I got to the control room I announced, "Coming on deck." I stood there wondering where Grudziński was.

Lieutenant Piasecki was looking over charts with Lieutenant Mokrski. He turned to look at me. "What is it Blackie?"

"Sir, I have a message from the captain."

"Oh? What is it?"

"The captain wants to speak with Grudziński in the Officer's Wardroom."

"Immediately?"

"I believe so sir."

"OK Blackie, anything else to report?"

"No sir. I've completed the inspection of the compressor and air system but nothing extra to report."

"That's good, thank you Blackie, Grudziński is on the bridge, I'll let him know. You're dismissed."

———————

Grudziński found Captain Kłoczkowski in the Wardroom, sitting at a table hunched over a glass of tea. He seemed to look more pained than ever.

"Sir, you wanted to see me?"

"Yes, sit down, we have to talk." As the captain straightened up to face Grudziński, he moved a hand over his abdomen as if to ease some pain there.

As Grudziński sat down, the captain continued. "How is everything? Is there anything to report?"

"Sir, we're currently running on the surface, charging batteries, according to your previous orders. We should be near Gotland after midnight. Otherwise, we await further orders. There may be some opportunity to intercept German vessels in the shipping lanes.

"Very good, Grudziński, we'll stand by when we get to Gotland." Kłoczkowski then massaged his stomach with both hands. "I need to talk to you about my health, it is not improving, if anything it is getting worse."

"But what are we going to do? You have been like this for days now."

"I need to get to a hospital."

"A hospital? So you want us to go back to Poland?"

"No, we need to pull into a neutral port. I want you to get Lieutenant Mokrski to give me the closest port."

"Sir, this is a surprise, a shock even. Can we just sail into a neutral port with no reason?"

"The reason is, I need a hospital. Under maritime law that is a valid reason."

"Sir, can we please check with command on what we should do?"

"Grudziński, I need a hospital and I do not want your obstruction on this. Now I want you to get Mokrski to locate a nearby port and I want him to do it immediately."

"Yes, sir, I will do that. However, Naval Command needs to know. Regulations require that they are informed of what we are doing."

"Damn regulations!" the captain slammed the table with his hand. "Soon there'll be no regulations – or Poland for that matter!"

Grudziński pulled back, startled by the captain's outburst.

Captain Kłoczkowski reached for his tea and took a long slurp. He then tore a sheet of paper from a notebook, scribbling a message which he handed to Grudziński.

"OK, contact command, send them this message, inform them of our location. Then tell Mokrski to bring his charts to the wardroom. We can talk more then." With that, he got up and walked slowly to his cabin.

———

Returning to the control room, Grudziński asked, "What's our status?"

"Continuing to cruise north, sir," Lieutenant Piasecki said. "We should be near Gotland by midnight."

"Any activity reported by the lookouts?"

"I checked with them a moment ago, there is no traffic or aircraft in sight."

Holding the captain's note in his hand, Grudziński slowly passed it towards Lieutenant Piasecki. "Andrzej," he said, using the Lieutenant's first name, "the captain says he needs hospitalization and has agreed to send this message to Naval Command."

Andrzej Piasecki read the message to himself.

'Captain Kłoczkowski is sick and needs hospitalization - request instructions'.

Looking up with surprise, Piasecki asked, "Klocz says he needs a hospital? Is he getting worse?"

"I think he is much the same," Grudziński replied. "He says he is worse, but I think it's because it is so prolonged."

"Is he handing over command?"

"No he hasn't, he is still second-in-command."

"Well OK sir, I'll get Kat to send this right away."

"Oh, and send it as a priority. And one more thing, where's the kid?"

"He should be off duty, he may be in his bunk."

Grudziński turned to petty officer Paul Gorny, "Go find Lieutenant Mokrski, and bring him here, on the double."

"Aye, sir."

———

Even though the message was sent as a priority, Naval Command took their time to respond. It was well after midnight before Grudziński got a response. If the Luftwaffe were living up to their name it would be surprising that naval offices were still intact. As for the radio stations to send and receive messages, it was even more surprising they continued to work. Poles however have a remarkable knack to survive under pressure.

The delayed response was probably because there had been no contact with the Orzeł for several days, and those at Naval Command had feared the Orzeł lost.

———

"So," Piasecki said, "here's the order from command."

Grudziński took the paper, typed by the cat.

'Either leave the captain in a neutral port and allow the executive officer to take over. Or return to Hel for a replacement commander. You decide'.

"So what are you going to do?" Piasecki asked.

"I'll give this to the captain, he's still in charge so it's up to him," said Grudziński.

"Well I think he'll opt for Sweden," Piasecki concluded.

"Mokrski," Grudziński ordered, "follow me, and bring your charts."

"Piasecki, take command while I'm with the captain."

Grudziński knocked on Captain Kłoczkowski's cabin. He and Mokrski then seated themselves at a table in the officer's wardroom, waiting for the captain to appear. As usual, the wait was longer than expected. "Maybe he is asleep. Should I go get him?" Mokrski asked.

With that, the captain appeared and seated himself at the table in front of Grudziński and Mokrski.   "Gentlemen, thank you for coming," he said, then asked, "have you talked with command?"

"Yes sir," Grudziński replied. "Command says either to return to base in Hel or to proceed to a neutral port. Here is the transcript. As you can see, they leave the decision with you."

Captain Kłoczkowski read the transcript carefully before saying, "Thank you, men." Then he continued. "So now, where can we go?"

Lieutenant Mokrski laid out a chart of the northern Baltic, unrolling it like a treasure map onto the table before them. He then turned it the other way round so the captain would be able to see the map the right way up.

"Sir, we spent the night here." Mokrski pointed with his finger to a position on the map. He looked at his watch and then said, "I think we are probably about here, "again pointing. "Now I understand you need a port with a nearby hospital, and the closest ones are here on Gotland is the port of Visby, then on the Swedish mainland there is Kalmar, Vastervik, Norrkoping, or even the ports that serve Stockholm, which is a little further north."

The captain looked at the map, considering the Swedish options. Then after some thought said, "What about here?" pointing at Tallinn in Estonia.

"Sir, that is Tallinn," Mokrski said, stating the obvious.

"Yes, I know," the captain replied, "what about it?"

"Well, that's a lot further. I thought you needed to go to the hospital?"

"Sir," Grudziński responded, "Tallinn is at least twice as far as Stockholm and as the Kid says, there are many more Swedish ports that are closer."

"Set a course for Tallinn," the captain said.

"Sir, but why Tallinn?" Grudziński asked.

"I have contacts in Tallinn and I believe we will be well received there."

"Sir, as it is closer, I think Sweden would be easier for us."

"Grudziński, are you trying to block me again?" the captain asked.

"No, sir."

"So, I order you and Mokrski to set a course for Tallinn."

"If those are your orders, then aye sir."

6 News from Poland

Ship's Log entered by: Lieutenant Jan Grudziński
Date: September 13, 1939
Location: Northern Baltic
Entry: The Captain is temporarily indisposed. Heading towards Estonia according to Captain's orders.

I rushed through the Orzeł, jumping feet first through each hatchway.

"Is there an emergency?" someone asked as I rushed by.

"It's my dinner," I shouted as I jumped through a hatch. "I'm heading to the mess room." I poked my head back through the hatch. "The news is on from Poland, I want to hear the latest!"

I rushed into the mess room and bumped into Alex, almost knocking him into the next person standing in line for food. "Do you have to be such a clumsy klutz?" he said.

"Sorry buddy, I just want to know what's happening on the news," I said.

"Be quiet you two!" Tom Przadka said. He was sitting at a table with Stanley Uliczny as they ate their dinner.

"We're trying to listen to the news," Stanley added, "they're talking about the battle at the Bzura River."

"That's what I came to listen to!" I said.

"Ssshhh!" Everyone shushed me at once, urging me to be silent. I felt a little embarrassed, but I suppose I was a little noisy, causing a big distraction. Radio Warsaw was reporting on what they were now calling Phase 2 of the Battle of the Bzura River. The battle had been raging for a few days, with significant losses reported by the Germans.

The battle had begun when Polish divisions from Poznan took advantage of weak German flanks and overstretched supply lines. The battle of Bzura had halted the German advance on Warsaw. It even seemed to be developing into a decisive victory. Polish infantry divisions were amassing near the city of Łowicz, ready to recapture it from the Germans. There was even talk that German Panzer divisions were being pulled back from the outskirts of Warsaw, to protect their flanks.

"This is great news!" Tom said enthusiastically. "At last we're showing the Germans how we can fight! We're hitting them back, and hard. I think we'll stop them in their tracks!"

"Are you kidding me?" Alex scoffed, "the Germans will regroup in no time."

"The trouble with you, Alex," Tom said, pointing his finger, "is you have no faith in the Polish fighting spirit. Didn't you hear? The radio said the Germans are pulling back from Warsaw,"

"I have plenty of faith in realism," Alex said. "I heard the radio said the German Panzers are pulling back from Warsaw. They are modern, heavy-armored tanks, and they move fast. That's why they call it the Blitzkrieg. Our tanks only have machine guns."

"We have artillery," Tom countered.

"Horse-drawn artillery," Alex scoffed.

"It's not the weapon you have, it's how you use it," Stanley said. "So far we've been very good with our artillery. Our armies know how to use what they have."

Alex shook his head as he took his tray of food from the serving hatch. I grabbed my tray and followed him to sit down. As we sat down opposite Tom and Stanley, Tom asked, "Why are you such a pessimist?"

"I told you, I'm a realist," Alex said. "We've already seen what those Panzers can do. I think this is only a temporary victory for us."

"That may be so," I said, "but whatever happens it buys us time until the British and French join the fight."

"Don't talk to me about the British," Alex said, "they've invented a new phrase for this war."

"Oh? What's that?" we all asked together.

"Because nothing is happening on their side of Europe, they call it, the Phony War."

7 Docking in Tallinn

Ship's Log entered by: Captain Henry Kłoczkowski
Date: September 14, 1939
Location: Tallinn, Estonia
Entry: We are nearing the approach to the port of Tallinn, Estonia.

"Up periscope," Grudziński ordered.

Lieutenant Grudziński caught the periscope handles as they came up, fixing his eyes to the sights. He circled twice, looking for any threats. "Looks clear," he said, scanning more slowly. "I see the coast."

Nods of approval went around the control room.

"All Stop," Grudziński ordered.

Piasecki rang the engine telegraph to relay Grudziński's order to the engine room.

"Get the Kid," Grudziński added.

Lieutenant Mokrski, the Kid, was brought to the control room.

"Get the chart for Tallinn, I need to get a bearing," Grudziński ordered. "I think we're on the western approach."

The Kid unfurled the chart onto the table.

Looking through the periscope, Grudziński said, "I see Naissaar Island to the east and Suurupi point to the south, ready on my mark."

"Ready sir," the midshipman called.

"Naissaar lighthouse, mark."

"Eight, two degrees." The midshipman called out the readings.

Then turning the periscope, Grudziński called, "Suurupi point, mark."

"One, five, five degrees," the midshipman called.

"Down periscope," Grudziński ordered.

The Kid fiddled with his protractor and compass on the chart before calling out, "That puts us at 59 degrees, 35 minutes and 39.1 seconds north, 24 degrees, 18 minutes and 14.5 seconds east, right there," he said, proudly pointing at the chart.

"Good work, Kid, your navigation is impeccable. You got to the right spot!" Grudziński congratulated Mokrski. "You certainly earned your pay for that!"

"Grudziński!" Captain Kłoczkowski shouted as he entered the control room, "Why have we stopped?"

"Ah, sir, I was about to call for you. We have arrived at the western approach to Tallinn."

"Very good," the captain said, looking at his watch. "It's not eighteen hundred hours yet, so the sun is still up. We need to remain submerged. What's our position?"

"About six miles due west of Naissaar point, sir," Grudziński replied.

"Very good, we'll hold this position. What's our sea depth?"

"About eighty meters, sir," Piasecki replied.

"Chart says the bottom is mud and gravel," Mokrski said. "Will we sit on the bottom?"

Captain Kłoczkowski looked at the chart. "No. We need to keep away from shipping until we can radio the harbormaster. We should be out of the way if we stay here between the main shipping lanes."

The captain then winced and held his stomach.

"Are you OK sir?" Grudziński asked. "Maybe we should radio now and enter the port before nightfall?"

"No. We stay submerged and hold our position until nightfall. It will be safer that way."

"Aye, sir."

"Piasecki."

"Aye, sir?"

"Maintain a watch on the periscope, every fifteen minutes."

"Aye, sir."

"Grudziński."

"Aye, sir?"

"Hold this position, minimum speed, circle if necessary. Keep our distance from everything."

"Aye, sir."

With one hand on his stomach, Captain Kłoczkowski hobbled off to his quarters.

————

"Sir, it's Grudziński," the lieutenant announced as he knocked on the captain's door.

"What do you want?"

"It's been dark now for an hour. We are maintaining our position at periscope depth as ordered. I'm asking if you are ready to radio the harbormaster in Tallinn, to request entry."

"Just a moment Grudziński."

While he waited, the captain kept his door closed, but Grudziński could hear a lot of shuffling in his quarters as if things were being hastily put away and packed.

Why is the captain so secretive? Grudziński thought.

"Grudziński," the captain said through the closed door.

"Aye, sir?"

"Surface and radio the harbormaster to request entry."

"Aye, sir."

"State the reason of repairs and medical assistance as specified under Articles Nineteen and Twelve of the Hague Convention."

"Aye, sir. Repairs and medical assistance. Articles Nineteen and Twelve."

"Inform me of their response."

"Aye, sir."

Ship's Log (supplemental): Lieutenant Jan Grudziński
Date: September 14, 1939
Location: Western approach to Tallinn, Estonia
Entry: Requesting entry to neutral port of Tallinn to conduct repairs and request medical attention for the captain.

With the Orzeł cruising slowly on the surface, the request to enter Tallinn was radioed to the harbormaster. There was some delay before a response was received.

"Lieutenant Grudziński," said the radio operator Henry Kotecki as he entered the control room, "I have a response from Tallinn. They have provided coordinates where we are to rendezvous with the harbor pilot for entry into the harbor. This says we must be there in one hour."

Grudziński took the message, examining the coordinates. Leaning over the chart table, he studied the location. "Yes, we can easily be there in under an hour."

"Shall I call the captain?" Piasecki asked.

"Yes, inform the captain that we've been instructed to rendezvous with a harbor pilot to enter the port. Also, I am plotting a course to that location."

"Aye, sir."

Piasecki strode off towards the captain's quarters while Grudziński conferred with the helmsman and navigator.

The darkness was complete. Without the moon, the inky blackness of the sea blended with the sky. Speckles of stars twinkled on the salty waves. Estonia was not at war. Without civil blackout, the coastal lights created an iridescent band as the Orzeł entered Tallinn Bay.

Standing on the bridge with the helmsman, Piasecki said, "Lieutenant, we are approaching the rendezvous point, about three miles dead ahead."

Grudziński raised his binoculars to scan the darkness ahead. "That's good, I think I can see the pilot launch ahead. Go and get the captain. By the time he gets up here, we should be there."

"Aye, sir."

As Piasecki climbed down to the control room, Grudziński instructed the helmsman to stay on course to the rendezvous point. Then he stepped up onto the podium, where he could see the four lookouts on the cigarette deck behind the bridge. "Alex!" he called.

"Aye, sir."

"Use the lantern to send a recognition signal to that launch ahead."

"Aye, sir."

Bosun Alex Kamecki took the lantern and started sending the Morse code signal to the distant launch.

Grudziński kept his binoculars aimed at the launch ahead while Alex kept repeating the signal. After some delay, the launch returned the recognition signal. "Ah, that's them alright," Grudziński said, to no one in particular. "Helmsman, continue on course."

"Aye, sir, continuing on course."

As the Orzeł neared the launch, Lieutenant Piasecki and Captain Kłoczkowski, climbed up into the bridge. "OK, Grudziński," the captain said, "report."

"Sir, we are approaching the pilot launch. We have exchanged recognition signals and they have confirmed that they are here to escort us back to the harbor."

"Very good, they will want to draw alongside to allow the pilot to board. Helmsman, slow our speed to three knots." The captain called into the control room, "Send up two deckhands to prepare to accept the pilot."

Moments later, four deckhands arrived on deck, in front of the conning tower. Two of them brought throw lines and boat hooks, while the two others carried the boarding plank.

The captain grabbed the megaphone as the pilot launch passed the Orzeł's port side with a wide birth. The launch then circled past the stern of the Orzeł, before pulling closer to the starboard side, keeping about thirty yards off the Orzeł.

Through the megaphone, the captain announced to the launch, "This is Captain Henryk Kłoczkowski, of the ORP Orzeł. Under Article Twelve and Article Nineteen of the Hague Convention, we request permission to enter the harbor."

There was no response from the launch as they slowly motored alongside each other. A crewman on the launch was standing at the stern, looking expressionless. The captain waited a moment before repeating his request. It seemed an eternity before an officer appeared from the cabin, he raised his megaphone and replied in Russian, "Heave to!"

"That's the signal," Captain Kłoczkowski said, "helmsman, steer into the waves," as the captain pointed windward. "Grudziński, order the engines to minimum revs, slow our speed to hold our position." He called down to the deckhands, "Prepare to accept the pilot."

The deckhands readied the boarding plank, two of them holding it upright using lines, ready to lower it when the launch approached. To either side of the plank, the two other deckhands attached the lines to deck cleats, ready to throw the lines to the launch.

The launch held its position, so Captain Kłoczkowski used his megaphone to hail the launch. Speaking in Russian he said, "We are ready." The only two men who were visible on the launch did nothing.

"You speak good Russian," Grudziński said, "I'm sure they understood you, but they don't seem in any hurry to bring us into port,"

Some moments later, a stout looking officer holding a pipe in his mouth emerged from the cabin. He stood on the deck with hands on his hips.

"That looks like the pilot," Kłoczkowski said.

Soon after another man appeared from the cabin. He was tall and thin, dressed in a smart naval uniform.

"Who is that?" Grudziński asked.

The naval officer then simply gestured with his hand towards the Orzeł. A seaman emerged from the cabin to take position on the bow of the launch, ready with throw lines.

The launch then moved closer alongside the Orzeł. Throw lines were caught and secured and the plank was lowered and secured. What appeared to be the pilot then approached the plank. "Permission to come aboard."

"Permission granted," Kłoczkowski replied.

The Estonian officer then walked across, saying, "Coming aboard."

Captain Kłoczkowski shared glances with Grudziński and Piasecki, before climbing down to meet with the pilot and officer.

The Estonian officer and Captain Kłoczkowski exchanged salutes, "I am Commander Rudolf Linnuste, Chief of Staff at Tallinn Navy Base. I assume it is acceptable for us to talk in Russian?"

"Yes, I and most officers on this boat speak Russian," Kłoczkowski replied in Russian. They continued their conversation in Russian...

"Very good. This is your pilot, Kristofer Talvik. He will guide you into port tonight. I am informed that you requested entry to Tallinn according to Articles Twelve and Nineteen of the Hague Convention, is that correct?"

"Yes, that is correct," Kłoczkowski replied.

"These articles cover repairs and attending the needs of the wounded or injuries, can you state what damage your boat has, and may I see the injured sailors?"

"We have a problem with our air compressor, and it is myself who needs medical attention."

"You do not look wounded."

"No Commander, I am not wounded. I have an illness and I need medical treatment by a doctor."

The commander regarded Kłoczkowski with a suspicious eye, looking him up and down.

Looking down from the bridge, Piasecki whispered to Grudziński, "I don't like the look of this."

"Very well Captain, we will assess the damage when we reach port. I will have our medical staff examine you to see what the problem is. In the meantime, we have to wait for the

EML Laine. She is an Estonian gunship who will escort you into port. I will remain on board with Talvik."

"Very well," Kłoczkowski replied, "would you both like to wait on the bridge while the Laine comes to meet us?"

"That will be acceptable."

As the EML Laine rendezvoused with the Orzeł, Grudziński looked at his watch, it was now 01:30. The five men stood shoulder to shoulder on the bridge.

"I will remain here on the bridge to oversee the entrance to our harbor," Commander Linnuste said. "The pilot, Talvik, will advise on the course to take but it is, of course, the captain's responsibility to issue any orders to the helmsman."

"That is understood as standard procedure," Kłoczkowski replied.

"Since the Laine is following astern, perhaps your lieutenant would be so kind to move to the rear, in case there are any signals that need to be relayed to us."

"Agreed," Kłoczkowski replied. "Grudziński, can you go to the cigarette deck at the back of the conning tower? Keep an eye open for any signals from the Laine."

"Aye, sir." Grudziński climbed down into the conning tower to transfer to the rear cigarette deck.

Over on the cigarette deck, Grudziński climbed up and joined the four lookouts still on duty there.

"Ah, sir, you've come to join us," Bosun Alex Kamecki commented.

"Yes, I didn't like the smell of that Estonian Commander, I think the air is fresher back here."

"Sir, we have a good view of that gunboat," Alex continued. "To be honest, I don't like the smell of them either. I thought Estonia was neutral and friendly."

Grudziński leveled his gaze at the following gunboat. Armed seamen were on deck and their forward gun looked ready for action. "Well, these are troubling times for everybody. I think they have to be careful and play by the book. Keep a close watch on them, if they send any signals we have to relay them immediately to the bridge."

"Aye, sir," all four lookouts echoed.

As the Orzeł sailed around the Paljassaare Peninsula, they approached the harbor. Entering slowly through the western gap of the breakwater, they passed the small lighthouse. The Laine continued to follow slowly behind them.

Passing the first dock Grudziński pointed to a tanker sitting idly. "Look, that's a German tanker, the Thalatta. Maybe that's what everyone is so jumpy about."

"Look! They're taking the Nazi flag down!" Alex cried, "And they're doing it on the double!"

"Looks like they're jumpier than the Estonians," Grudziński said.

"They look scared to me, sir."

Deckhands emerged from inside the Orzeł, ready with throw lines as she pulled up to the quayside. In front, already docked at the quay was an Estonian destroyer, the EML Izyaslav. As the Orzeł tied up, Estonian seamen connected lines from the destroyer to the bow of the Orzeł. As they did this the gunboat Laine docked immediately behind the Orzeł and also connected lines to the stern of the Orzeł.

"We are completely hemmed in front and back," Grudziński commented.

"I don't think they want us to play with the Germans," Alex added.

When the docking was completed, Captain Kłoczkowski escorted Commander Linnuste and his pilot, Kristofer Talvik, down the gangplank onto the quayside. Estonian guards began to take their posts around the Orzeł.

A staff car arrived and parked near Captain Kłoczkowski. The driver opened the rear doors, allowing two men to emerge. One was a smartly dressed naval officer, the other was a distinguished-looking man dressed in a suit. Captain Kłoczkowski saluted the officer and shook hands with the suited gentleman.

"Who are they?" Alex asked quietly.

"The officer is a commanding rank, probably some Naval Attaché," Grudziński said. "The other looks like some sort of diplomat."

"Well I hope he's a Polish diplomat," Alex said with a grin. "We can do with some good treatment here."

Moments later, Kłoczkowski walked back up the gangplank to the Orzeł, leaving the party of officials on the quayside. As he came back on deck he indicated to Grudziński to meet him inside the Orzeł.

As Grudziński stepped off the ladder into the control room, Kłoczkowski had already disappeared to his quarters. Piasecki held up his hand. "Wait here, the captain is getting some things from his quarters. He said he wants to talk with you."

"What's happening? Is he being admitted to hospital?"

Just then, Captain Kłoczkowski stepped into the control room carrying a large suitcase and a compact typewriter, in a handled case. "Yes I am," he announced, "They have given me permission to be checked over by a doctor. I'm leaving for the hospital now." Grudziński shuffled past his officers with his heavy suitcase. "We have also been granted leave to remain here in Tallinn, according to the terms of the Hague Convention."

"That's good news, sir, but there seems to be a lot of security around us."

Kłoczkowski paused as he started to climb up to the deck hatch. Turning towards Grudziński he said, "Follow me, I want you to meet with the Polish Ambassador. You can discuss these issues with him."

Climbing up to the deck through the conning tower, they stepped onto the gangplank. As Grudziński followed behind, he said, "Sir, you seem to be taking a lot of things. Are you expecting to stay long?"

"It's all just in case, lieutenant."

"Including the typewriter?"

"Grudziński," Kłoczkowski was irritated by these questions, "you know full well there may be hospital forms that I need to fill out."

Stepping onto the quayside, Captain Kłoczkowski placed his belongings on the cobbled ground before introducing Grudziński.

"Lieutenant, this is the Polish Military Attaché, Stanislaw Szystowski, from the Polish Embassy in Tallinn, Mr. Szystowski, this is my First Officer Grudziński."

Grudziński gave a formal salute, before shaking Mr. Szystowski's hand.

"My first officer is very fresh from the academy, but he will be your point of contact while I am indisposed."

"I understand, Captain."

Kłoczkowski then indicated towards Commander Linnuste. "Grudziński, you have already met the Chief of Staff on this base." Grudziński formally saluted Commander Linnuste, who returned a brief salute.

Finally, Kłoczkowski introduced Commander Valeva Mere. "Grudziński, this is the Commander of the Estonian Navy, Commander Mere. Commander Mere, this is my First Officer."

Grudziński stood to attention, and while holding his salute said, "It is my honor to meet such a distinguished officer."

Commander Mere returned a relaxed salute, and said, "Thank you, lieutenant. Commander Linnuste will be your primary contact during your stay here."

"What if I need to contact the embassy?" Grudziński asked.

"You can do that through me, lieutenant," Linnuste replied.

"The embassy is just a phone call away," Attaché Szystowski added. "I must remind you lieutenant, you and your crew are here under the auspices on the Hague Convention." Szystowski reached into his briefcase and handed a folder of papers to Grudziński. "These papers outline the restrictions imposed by the convention."

"Thank you, sir." Grudziński accepted the paper folder. "Our crew are very tired and do need a wash facility. Are we allowed to exercise on the dockside? And is there a washroom that my crew can use?"

"Absolutely," Linnuste replied. "There is an officer's restroom by the harbor office and a workman's washroom by warehouse number one, which your crew can use. The German ship is heavily guarded and there is no way to leave the dockyard without my permission. However, may I suggest you restrict your crew's movements to small groups, say five men at most."

"Thank you, sir, that is perfectly acceptable," Grudziński affirmed.

"Guards will remain posted. You are not our prisoners, provided your crew behaves according to the restrictions of the Hague Convention.

After the formalities to close the conversation, Captain Kłoczkowski got into the staff car with Attaché Szystowski and departed for the hospital in Tallinn.

8 Interned in Tallinn

Ship's Log entered by: Lieutenant Jan Grudziński
Date: September 15, 1939
Location: Tallinn, Estonia
Entry: Entered port to admit Captain Kłoczkowski to hospital and assess compressor issues.

At dawn, Grudziński allowed the crew to rotate onto the deck for fresh air and to smoke cigarettes.

"The morning sunlight will be good to raise the crew's spirits," Grudziński said to Piasecki. As the two officers strolled around the submarine deck, they noticed the Estonian guards on the quayside were very relaxed.

Grudziński walked down the aft gangplank. Standing on the quayside was Stanley Uliczny, who was chatting to one of the Estonian guards. Both men were smoking cigarettes.

"Good morning, sir," Stanley saluted.

The Estonian also saluted, "Good morning, sir," he said in Polish, "I speak a little Polish."

"Good morning," Grudziński acknowledged their salutes.

The Estonian had his rifle slung over his shoulder, and he shuffled lazily from foot to foot. Grudziński noticed that the breech on his rifle was open and empty, indicating that his rifle wasn't even loaded.

"So, you had a nice chat in Polish?" Grudziński asked.

"Yes, I give Stanley my cigarette, and Stanley give me his cigarette, and we talk in Polish."

Grudziński gave them his wide, disarming smile. "That's good to hear. Stanley, I think you need to get some breakfast, follow me back up the plank."

"Thank you, sir."

"You have good breakfast," the Estonian said, as the two men walked back up the plank. When they both got back on deck Grudziński asked, "Did that guard tell you anything interesting?"

"Not really, but he's not properly guarding. He kept saying he had to watch us. He also kept saying that we'll like it here."

"He said, that?"

"Yeah, he was acting as if we're here on vacation."

"OK, go and get yourself some breakfast."

"Thank you, sir."

————

Grudziński looked around at everyone's relaxed attitudes, both on deck and the quayside. Blackie and Alex were standing nearby smoking cigarettes. Approaching them, Grudziński asked, "Do either of you speak Russian?"

"No sir," Alex responded.

"A little," I said, "my mother is Ukrainian."

"Very good. Blackie, I have a job for you."

"Yes, sir. What is it?"

"I want you to stand at the bottom of the gangplank and act as a guard."

"Sir?"

I've relieved Stanley, and he needs to be replaced. The guard is friendly, so while you are there I want you to find out everything you can."

"Like a spy?"

"Yes, like a spy, find out what is going on here."

"Aye, sir. That's very easy for me."

Grudziński reached into his pocket and pulled out a packet of cigarettes. "Take these, Stanley told me that he likes to swap cigarettes."

"Aye, sir."

————

Grudziński stood on the cigarette deck watching for any activity on the quayside. Other than small groups walking to and from the washrooms, very little was happening.

Lieutenant Andrey Piasecki climbed up from the control room.

"Anything to report?" Grudziński asked.

"We've received confirmation from our base in Hel that we are in Tallinn, but only confirmation, no other news. We've replenished our water tanks, and I've made sure everything is stored, ready for our departure."

"Thank you, Andrey, but I don't think we'll be leaving any time soon."

"Oh? I think we can manage at sea with the compressor. I just want to be ready when the captain returns."

"It's not the compressor I'm worried about or the captain."

"What is it then?"

At that moment, Grudziński indicated the approach of the Estonian staff car driving up the quayside.

"Maybe they will tell us something. Let's go down to the quay to see what they have to say."

Both men climbed down from the conning tower. They then walked down the aft gangplank in time to meet Commander Linnuste who had just emerged from the car.

Commander Linnuste saluted. "Good morning, lieutenant, may we speak in Russian?"

Lieutenant Grudziński and Lieutenant Piasecki both returned salutes.

"Yes, as I said last night, I speak Russian and so does Lieutenant Piasecki."

"Very good," Commander Linnuste continued. "I have some good news for you, lieutenant. Your captain is being cared for and has been transferred from our base infirmary to the city hospital. He will be cared for by the best doctors in Estonia."

"I'm glad to hear that, commander. Is there any indication of what is wrong with him?"

"Our doctors have told me nothing. With the weekend now beginning, I don't think we will hear any more until Monday."

"Monday?" Grudziński looked wide-eyed. "I don't think we have rights to remain in port for that long."

"Ah…" the commander raised his finger, indicating he was going to say something of importance. "That brings me to the second piece of news."

As the commander paused, Grudziński exchanged glances with Piasecki.

"You are of course aware of the presence of the German freighter, the Thalatta?"

"Yes, of course," Grudziński confirmed.

"Well, Article Sixteen of the Hague Convention contains a contingency for situations like this. Any armed belligerent must allow any unarmed belligerent to leave the port and reach a distance of safety. In other words, you must remain here in port for 24 hours after the German ship leaves."

"That is understood, commander, and we will comply with maritime law."

"Yes, we will make sure you do comply, but I must say that there are strong forces at large that were very surprised at the timing of your arrival."

"What do you mean surprised? We gave reasons for our arrival."

"These are very difficult times for everyone, Lieutenant Grudziński. We must balance our diplomacy appropriately."

"Are you saying we are under suspicion?"

"All I'm saying is you have an extended leave of stay."

"Are we being imprisoned?"

"No, you are not imprisoned, you are free to move about, as we have agreed. My dock guards will of course prevent you or your crew from approaching the Thalatta. I must also warn you that armed guards will be posted around the Thalatta, while they remain in port. I will ensure the safety of the Thalatta."

"We will not make any attempt to approach them. I assure you that their presence was also a surprise to us."

"Very well, lieutenant, that is all I need to inform you of that this time. If you have any questions you can approach the harbor office at the head of the quay over there." The commander indicated the office in the distance.

"Thank you, commander, I'll keep that in mind," Grudziński nodded.

"Very good," Commander Linnuste said. "I'll wish you an enjoyable stay."

They exchanged salutes and handshakes before the commander returned to his car. As he drove away, Piasecki said, "Well, it looks like we are stuck here for a while."

"I smell a rat," Grudziński snarled. "Linnuste said there are 'strong forces' at large. I wonder what he meant by that? I want you to stay on deck and keep a close watch on anything that happens. I'll go and contact Naval HQ again and see if they have anything to say."

"Aye, sir."

Grudziński hadn't finished his lunch when Stanley came running into the wardroom.

"Sir, Lieutenant Piasecki wants you topside in the bridge! He said it's urgent."

"Thank you." Grudziński smiled in his casual way, as he rose from the table, wiping his mouth with his napkin. He turned to Stanley. "Please clear these plates away for me. We must maintain a clean boat."

"Aye, sir."

Up on the bridge, Piasecki handed a set of binoculars to Grudziński. "Have a look at the dockside office, something is going on there."

Parked outside the office was a large, black Mercedes, with Nazi flags on the front. Sitting in the driving seat was a chauffeur.

"That arrived a few minutes ago. There were three men who went into the office. One looked like a diplomat, the second was a uniformed naval officer, and I'll bet the third was a Gestapo officer."

Grudziński peered through the binoculars longer, looking for activity, when a second car arrived.

"Sir, those are Russian flags on the front."

At that moment the chauffeur stepped out to open the door for a suited man.

"Hm, that looks like a diplomat," Grudziński said.

"Yes, and I'm wondering what the Russians are doing here..."

"I think those are the rats I smelled."

"The 'strong forces' at large," Piasecki mumbled.

Moments later a third car arrived.

"That is Commander Mere, of the Estonian Navy," Grudziński snarled. "I think there's a party going on there." Grudziński turned to Piasecki. "I don't like the look of this, and I think this is a trap."

"But sir, we're under the Hague Convention."

"Do you think any of those Germans or Russians care about conventions? Do you think the Estonians have any power to stand up to them? I fear the worst! Get below Piasecki, and gather all codebooks and secret documents together, everything. Prepare to destroy them on my order. On the double!"

"Aye, sir!"

Piasecki practically flew down the ladder into the control room.

Grudziński stayed on the bridge observing the office. *I wonder what they are planning for us*, he thought to himself, *but why are the Russians involved?* Moments later a platoon of Estonian naval guards marched up to the office. They stood at ease on order from their chief and waited.

That looks like they're going to make a move on us, Grudziński thought. Climbing down into the control room, he gave Piasecki the order to stand by the codebooks and all secret documents. Piasecki clutched the documents in his arms, indicating his readiness to burn them. The others in the room reflected fear in their faces. What emergency was heading their way to warrant the destruction of these papers? Without codebooks, how could they communicate with Naval Command?

Grudziński then went out on deck for the arrival of the Estonian officers. He didn't have to wait long. The Estonian staff car brought Commanders Linnuste and Mere to the quayside by the Orzeł. They waited in the car as the additional guards marched across the quayside towards the Orzeł. Outside the office, Grudziński could see the German and Russian officials standing in the distance, observing the Orzeł with an arrogant posture.

Grudziński perceived oncoming doom. *This is more frightening than depth charges*, he thought. *An underwater explosion is instant death but this is slow motion, this is a real fear. How can I protect my submarine and my men from what I see coming? I will just have to play it by the book. How can a book protect us now? I hope I haven't misread the situation. If I destroy the codebooks prematurely, we are effectively isolated from Naval HQ. On the other hand, if they do get their hands on those codes then a lot more lives will be at stake. We are stuck between the devil and the deep blue sea! We are trapped here… and they have the upper hand.*

Grudziński stood on deck by the conning tower with his feet apart and fists on his hips, trying to look formidable.

As the platoon of guards approached the Orzeł, Commander Linnuste emerged from the car and indicated the guards to stand ready at both gangplanks. The Estonian guards posted earlier simply stood aside. The Polish crewmen standing at the bottom of the gangplank looked towards Grudziński for guidance.

Piasecki was leaning out of the conning tower hatchway, waiting for the order.

Commander Mere, the Estonian Naval Attaché, emerged from the far side of the car, and slowly sauntered to the quayside. He too stood with his feet apart and hands on hips before shouting up to the Orzeł, "Lieutenant Grudziński!" He then pointed with one finger towards the ground in front of him, indicating that the Polish Lieutenant should come down to the quayside.

Grudziński turned his head towards Piasecki and said, "Burn the codes and all the papers."

"Yes, sir!" Piasecki disappeared inside, slamming the hatch shut.

Grudziński swallowed hard. He turned and walked towards the gangplank, keeping a straight spine and looking firmly ahead. *I feel as if I'm walking to my execution*, he thought. *Whatever befalls us I will play it by the book, I will follow the law, but above all, I will do it with the pride of a Polish officer.*

Standing on the quayside, Commander Mere addressed Grudziński in Russian. "Lieutenant Jan Grudziński, as you are the acting commander of the ORP Orzeł, I am presenting you with this official communique from the government of Estonia."

"What does it say?" Grudziński asked, taking the sealed letter.

"The Orzeł is to be interned here in Tallinn. The order is effective immediately."

"Interned? I object to this in the strongest of terms! We are here under the terms of the Hague Convention and we have rights under maritime law. You have no grounds to intern us."

"To the contrary, lieutenant, we have very good grounds. We believe that you entered this port under false pretenses. Hence, we have decided to intern you."

"Who exactly are we?"

"We, meaning the government of Estonia."

"Did you have any help from the Germans over there?"

"They have no input on our decisions, they are simply concerned about their merchantmen in our harbor."

"On exactly what grounds are you interning the Orzeł?"

"Your request cited two articles of the Hague Convention, which refer to ship repairs and medical assistance."

"Yes, that is correct."

"Your repairs are concerned with the compressor, and we do not consider this to be essential. If the compressor was completely inoperable, the Orzeł could still sail to a homeport for repairs."

"What about medical assistance?"

"Again, we consider this to be inessential. Your captain has been complaining of an illness, but our doctors have not been able to find anything wrong with him."

"Where is our captain? Is he being detained?"

Commander Linnuste stepped forward. "Captain Kłoczkowski is still in hospital and remains in our care. He is safe and well, he is not being harmed."

"What will become of my crew if I allow this to happen?"

"Your crew will also be safe and well cared for." Commander Linnuste held up a reassuring hand as he said this. "You will all be taken out of this war. You can all remain here until the fighting is over. You are not being imprisoned, you are simply being interned."

"I wish to speak with the Polish ambassador," Grudziński said with folded arms.

"We can call your ambassador, but he will be of no help." Now he held up both hands.

It looks like Linnuste is surrendering, Grudziński thought, *but to whom is he surrendering?*

"Lieutenant," Commander Mere looked sternly at Grudziński, "your ambassador has no authority here. The bottom line is, you, your crew and the Orzeł will be interned, and that order is effective immediately. If you oppose us in any way, we will use force if necessary."

Grudziński thought, *what can I do to buy more time?* "OK, I do not want bloodshed, but I do want to follow strict procedures."

"Procedures are good." Mere smiled.

"So what happens next?"

"Oh that is very simple," Linnuste stepped in. "All we need to do at this time is to board your boat and inspect it to make sure it is not a threat to the German ship or the port of Tallinn."

"OK," Grudziński nodded. "I have one strict procedure
that must be followed."

"You may make a request," Mere said.

"What is it you want?" Linnuste asked.

"Not all my crew speak Russian, so as you inspect my
boat, I insist you are accompanied by a crew member who
can translate Russian to Polish."

"I think that is a fair request. Granted. Now, can we
proceed?"

As the entourage came onto the Orzeł's deck,
Commander Mere stopped and said, "Before we proceed
with the inspection, we must disable the deck gun."

"What!?" Grudziński exclaimed. "You cannot disable my
boat!"

"Let me remind you that we must make sure the Orzeł is
not a threat to the German ship or the port of Tallinn. This
includes the 105mm deck gun and the 40mm anti-aircraft
gun."

"You seem to know a lot about our boat."

"We know enough about what we have to do."

Before continuing through the boat, Mere stationed an
Estonian guard on the Orzeł's bridge and in the control
room. "These men will remain here as a precaution,"
Commander Mere said. "We will change them every four
hours. Small arms must be surrendered, my purser will collect
these and complete any documentation."

Both Foterek and I were in the engine room. We could
not talk because the diesel engines were running. If we did
talk, it was only through sign language. We were charging the
batteries and ventilating the submarine. We did not know the
Orzeł had been interned, let alone, that the Estonians had
boarded our boat.

A tall, pompous, well-decorated and officious looking
Estonian naval officer entered the engine room. As he stood
upright, Foterek turned to face him. Another officious

looking Estonian struggled through the watertight door, closely followed by an armed guard.

Foterek reacted immediately picking up a heavy spanner in his right hand, twirling it as if he were a gunslinger in an American Western movie. As he glanced around, Foterek also picked up a large screwdriver, laying by his side. He then moved forward to defend his engine room. He was ready to kill any foreigner who dared enter his sacred domain.

The sight of Foterek must have stunned the Estonians, because they stopped and held back, with looks of apprehension on their faces.

Lieutenant Grudziński followed them in. Our lieutenant was quite the gentleman, often waving people to pass through a doorway before him. I think this time he did it on purpose.

Grudziński held up his hand to calm Foterek. He then grinned his girlish smirk towards Foterek and nodded.

Foterek quickly holstered the screwdriver from his right hand to his back pocket. His left hand hid the spanner he was clutching between the gaps of the diesel engine. He then leaned on the spanner as if to look nonchalant.

"Hello, gentleman," Foterek greeted, "is there anything I can do for you?"

I stood behind Foterek, looking quizzical.

"We have to shut your engines down," shouted Commander Mere.

Foterek feigned deafness and cupped his hand to his ear.

"We have to shut your engines down," Mere repeated.

Foterek shook his head negatively, leaning forward with his hand cupped over his ear.

"Shut the damn engine down!" demanded Mere, this time with visible frustration.

Grudziński indicated silently with a wave of his hand to stop the engine.

Foterek nodded and turned towards his diesel. He began to shut down the engines, silently and slowly. The engine began to idle while Foterek bled air from some valves while slowing down oil flow with other valves. He paused as he listened to the slowing revs of the engine. He then indicated to me to transfer to battery power.

I moved all the switches on the electrical board to transfer all boat power to the batteries.

Foterek gave me the thumbs up.

The engine idled its way down to its slowest cycle, before thumping its way to a complete halt. Lieutenant Foterek then stood proudly alongside the huge engine, grinning proudly.

Grudziński rolled his eyes and shook his head.

"Is that the best you could do?" Commodore Mere asked.

"Under the circumstances, yes," Foterek replied. He then leaned towards me and said, "Good work, Blackie."

Of course, those of us who knew realized that the engine could be stopped much faster. After all, how else could a submarine handle an emergency dive and switch over to electric motors? However, Foterek was performing for his uninvited audience.

"Are you the chief engineer?" Mere asked.

"Of course, Warrant Officer, Wacław Foterek, at your service!" Foterek bowed theatrically.

"We will disable your engines," Mere said. "This must be done immediately."

This was like saying to Foterek, 'You must die!' I began to feel afraid for what he might do next.

"Not possible!" he stated. "These engines are the living heart and soul of the Orzeł, if they are disabled, there will be no Orzeł!"

Foterek moved closer to Commander Mere, staring him in the eyes. "Do you feel hot? Perhaps a little perspiration? How about your breathing?"

Perspiration was prominent on Mere's brow, hardly surprising since he was standing next to a hot engine.

"The air on this boat needs to be circulated. How long do you think a man can survive in a steel tube without fresh air?"

"As I have informed Lieutenant Grudziński, this boat is now being interned by Estonia, under the rules of maritime law."

Foterek moved frighteningly close to Mere. "I don't care whose rules you follow, this engine must, and will, remain operational."

Grudziński interjected, "Commander, what my chief engineer says is true. We require the engines to remain operational to enable all systems on this boat, the most important of which is air circulation. In case you didn't realize, we do not have any windows."

Mere scoffed in frustration. "These engines must be disabled. I do not want any attempts to leave this port."

"How can we possibly leave?" Grudziński asked. "We are tied not only to the quay but also to a destroyer and a gunboat!"

"What about batteries?" Mere asked. "Can we disable the engine and let you run on batteries?"

This time Foterek rolled his eyes and shook his head.

"That's not practical," Grudziński said. "Batteries have a limited life and need the engines to be recharged." Grudziński now stood as firm as Foterek. "These engines must remain operational, at least for the time being."

"Very well," Mere said. "We will leave your precious engines for now, but we will soon see what happens to them. In addition, maybe we will see what happens to you, Warrant Officer! Now let us continue with the inspection."

———

Well, I must tell you, being inspected like that had a crippling effect on morale. After they left the engine room, I watched as my chief, Foterek had a fit of anger, kicking could the bulkheads with his heavy boots.

"Sir, calm down," was all I could say.

It took many moments, but when Foterek finally calmed down, he grabbed his rag and started polishing his engine. "They want to shut me down," he kept mumbling. "If only the captain was here."

I could not console him, because I felt the same way. I felt as if I was being fired from my job. I also felt that we were now out of the war. Maybe that's why the captain brought us here, to take us out of the war. Whatever it was, I had a sickening feeling in my stomach.

Since we were now running on batteries, I didn't think there was much I needed to do in the engine room, so I wandered slowly around the boat, as I followed in the wake of this so-called inspection by the Estonian commander. Whenever he paused to ask questions of the crew, he would leave those men dumbfounded. When I passed them, I saw their ghost-like faces.

I heard Boson Alex Kamecki mumble, "We're finished."

I passed Master Seaman Tom Przadka. All he could say was, "Where's the captain?"

I don't know why, but I felt that I was following a Nazi agent. He was invading our boat, just as the German Wehrmacht was invading Poland. I felt this so strongly that I imagined a Swastika on his back. *Why would an Estonian want to close us down so badly?* I thought. *Estonia used to be friendly to Poland, why would they abandon us?*

————————

After seeing what happened in the engine room, I didn't think my heart could be broken anymore. But what I saw in the control room shattered it.

The Estonian commander removed all calculating equipment for the firing of torpedoes. This included the all-important 'Is-Was', which is a slide rule type of device used to calculate the angle to fire a torpedo. A submarine and its target both move on their own courses, often at different speeds. A torpedo thus needs to be fired ahead of a targeted ship to strike it and not miss. Such geometrical calculations are quite complex and the slide rule does it all for you. Without it, we were unable to shoot with accuracy.

But this was not what broke my heart.

Mere demanded that all navigational equipment be removed. All the charts, maps, and documents that we needed to find our way were confiscated. The heartbreak was when the commander made Lieutenant Marian Mokrski carry these things off the boat and over to the harbor office.

I watched as the Kid carried his beloved charts and maps along the quay towards the office. Lieutenant Piasecki stood on the deck next to me. "He looks like a mother who held her baby, knowing they will be parted forever," he said.

That description caused my throat tighten, as if I would cry. It took all my strength to not scream and curse at the evil agent who was stealing Mokrski's baby.

The Kid disappeared into the office, leaving Piasecki and me to stand on the deck in silence. Now we both had nothing to do. There was nothing left for him to command, and the engines no longer had a use for me. The war was over for us.

Moments later we watched as the Kid left the office and returned to the Orzeł, unaccompanied. There was something strange about him as he walked back. He almost looked as if he was skipping. Could a mother possibly be happy after leaving her baby?

Piasecki and I looked at each other as if to say, *are you seeing what I am seeing?*

The Kid walked up the gangplank and strode along the deck with a gleeful grin. As he passed us Piasecki asked, "Are you OK?"

The Kid simply tapped his hand on his heart and winked at us, before disappearing through the hatch into the conning tower.

"Sir?" I asked, "Could he be suffering some sort of shock?"

"I don't know, that's not how I expected the Kid to behave."

Ship's Log (supplemental): Lieutenant Jan Grudziński
Date: September 16, 1939
Location: Tallinn, Estonia
Entry: The ORP Orzeł has been interned by the Estonian authorities, we await their engineers to assist with the disabling of the deck gun and removal of torpedoes.

Lieutenant Grudziński climbed the ladders to the top of the conning tower. Lieutenant Piasecki was at the top, on the cigarette deck observing the activities on the quay, as he leaned on the gunwale.

"Captain." Piasecki stood straight as he acknowledged Grudziński.

Grudziński looked at him quizzically. "Funny you should call me that."

"Well, sir, according to regulations, in the absence of our captain, the second officer should assume command."

"This is not the sort of command I ever thought I would have. Handing over our vessel to a foreign nation."

"Sir, I am sorry that it has happened this way for you."

"Well, never mind that now." Grudziński looked out over the quay. "Where are they? Commander Mere said they would be here at 08:00, and it's now 09.45."

"Well sir, none of these Estonians seem to move with any hurry. That group down there look like the Estonian engineers, They've been sitting there for about half an hour."

"Ah, I think there's some movement up at the harbor office. That looks like Mere's car."

As the car drove across the quay and pulled up alongside the Orzeł, Grudziński thought about his command and the fate of his crew. *After this depressing end, will I or my crew see home again? Will Poland ever be the same again?*

Lieutenant Jerry Sosnowski and Warrant Officer Joseph Stelmaszyk were already waiting on the foredeck. Grudziński climbed down from the conning tower to meet with them.

"Sir!" They both saluted as Grudziński approached them.

"Gentlemen." Grudziński returned the salute. "Thank you for being ready this morning. As I explained earlier you both have unfortunate jobs to do."

Both men nodded at the ready.

"Gunnery officer Sosnowski, you must oversee the disablement of the deck gun."

"Aye, sir."

"Torpedo officer Stelmaszyk, you must oversee the removal of our torpedoes."

"Aye, sir."

"As I have explained, we are being interned here in Tallinn, so you both must be courteous to our Estonian hosts. But do not let them overreach their authority." Grudziński looked sternly at both of his officers. "Especially Commander Mere. He seems to have a penchant for degrading us."

"Aye, sir," they both acknowledged.

"What about the captain?" Joseph asked.

"He won't be returning. The important thing to remember is, you must perform your duties as a Polish Officer!" Grudziński paused. "If there are any questions of procedure or authority, then summon me. During this transition period, this is the ORP Orzeł. Any more questions?"

"Is there any way we can get out of this?" Sosnowski asked.

"I'm afraid not," Grudziński said, "we are under Estonian internship."

"Is this what our captain wanted?" Stelmaszyk asked.

"I can't answer for the captain. We are now in this situation, and we must handle it professionally as Polish Officers."

———

Lieutenant Sosnowski had the job of overseeing the dismantling of both deck guns. Both were manufactured in

Sweden. The main deck gun was a Bofors 105mm canon, the anti-aircraft gun was a twin-barreled Bofors 40mm machine gun. All they had to do was to remove the breech from the guns. A standard task which all artillery officers were required to be able to do.

The practicality of removing the Orzeł's gun breech turned out to be much more complicated.

Submarines tend to have deck-mounted guns that are open to the sea. The Orzeł's deck gun was protected by a turret, providing some protection to the gun operators in case of adverse sea conditions or close combat. Normally two crewmen would operate the gun within the turret, loading it and aiming it as appropriate. The presence of Estonian naval engineers, and the oversight of Commander Mere, crowded an already confined space.

"Lieutenant Grudziński, I must have a word with you."

"What is it Commander Mere?"

"We have a problem with dismantling the deck gun."

"I'm sure Lieutenant Sosnowski can be of better help than me?"

"That's the problem, I think Lieutenant Sosnowski has taken something."

"Meaning what?" Grudziński looked puzzled.

Lieutenant Sosnowski shrugged, with a silent question.

"We have removed the breech," the commander explained, "but there is an important component missing."

"What is missing?"

"The breech lever and retaining catch, and I think your subordinate Lieutenant has taken them."

Sosnowski stooped inside the hatch to the gun turret. "Sir, I do not have the breech lever or the retaining catch, and I do not know what happened to it."

"Commander, has the breech been removed?" Grudziński asked, "Is the gun now disabled?"

"Yes, of course, I have seen to that."

"Then why is the breech lever so important?"

"I must make sure all components of the gun are present and accounted for."

That sounds like he's following instructions. But whose instructions and why? Grudziński thought.

Grudziński stood there for a moment considering the situation. "If I don't have it, and you don't have it, and my lieutenant doesn't have it, that narrows the search options." Looking at the tool bags the Estonians were using, Grudziński then suggested, "Can we check through these bags to make sure it hasn't been misplaced?"

"Yes, but I don't think…" Mere stopped short.

One of the Estonian engineers began to check his tool bag. There in his hand, he pulled out the breech lever and retaining catch. He looked a little sheepish as he did so.

"OK, commander," Grudziński said, "I think this has just been a misunderstanding. You now have the breech mechanism with all its components. Will there be anything else you need from this gun?"

Mere tried not to look embarrassed. Instead, he looked towards his engineers who just shrugged. "No, lieutenant, I think I have everything we need."

Grudziński excused himself and left the turret. *What the hell was that all about?* he thought, *I thought he just wanted to disable the gun. Why does he need all components? Before he starts on the torpedoes, I need to talk with Stelmaszyk.*

Joseph Stelmaszyk was still on the foredeck with Stanley.

"Joe, can I have a word with you?"

"Sir?"

"I want you to delay the torpedoes' removal as much as possible."

"Sir? Is there something wrong?"

"I just need more time, so I want you and your men to work slowly."

"Should I have the aft torpedoes removed first?"

"That's a good idea but delay as much as you can on each torpedo."

"I can think of lots of excuses to work slowly."

"Good, keep it as slow as possible."

"Is there something happening that I should know about?"

"Maybe…" Grudziński scratched his chin. "I'll keep you informed as things develop."

Grudziński walked back to the conning tower, climbing up to the cigarette deck to meet with Piasecki.

"Having fun with your Estonian friends?" Piasecki asked.

"I think I learned something from them this morning."

"Oh? What's that?"

"I'm not too sure, but I know it's not good."

"Are you smelling more rats?"

"I think so." Grudziński looked around, trying to think. "If Mere wanted to disable the deck gun, would it matter if he lost a part of the breech mechanism?"

"Probably not, he could throw the entire breech into the harbor for all that mattered."

"So why would he be concerned about missing the breech lever and retaining catch?"

"Did someone steal it?"

"No, it turned up in an Estonian's bag. It just got misplaced. It was an innocent mishap. But the question remains, why was he so concerned?"

Piasecki thought for a moment. "I think it's obvious, he wants a working gun."

"That's exactly what I thought! And if he wants a working gun…" Grudziński didn't need to complete the sentence.

"…Then he wants a working submarine!" Piasecki completed the sentence for him.

There was a long pause before Piasecki continued. "Is that why the Germans are here?"

"I assume that the Germans want this submarine."

"So the Germans must have pressed the Estonians to intern us."

"That's exactly what I'm thinking, they must be trying to appease the Germans to stay out of harm's way."

"So what are we going to do? Do you have a plan?"

"I don't know yet." Grudziński clenched his fist. "But I'm not going to let those Germans get this boat! I'll scuttle her right here if I have to."

"That's no good!" Piasecki shook his head. "It's too shallow here, and they'll just refloat her. What about out in the channel? We could block the harbor there."

Grudziński looked out towards the open sea. "If we could get that far, we would have a chance to make a run for it."

"You mean to escape?"

"Yes! Why not?" Grudziński grinned. "If they sink us, we block the channel. If we escape, we're back in the fight. Either way, we spit in their eyes!"

"That's crazy enough to work! Do we go tonight?"

"We need to plan this out. I also want only volunteers from the crew, I don't want to waste lives needlessly."

"OK, I can talk to the men, I'm sure we'll get plenty of volunteers."

"Be careful how you pass the word, we have a guard in the control room and the bridge. They must not get wind of this. There's also that sand bar in the harbor, and we don't have the knowledge of the Estonian pilot. If we get caught on that mud bank, we're sitting ducks."

"Hm…" Piasecki looked thoughtful. "I think I know a fisherman who may be able to help with that."

———

Within an hour, everyone on the Orzeł was greeting each other with the two-fingered salute. As they passed in the corridors or entered a compartment, men greeted each other silently. Sometimes they even winked and smiled.

Selected crew were instructed to walk around the quay, only a few at a time. As they walked, they pretended to be in quiet conversation so as not to attract attention. The Estonians did not question them. After all, the Poles were not going anywhere. The purpose of this casual walking was twofold. First, to observe what was around the quay, and second, to count the steps to different locations and work out the time to get from point to point. If they happened to pass each other they would offer the two-fingered salute.

Petty Officer Vlad Narkiewicz somehow managed to borrow a dingy from some harbor workers. He set off rowing around the harbor, whistling to himself while quietly casting his fishing rod. Seaman Stanley Uliczny and Warrant Officer Joseph Stelmaszyk were still working with the Estonians to remove the aft torpedoes.

"Where's he going?" one of the Estonians asked.

"He's going fishing," said, Joseph.

"Yeah, he told me he's after some flounders," said Stanley as he gave the salute. "It's Saturday and we hope to have a nice dinner tonight."

The Estonian looked doubtful. "So what's with all this saluting?" he asked.

"Oh, you mean this?" Stanley saluted. "it's a Polish tradition."

"What tradition is that?"

"Saturday the sixteenth of September, it's Victor's name day."

"Who's Victor?"

"Pope Victor the First, he was very religious you know," Stanley added with a nod. "He used to touch his halo when he blessed someone."

"You Poles are crazy."

"Maybe we're just crazy about religion. You can do it too," Stanley invited the Estonian with a salute.

"Like this?" the Estonian saluted.

"Yes, that's it!" Stanley smiled. "Now pass it on."

Pretty soon all the Estonians and Poles were saluting each other, laughing and joking as they did so.

Stanley turned to Officer Stelmaszyk and said, "You see, I even have the Estonians helping us."

———————

On Sunday morning Grudziński entered the control room with a cup of coffee in hand.

"Sir." Piasecki saluted him. Even the Estonian on duty saluted with a smile.

"Whose name day is it today?" Grudziński asked.

"I think it's Saint Justin, sir," Piasecki responded.

"Perhaps a day of rest," the Estonian said in broken Polish.

"We can always hope," Grudziński smiled.

There was a commotion in the radio room. Grudziński put his cup down and went to see what was happening. Henry Kotecki, 'The Kat' was standing in the confined room banging his radio with one hand and turning the dial with his other.

"Kotecki," Grudziński said, but the Kat ignored him while he continued to fuss noisily.

"Kotecki!" Grudziński repeated.

"He has his headphones on," Piasecki said from behind.

Grudziński grabbed Kat's arm. "Henry, what is wrong?"

"This is wrong!" the Kat cried, "Everything's wrong!" The Cat continued to fuss, knocking papers to the floor.

"What is wrong?" Grudziński demanded.

"The news, the news," was all Kat could say.

"Kotecki! Stand to attention!" Grudziński ordered.

Kotecki snapped to attention but the pain on his face was unmistakable.

"Take those headphones off," Grudziński said more quietly.

Kotecki removed them and placed them on his radio desk.

"Now, tell me what's wrong."

"Sir," he began with a stammer, "I was listening to the news, as I always do every morning, and I heard something terrible."

"What did you hear?"

"Russia has invaded."

"Russia has invaded who?"

"Poland! Russia has invaded Poland!" Tears were in Kat's eyes. "I am from Vilnius, and my family are there. Vilnius is near the Russian border."

Grudziński stepped back in shock. Piasecki stood speechless. The radio room was adjacent to the control room so everyone in the control room also heard. Some shook their heads in disbelief, but no one made a sound. The only person to break the stunned silence was the Estonian.

"I don't understand, but this is bad. No?"

"We leave tonight!" Grudziński whispered through clenched teeth to Piasecki, before marching out towards the engine room.

———

"Blackie!" Grudziński called as he entered the engine room through the hatch.

"Yes, sir?"

"I want a hacksaw."

"Yes, sir, I have one here," Blackie said as he offered him the saw from his tool bag. "Can I ask what you need it for?"

"Torpedoes," was all Grudziński said as he turned to head towards the bow.

"What was all that about?" Foterek asked.

"I'm not sure."

"What did he want?"

"My hacksaw."

"What for?"

"Torpedoes, was all he said."

Neither of us could fathom what Grudziński was going to do.

———

In the forward torpedo room, the crew were getting ready to finish removing the torpedoes. A few had been removed the previous afternoon before work stopped for the day. Each torpedo was secured on its rack, like a steel stretcher, stacked on the port and starboard walls. When the ship was ready to fire, the movable rack was slid out from the wall and lined up with the torpedo tube. The torpedo could then be slid into the tube in preparation.

Loading torpedoes was a similar operation. There was an angled hatch in the ceiling of the torpedo room leading out to the open deck above. Through this hatch, torpedoes could be winched slowly down a slide into the submarine and positioned carefully on their respective racks. When placed safely and secured with straps, the rack could then be slid into its storage position.

What the crew now prepared for was the reverse of that operation.

When Grudziński walked into the torpedo room, the news of the Russian invasion had already reached them. The men just stood there silently, no one offering a salute. What use were words when two armies were marching across your homeland?

Above them, a voice echoed down through the torpedo hatch. "Hey you down there, we're almost ready up here. I'm sending the cable down."

A clanking sound signaled that the steel cable was being slowly lowered down through the sloping hatch.

Stanley stepped forward. "That's Stelmaszyk up on deck and he's overseeing the Estonians. He won't have heard the news yet, it's only us down here that know."

The cable stopped in place, ready for a torpedo. Grudziński stepped forward, brandishing the hacksaw. Placing one hand on the cable to hold it still, he began to saw the cable with his other hand.

Stanley stepped forward. "Sir! What are you doing?"

"I need these torpedoes."

"Sir, if you do this the Germans will probably shoot you."

"I need to keep these torpedoes because we're leaving tonight. I need to delay the Estonians a little longer."

"Sir, please, this is not the way."

"So what else do you suggest?"

"Sir, if you use that hacksaw, they will know someone cut the cable. If you want to break the cable, that is not the way to do it."

"I have no other choice."

"Yes you do, let me do it."

"So you get shot? I'm responsible here if anyone gets shot it'll be me."

"Sir, no one has to get shot. Forget the hacksaw, I know how to sabotage the cable so they will think it simply broke."

"You can do that?" Grudziński looked surprised.

Stanley stood back with hands-on-hips and said, "Hey, I'm not just a pretty face."

"OK, then, the job is yours." Grudziński handed the hacksaw to Stanley. "But first, take this hacksaw back to Blackie, it belongs to him."

They saluted each other as Grudziński left.

————

Climbing up through the conning tower, Grudziński walked to the foredeck. The hoist and winch were in place, ready to pull torpedoes out of the Orzeł. The Estonians were huddled around the torpedo hatch waiting to start. Warrant Officer Stelmaszyk was looking out over the quay, waiting for the mobile crane to arrive. Without the crane, work could not commence as the crane was heeded to hoist the torpedoes onto the back of a waiting truck.

As Grudziński approached, he said to Stelmaszyk, "Can I have a word with you?"

"Ah, Captain, I can report that we are working with appropriate efficiency," Stelmaszyk saluted.

"There is an Estonian guard in the bridge above us, so I don't want to speak too loudly, but there are a couple of things I need to tell you."

"Yes, sir. What is it?"

"First thing is, we are leaving tonight."

"Excellent news sir, we are all behind you!"

"Stanley has a plan to sabotage the hoist, I want you to talk with him because I don't want any Estonians injured."

"Yes, I'll check with him and we'll be careful," Stelmaszyk nodded. "I have nothing against these fellows, they are all good, honest men."

"There is one other thing."

"What is it, sir?"

"I must be blunt. The news has spread to everyone inside the Orzeł, but it seems that no one on deck or even the Estonians on the quayside know yet."

"Know what?"

Grudziński paused. He felt as if he were delivering news about a death in the family. "This morning, we received news that Russia is also invading Poland."

Stelmaszyk did not immediately respond but cocked his head in a questioning manner. Eventually, he said, "Why?"

Grudziński shrugged and shook his head. "If you want to be relieved, that's OK, but I need you working here with Stanley to safeguard these torpedoes. We need to keep some torpedoes when we leave."

"I understand, but I don't understand why Poland is being treated this way."

"Never mind why." Grudziński gripped Stelmaszyk's arm. "What we do now, we do for Poland, and I need you to stay on station as a Polish officer."

Stelmaszyk stood upright with pride. "I understand sir." Saluting, he said, "I will do my duty."

"Good man, carry on!" Grudziński saluted back.

———

Stelmaszyk returned to his post on deck, to oversee the hoisting of torpedoes out of Orzeł's bow. He now knew what Seaman Stanley Uliczny was planning. *This will be a grand performance*, he thought to himself. *The Estonians will never suspect a thing. I just hope that damned commander doesn't get too nosey.*

Everyone was now ready to hoist the first torpedo of the morning. Stelmaszyk continued with his delaying tactics, trying to slow down every step of the operation. "Is everyone ready?" he asked the Estonians in Russian.

"Da," they all responded.

"Is everyone ready down below?" Stelmaszyk shouted down the torpedo hatch in Polish.

"All good down here sir," came Stanley's reply.

Stelmaszyk indicated for the winch to start hauling the torpedo up through the hatch. Occasionally he would signal to stop hauling, allowing him to inspect the progress of the torpedo. This was a normal procedure, but Stelmaszyk did this more than needed to delay as much as possible.

Soon the torpedo was clear of the hatch, where the Estonians secured it into a lifting basket. Stelmaszyk was careful to inspect the securing straps, pulling on each one meticulously. When he was satisfied, he signaled to the waiting crane on the quayside to lift the torpedo from the deck, and onto a waiting truck. Even this part wasn't without delay as Stelmaszyk kept ordering the crane to pause while he complained about the balance of the basket.

Stelmasyk made a procedure that should have taken much less than an hour take over an hour and a half. One more torpedo was withdrawn, wasting the entire morning. When lifting the third torpedo, Stanley gave the signal to Stelmaszyk in Polish, "Be careful with this one!"

Once again Stelmaszyk indicated for the winch to start hauling the torpedo. After a couple of feet, the torpedo seemed to get stuck.

"Come on, pull!" Stelmaszyk shouted in Russian.

The winch operator increased the power.

"Come on, pull harder!" Stelmaszyk ordered.

As the Estonian powered the winch even more there was a terrific snap as the cable recoiled out of the hatch. The torpedo clanked down the couple of feet to the bottom of the hatch. The Estonians dived for cover expecting an explosion.

"What the hell happened?" Stelmaszyk began shouting.

Stelmaszyk, who was the only one left standing on deck, moved towards the hatch. "Is everything OK down there?"

"We're fine," replied Stanley, "it looks like the cable snapped."

Stelmaszyk looked toward the steel cable which was lying on the deck in front of the winch. Picking it up, he examined the broken end. "This cable has snapped! What's the meaning of this?" he exclaimed as he looked at the winch operator.

"I don't know," replied the Estonian, "this was a strong cable."

"You can see that this is not a good cable," Stelmaszyk retorted. "Look at how it has snapped!"

"It was a good cable," the Estonian repeated.

"You could have blown up the whole ship! You could have killed us all!"

The other Estonians now moved towards their beleaguered colleague, as Stelmaszyk ranted about how delicate the torpedoes were. That's when Grudziński came on deck. "What's going on here? What's all this noise about?"

"Sir!" Stelmaszyk replied, "the winch cable has snapped, causing the torpedo to slide back down the hatch. They could have blown us all sky high!" Stelmaszyk threw his arms upwards in a dramatic gesture, dropping the cable to the deck.

Grudziński picked it up and examined it carefully. "This has snapped," he said, nodding his head, "it looks like an old cable to me."

"No, no, this was good cable," The winch operator was now pleading.

"This does not look like a good cable to me, and Stelmaszyk is correct, there could have been a serious accident," Grudziński said.

Commander Mere heard the commotion from where he was on the quayside. He rushed up the forward gangplank. "What's going on here? Why has work stopped?"

The winch operator started talking excitedly in Estonian to the commander, the other Estonians also joined in all talking at once, shrugging their shoulders and pointing towards the cable which Grudziński still clutched in his hand."

Stelmaszyk began swearing and gesticulating. Stanley poked his head sheepishly out of a deck hatch to watch the commotion.

"Commander," Grudziński said, holding his hand up to quell the noise. "Allow me to explain. As you can see, the winch cable has snapped while they were pulling a torpedo out from below deck. When it snapped, the torpedo then slid back down the chute. Lucky for us it was only partway up, otherwise it could have been a very serious accident." Grudziński brandished the cable towards Commander Mere.

"I thought you had disarmed the torpedoes?" Mere asked.

"Yes, of course, we have," replied Stelmaszyk, "but they are still loaded with heavy explosives."

Mere examined the cable. "It does seem to have snapped. My men will replace the cable and we can restart work within an hour."

"Commander," Grudziński said, "my men are exhausted, we have been at sea for over two weeks. We are now being interned and forced to disarm our submarine. My men need a rest."

"Lieutenant, I cannot allow any shore leave. That is out of the question."

"I am not requesting shore leave. We have also learned this morning that Russia has joined the invasion of Poland."

"Yes, I have also heard the news."

"My men are not only exhausted, but they are also completely demoralized, they need to rest."

"What are you suggesting lieutenant?"

"Today is Sunday. I would like my men to be able to rest for the day. Perhaps we can gather our thoughts in prayer. We could even hold a mass."

Commander Mere looked around with his hands on his hips. He could see that every Polish face looked sullen and dejected. "Very well Grudziński, you can have your day of rest. You may hold a mass on the quayside if you wish. My men will not intrude on your peace. However, we must restart work tomorrow morning."

"My men will feel better in the morning, I can promise you that."

"In the meantime, my men will get this winch out of your way and replace the cable."

"Thank you, Commander." Grudziński and Mere then exchanged salutes.

9 Sunday Mass

Ship's Log entered by: Lieutenant Jan Grudziński
Date: September 17, 1939
Location: Port of Tallinn, Estonia
Entry: Although the Orzeł is interned, we have managed to save some torpedoes. The bad news of the Soviet invasion of Poland has deeply affected our morale, but the Estonians have allowed us this Sunday to rest.

When I heard we had the day off for Sunday, I was very relieved. We all knew something was going to happen to stop the Estonians from stealing all our torpedoes, but we didn't know exactly what. We all knew that the Germans were behind this devious plot to intern us. We learned that the Russians were now invading Poland. It seemed that the world was against us. We had a plan to keep fighting, but I thought our chances were very slim.

I was tired, worried, and I needed to rest. Luckily, I was able to find an empty bunk to lay down on, so I could relax, and maybe even sleep.

Rebi, or Petty Officer Henry Rebizant, our electrician was also lying on a nearby bunk.

"Hey, Blackie, I hear the Estonians need a new cable for their crane," he said.

"Yes, I heard, that's why we got the day off." I yawned, longing for some rest.

"What's up Blackie?" Rebi asked. "You don't look good."

"I'm worried the Estonians could catch on to our plan."

"Don't worry, they won't," Rebi reassured me.

"What about the Germans?" I asked. "They have eyes and ears everywhere. I'm worried about this subterfuge. I don't mind fighting at sea, but I'm worried about being caught and imprisoned by the Germans."

Before Rebi could answer, Foterek came by. "So that's where you two have been hiding," he said. "I want you both to smarten yourselves up, the captain is calling for a Mass today at noon on the quayside."

Rebi and I looked at each other, then down at ourselves, as if to inspect our uniforms.

"Get cleaned up and be topside in one hour, you can use the washrooms on the dockside," Foterek ordered. "Put your dress tunics on, I want my engineers looking proud."

"Yes, sir," Rebi said, as he raised himself from his bunk.

"Aye, sir," I echoed, as I started to roll out of my bunk.

Foterek reminded me of how my mother used to be on Sunday mornings. She would wash us and dress us, and boss us around to make sure we were the cleanest and best-behaved children in the village. Throughout the morning she would be angry, shouting at everyone, telling us all to hurry up. My father had to prepare the horse and cart for us all to ride into the village, while my mother spread clean blankets on the benches in the cart so we wouldn't get our clothes dirty. As a final touch, she would pick flowers from her garden to adorn the horse. During winter she would use sprigs taken from pine trees.

As my father drove us to church in the cart, my mother would sit erect beside him watching the lane ahead. "Watch those potholes!" she would command. "We are not sacks of potatoes! We are a family going to church!"

So there I was, commanded yet again to attend Mass.

Just like on any Sunday, in any Polish village or town, we gathered for Mass. We mingled on the quayside as a crowd, exchanging pleasantries, all without jokes or loud talking. We smiled at each other and shook hands as if it was just another Sunday afternoon.

Eventually, Lieutenant Grudziński emerged onto the deck of the Orzeł, followed by Lieutenant Piasecki and other officers from the control room. They walked single file to the front of our crowd, just like a priest followed by his altar boys. There was no organ music to accompany them, only the calls of the seagulls.

Foterek raised his hand in the air, snapping his fingers. Rebi and I looked at him, as Foterek gesticulated for us to stand around him as a family of engineers. Other groups did the same and we all quietly assembled into our families of subcommands.

Grudziński gathered a few crewmen together at the front of the waiting crowd. I couldn't hear what they were saying to each other, but eventually, they began to sing 'Serdeczna Matko'. They sang nervously together and quietly, but as Grudziński encouraged them they began to sing as a whole unit. We now had a choir. Some of us began to sing along, even if only in subdued tones.

Even for a submariner, Lieutenant Grudziński was short and petite, so Lieutenant Piasecki pulled a crate over to act as a podium. Grudziński nodded towards Piasecki in thanks and stood on the crate so we could all see him. He stood there for a while, not even trying to gather attention from his audience. He was like a priest in meditation on the altar.

The singing came to a slow halt, while the murmur of conversation slowly subsided as the crew of the Orzeł slowly realized that Grudziński stood waiting before us. Foterek whispered to us, "Men, face forward, our commander is about to speak."

Grudziński then took a deep breath and spoke loudly so all could hear.

"Men, we have come a long way to get here, and I am proud of you all to make this journey possible. Today is Sunday, a blessed day of rest, let us all be thankful for that."

We all nodded in agreement. Even if the Estonians realize we sabotaged the crane cable, at least we got a day off.

Grudziński continued, "Today I will lead you all in prayer, to give thanks for what we have. Tomorrow promises hardships for us, and it may be some time before we see our homes again. Let us not forget that it is our country, our homes, and our families that we fight for."

There was total silence from the crew, I don't think I was the only one to wonder if we would ever see our home again.

Grudziński took a deep breath and looked skyward. "Allow me to lead you in the Lord's Prayer."

We all knelt, bowing our heads, and chanted together the well-known words.

Our Father who art in heaven,
hallowed be thy name...

As we prayed, I noticed that the Estonian guards kept a respectable distance from the Orzeł, were also kneeling, and held their heads down in prayer. I felt good that they were part of our Mass.

We all finished the prayer with a loud "Amen". We then stood up and waited for Grudziński to continue.

"Now is the time for us to break bread together," Grudziński announced, as he gestured for Freckles to move forward with his basket of bread. "We don't have *opłatek*, but our ship's cook will give you all rye bread to share."

Opłatek is the Holy Eucharist that the priest gives out at Communion. The thin wafers of unleavened bread are embossed with religious scenes. My family would always have it at home at Christmas and we would share it just before Vigilia, our traditional Christmas Eve feast. This was our Christmas vigil as we waited for the first star to appear. It was during that time that we would share the Opłatek, giving thanks to each other as we did.

As Freckles came by with his basket, he broke off a chunk of bread from one of his loaves. Handing the chunk to me he said, "Peace be with you."

"And also with you," I responded.

Freckles then gave some bread to Rebi and Foterek who were both standing with me. "Peace be with you," I said, as I shared bread with Rebi.

"This reminds me of Christmas at home," he said.

"I was thinking the same thing, I miss my mother's borsch and baked fish on Vigilia. I don't think we'll be home this Christmas."

Foterek stepped in, breaking bread with me. "Blackie, I'm glad you're on my team. We may not be home this Christmas, but we'll get through this and we'll all be home for the next Christmas."

I smiled and broke bread with him. "Thank you, and peace be with you."

"And with you," Foterek returned with a smile.

As we all mingled, breaking bread with the rest of the crew, I felt the warmth and camaraderie we all had for each other. Something at the back of my mind kept haunting me with a nagging feeling of doom. Yes, it was fear, but not the usual fears of a submariner. It was not fear of being underwater, or being chased by hunter-killers. It was a fear worse than death. It was the fear of being imprisoned. Officially we were interned in Tallinn. If the Estonians discovered our plans to escape, what would happens then? It would be yet another defeat for Poland, our precious Orzeł would be given to Germany or Russia, while my shipmates and I rotted inside of some dank prison, never to see our homes again.

As I shared bread with my crewmates, I met Józef. He was taller than most of the crew, lean and strong. He wore a traditional necklace, typical of the Tatra Mountain men, so I had to ask him, "Where is your home in Poland?"

"Zakopane, my family have a small farm outside of the town."

"I recognize the necklace you always wear."

"Yes, my father made that for me, he said it will bring me good luck."

"So why is a mountain man serving on a submarine?" I asked.

"Why not?" He shrugged his shoulders. "I fight for Poland. It doesn't matter if I fight on the mountain or in the water, what matters is I fight."

"You mountain men always seem fearless."

"Oh, that's not true, we have many fears, mostly we fear God, and sometimes the weather." He winked and smiled as we broke bread.

Lieutenant Grudziński called out for everyone's attention.

The crew slowly turned, still clasping chunks of bread in our hands. "It's time for a sermon," Rebi whispered to me jokingly.

"Yesterday," Grudziński announced, "the British Naval Attaché came to visit us from the British Embassy."

Both Rebi and I looked at each other, wide-eyed! We expected some fantastic news. Maybe the British would save us from internment!

"The attaché was stopped at the gate and was not allowed to enter the dock. He was allowed to pass us this note, on a small card."

Grudziński held the small card above his head just like that British Prime Minister who declared "Peace in our time".

"The message says, 'Good luck and God bless you'."

I looked at Rebi who just scoffed. "The British, do you see how much they care about us?"

"This message," Grudziński continued, "can only mean one thing. The British cannot help us, but they stand with us."

Rebi looked at the ground. "What good does that do?"

"We stand here by ourselves, but we are not alone!" Grudziński stated. "We need help, but we are not helpless. We have a dark night ahead of us, but our resolve will light our way! We all know what we have to do, but let us not forget why we have to do it."

Grudziński paused while the crew looked up at him. I was worried he would now say too much about our planned escape, while the Estonians listened.

"We do what we must do for Poland, we do it for our homes and our families. The coming night will be the darkest, but if we stand together, the morning will be the brightest for us all."

Grudziński held up his hand as if to signal a stop. "I want to remind you all that we are submariners. Because of what we are I want you all to join me in a hymn that is very dear to my heart. The 'Hymn to the Baltic'!"

All our hearts lifted, even Rebi looked up, wide-eyed. "I love this hymn!" he exclaimed.

This hymn was the anthem of our small but proud Polish navy. Written in 1919 after World War One, when Poland was freed from the shackles of partition and became an independent country once more. We all started to sing, quietly at first.

Cordial mother, protector of people
Let the crying of the orphans arouse you to pity...

I had that choking feeling in my throat as if I wanted to cry. I noticed that Rebi's voice was broken, so he must have felt the same as me. I put my hand on his shoulder, he looked at me and we both seemed to gather strength. After the first verse, we both began to sing with full voices. The entire crew of the Orzeł sang loud, our voices filled with pride.

After the mass, I watched as Alex took a chunk of bread to one of the Estonian guards who had been watching the mass from a distance. As he gave a chunk of bread to the guard he said in Russian, "Let us share bread, and wish peace for each other."

"What do you mean? I am guarding you, you are my captive! Why do you wish me peace?"

"You are following orders, just as I am. We are both men of flesh and blood, if it was not for this war, we would both be at peace. So let us wish that we can both return to peace."

The guard lent his rifle against the wall as they both shared bread smiling and joking with each other.

10 Escape from Tallinn

Ship's Log entered by: Lieutenant Jan Grudziński
Date: September 17, 1939
Location: Port of Tallinn, Estonia
Entry: The night is quiet. I have ordered the crew to begin our escape plan. God help us.

It was approaching midnight and I was nervous. Strangely, Alex seemed very calm.

"Come on, Blackie, follow me. Whatever happens up there, just follow my lead."

I followed Alex to the control room.

"Did you bring your knife?"

"Yes," I said. "That's the third time you asked me."

"Well, give it to me," Alex said. Then he asked, "Did you bring cigarettes?"

"Of course. I also have matches."

As we entered the control room, I saluted Lieutenant Piasecki. "Sir, requesting permission for me and Alex to go up top for a cigarette."

Piasecki looked at his watch and said, "Granted."

As Alex and I both climbed up into the conning tower, we could hear the Estonian guard in the control room say, "Everyone here seems to smoke so much, is that usual?"

"They just came off their shift and there's not much else to do on a tiny boat like this," Piasecki said.

We climbed up into the bridge, where the second Estonian guard was on watch. "What are you doing up here?" he asked, pulling his rifle from his shoulder, holding it nervously towards us.

"Hey, stand at ease, we're only coming up here for a smoke." I waved my packet of cigarettes at him as I climbed off the ladder.

"Yeah," Alex said as he also climbed up. "It is better to smoke in here at night because it's out of the wind. We call it 'coming up for fresh air'."

"Smoking is fresh air?" The Estonian looked surprised.

"Have you been below?" Alex asked.

"Yes," the guard confirmed.

"So you will know what I mean by fresh air."

"Would you like to smoke with us?" I asked, offering the guard a cigarette. The guard looked around to see if anyone was watching from the quayside, before he turned back to me and said, "Yes."

———

Lieutenant Grudziński entered the control room and looked at his watch. It was time. "Piasecki."

"Aye, sir."

"We need more ventilation in here, it's getting very stuffy."

"Aye, sir." He then passed the order onto Master Seaman Jan Olejnik. "Olejnik!" he ordered, "open all vents and run the fans at maximum."

"Aye, sir."

This order was not just to ventilate the submarine. It was a signal to the whole crew that the escape plan was now active and in progress. All crew now had to be ready at their stations. There was also a second reason for the order. Olejnik also started the boat's gyroscope. The motors that ran these were not exactly silent, but with ventilation at maximum, the sound blended with the vents' noise. Our hope was that the Estonian guard in the control room would not question what was happening.

"Ventilation is good, no?" the guard said.

"Yes, we have no windows on this boat," Piasecki confirmed.

———

The Orzeł's ventilation system did not extend to the bridge, but with the hatch open, I could now hear the vents below blowing air throughout the boat. Both Alex and I knew this was the signal.

"So where do you come from?" Alex asked the guard.

"I come from a village on the peninsula."

"Oh, can you see it from here? Do you mean that peninsula over there?" Alex asked.

The guard moved to the seaward side of the bridge. "No, that is the peninsula, but you cannot see my village. It is called Lubja."

As Alex kept the guard's attention out towards the sea and the distant peninsula, I stood on the podium with my head above the bridge. From there, I gave the signal to the two men about to embark on their quayside mission. I did so by puffing heavily on my cigarette, using the little red flashes of the burning ember to indicate that the coast was clear.

———

Paul Gieldon stood at the top of the ladder of the aft deck's hatch, pushing the hatch slowly open, just enough so he could see the top of the conning tower. He waited for the signal. When he saw the red flashes of the puffing cigarette, he instructed his two comrades to go.

"Remember what you have to do," Paul whispered. "Be quick and hurry back."

Master Seamen Jan Torbus climbed quietly from the hatch, crawling slowly across the deck towards the gangplank. Master Seamen Tom Prządka also crawled close behind. Both men kept low and moved slowly so as not to attract attention.

Each man was armed with a fire axe. As they crept along, the trick was to keep the metal head of the axe from clanging on the Orzeł's steel deck.

After creeping down the gangplank, they then had to walk upright across the open quayside. They walked the shortest route to the cover of a nearby warehouse. The swift movement of a sprint may have attracted the attention of other Estonian guards, so the plan was to walk slowly but steadily with their heads held low. The axes they carried had to be close by their sides, swinging in time with their legs, so their silhouette would look like they carried nothing.

When they reached the warehouse, Jan turned left while Tom turned right. They could now use the building as cover, sneaking quickly along its edges using crates and other equipment to conceal themselves. Jan and Tom had an advantage because, during the night, the Estonian guards protected the gates and perimeter of the docks. Estonian security relied on the two guards they had watching the Orzeł. As long as they were occupied with that, Jan and Tom had the element of surprise on their side.

Their respective targets were previously identified by the Polish crew who had scouted the dock area during the day. they had carefully identified two important targets for a successful escape. The telephone lines and the power lines had to be cut to increase the cover of darkness and prevent an alarm from being raised.

Jan had the closest target of the telephone lines, probably the riskiest. These were connected to the back of the harbor office and had to be cut first. He had to avoid being seen by any guard who happened to be in the office. Jan used the shadows to silently cross an alleyway that ran from the warehouse to the back of the office. There he crouched behind a parked truck. From his hiding place he could see the power lines in the distance while waiting for Tom to get into his own position.

Tom had the farthest to go to the power lines. Although he passed through dark alleys with plenty of cover, his path was not without risk. There could be a random guard patrol, so he had to creep along silently, listening for any threats. Crossing the distance stealthily took a lot longer, and he was out of breath from carrying the heavy axe.

The moon was a waxing crescent moving in and out from behind scattered clouds. Their targets were near the fence protecting the perimeter of the harbor. A single telegraph pole stood at the corner of a warehouse. Several electric cables, wrapped in a thick sheath, climbed the pole. At the top, they branched into individual cables before crossing high above the perimeter fence to another pole outside the harbor area. The rising cable was his target, but the protective steel sheath rose to a point far above his head.

Damn, I hope I can swing hard enough to hit that high! Tom thought.

That was not his only problem. Although the night was dark with only partial moonlight, there were lights along the length of the perimeter and many more lights beyond the perimeter in other warehouses and roads. They all combined to illuminate the telegraph pole. He would be visible if he tried to cut the cable.

When I saw that Jan Torbus and Tom Przadka had cleared the Orzeł and disappeared beyond the warehouse, I flicked my cigarette into the water and climbed down off the podium. My action signaled to Alex that Jan and Tom were clear. "Hey, I want another cigarette," I said. "Who's going to join me?"

"I think you like fresh air, no?" The guard asked with a grin.

"Hey, maybe I can get Freckles to bring us our ration of vodka!" Alex exclaimed.

"What is this Freckles? I don't understand," the guard asked, now puzzled.

"Freckles is our cook, and we all get a ration of vodka every day," Alex replied.

"You all drink vodka every day? I think you Polish always have surprises."

"That sure is the truth," I said.

Jan Torbus was still crouched behind the truck looking out towards the power line, waiting for Tom to get into position. *He is taking a long time. Maybe he got caught? Should I run back to the Orzeł?* Many questions crossed his mind while he waited anxiously. *I'll hang on for another moment, just another moment,* Jan kept thinking, when suddenly Tom appeared next to a telegraph pole, waving his arms several times, and seeming to look straight at Jan.

Jan poked his head above the front of the truck, then waved back to return the signal. With Jan's wave, Tom disappeared back out of sight.

That's the signal, Jan thought, *now it is up to me.* Jan looked carefully around and listened for any footsteps. When he was satisfied the coast was clear, he lifted his axe and prepared to cut the telephone cable.

———

Tom looked towards the harbor office but did not see Jan. All he saw was an old truck parked behind the building in the shadows. *Where the hell is he? I can't see him, the only way for him to see me is to step out of the shadows.*

With that thought, Tom checked the coast was clear and stepped into the dim light next to the telegraph pole. Looking towards the harbor office, he could not see Jan. All he saw was the old truck and dark shadows behind it. Tom waved, hoping he could get Jan to wave back, but still he saw nothing.

He jumped back into the shadows. *What the hell do I do now? Maybe Jan was caught,* Tom thought. *If he was caught, then the alarm has already been raised. My only chance now is to signal the escape by cutting the lights. Jan and I will probably end up in an Estonian prison, but at least the Orzeł gets away.*

With that thought, and determination to free the Orzeł, Tom stood up and gripped his axe tightly.

"I am an ancient Polish Hajduk warrior chopping down the enemy with my axe!" Tom shouted. He ran six steps into the light, turned quickly, and dashed towards the telegraph pole. Swinging his axe over his head, trying to get the maximum height, he leapt with full force to swing the sharp axe, embedding its blade in the exposed power cables.

There was a sharp cracking sound with an explosion of sparks, as the steel blade shorted the power lines, embedding itself into the wooden pole. Tom crashed sideways into the corrugated wall of the warehouse with an enormous bang, and fell backward onto the hard, paved ground.

The entire dockside was suddenly plunged into darkness. The only light that bathed Tom now was the crescent moon and the lights still burning beyond the perimeter of the blackout.

I've got to get moving, he thought, as he stared up at the embedded axe above his head. Just then he heard a distant thump. Then a moment later, he heard another thump. Rolling onto his side and looking towards the noise, he saw Jan running out from behind the harbor office, throwing his axe to the ground.

There he is, thought Tom. *Looks like he's cut the phone lines.* Getting up with a grimace, Tom began to hobble towards the Orzeł. Who cared about stealth now? With a bruised arm and bruised thigh, Tom quickened to a slow jog, then a slow run.

———

"What the hell?" Alex heard the guard on the bridge exclaim as the lights went out all around the dockyard. The red deck light inside the bridge was the only illumination now, to the guard's obvious surprise. "The lights went out! Is it a power cut?"

"No! It's another Polish surprise!" With one hand, Alex flicked his cigarette away, as he withdrew his other from his coat pocket. He was holding a knife. He pressed the deadly blade against the guard's throat.

"Be quiet! Do as I say or Blackie has to clean up a bloody mess!"

With that order from Alex, the Estonian froze.

"The guard below, what is his name?" Alex asked.

"Markus."

"OK, shout down the hatch and tell Markus to send up some vodka," Alex ordered.

"What?"

"Do it!" Alex tightened his grip on the Estonian's throat and forced him to kneel close to the hatch.

"Ok, Ok," the guard complied. "Hey, Markus!"

———

Down below in the control room, Markus heard the guard above calling to him. Yet the guard hadn't blown his whistle, so it didn't sound like an emergency. Markus simply moved to the hatch, looked up, and asked, "What?"

"Send up some vodka."

"What?" Suddenly Markus felt a cold steel blade press into his throat. "Don't move," Olejnik said, as he held his knife to the guard's throat. Grudziński quickly relieved the guard of his rifle while Piasecki bound the guard's hands behind his back.

"Olejnik, keep him in the mess room and stay with him and guard him well."

"Aye, Captain!" Olejnik replied, marching the guard off to the mess room.

"We're coming down!" shouted Alex, as he helped the second guard down the ladder. "He's not bound but he is disarmed, and I took his whistle."

"This is a stupid Polish trick!" the guard protested, as he stepped down into the control room. "This will be big trouble for you!"

"It'll be even bigger trouble for you if you don't do as we tell you," Piasecki said as he bound the guard's hands. "Alex, take him to the mess room with the other guard. You and Olejnik will keep an eye on them both."

"Aye, sir."

"Where's Blackie?"

"He's up top wearing the guard's coat and hat just in case he's spotted."

"Good thinking," Grudziński said. "Helmsman, get up to the bridge and prepare to pull out." Grudziński pulled the engine telegraph to signal to start of the engines and stand by.

———————

Paul Gieldon was still at the aft deck hatch when the engines started. "Come on men that's the signal to cast off!" He pushed the hatch open fully and climbed out. "Come on, let's go!" He was followed by three other seamen, who clambered out of the forward deck hatch and began casting off the lines securing the Orzeł to the dock and the adjacent gunboat and destroyer.

Diesel fumes shrouded the aft section of the Orzeł as the engines powered into life.

Paul threw the aft gangplank into the water where it sank. Other men pushed the forward gangplank into the water where it also disappeared.

I shouted from the bridge, "Torbus and Tom aren't back yet!" I pointed towards a figure I saw running across the quay."

———

The harbormaster on duty sat at his desk, leaning back in his chair with his feet on the desk. He enjoyed the night shift as it was usually quiet. As he read his book he appreciated the fact that he didn't have to deal with the daytime duties, and all those troublesome officials dealing with that Polish submarine. Even the guard who was on duty snoozed quietly on the other side of the office.

When the lights went out, he swore. *Those damned fuses, they need changing every week!* He searched his pocket for matches as he stumbled across the office, heading for the fuse box. In the darkness, he bumped into a nearby desk. *Wait a minute,* he thought, *there's no light outside either…*

As he looked out the window, trying to see if there were any lights on the dock, he was startled by a loud thump on the back wall. "What the hell was that?" A moment later there was a second loud thump.

"Mikael, wake up!" he shouted at the guard. There was no response, so he kicked the guard's leg, pushing it off the desk where it rested.

"What the hell!" Mikael exclaimed, angry that he had been woken up so rudely. "Why is it so dark?"

"I don't know, there are no lights anywhere! You're the guard, you need to go and find out!"

They both went to the window to see if any lights were working. That's when they saw a figure sprinting across the quay.

"Who the hell is that?" the harbormaster asked.

"Oh, shit!" The guard scrambled back to the desk to find his gun in the dark. The harbormaster went to his desk and using the phone, tried to call the guard commander. "The God damn phone is dead!" was all he could shout.

———

From my position on the bridge, I could see Jan running as fast as he could across the open quayside towards us. The helmsman and Vlad came up to the bridge and also saw Jan heading towards us at a sprint.

I stood up on the podium to get a better view. "Run!" I shouted.

All the noise was attracting the attention of seamen on the destroyer Izyaslav. First, one head looked over the gunwale, followed by a second. They looked curious more than anything so I waved my cap towards them. Since I was wearing the Estonian guard's jacket and cap, my action seemed to reassure them. However, they started pointing at the dock lines, or should I say *lack of* dock lines, because they were detached and we were gently drifting by the side of the quay.

Jan ran towards the aft of the Orzeł where the seamen who released the lines were waiting. This was good because it was farthest from the prying eyes on the Izyaslav, but I now saw faces appearing on the bridge of the gunboat behind us.

Grudziński now appeared on the bridge. Seeing that Jan was running, he yelled, "Jump!"

At that moment, Jan reached the edge of the quay and jumped with his long legs stretched wide. The deck was about the same level as the quay. Jan landed squarely on the narrow deck and the waiting seamen arrested his momentum to stop him from falling into the water beyond.

Cheers arose from the men on the Orzeł's deck, but standing on the podium, I could see growing concern on the faces aboard the Izyaslav in front and the gunboat behind us.

"Sir, I think we have some trouble," I called down to Grudziński, who climbed up to the podium to see.

He immediately understood the gravity of the situation. "Where's Tom?" he asked.

"Over there." I pointed to the figure running from the corner of the warehouse. Tom was running but not nearly as fast as Jan had. He ran with a limp which made him look like a horse cantering to the finish line.

"He looks wounded!" I said.

That's when a guard appeared from the harbor office. He raised his arm straight into the air and fired a shot from his pistol.

Tom tried to run faster, but I was now worried that a full alarm would be raised and that Tom could be shot from the gunboat or destroyer. "Run!" I pleaded aloud.

"He won't make the jump!" Grudziński shouted down to the deck. "Form a human ladder down the side of the boat and pull him up!"

Men from the foredeck ran to help those on the aft deck. The hull of the Orzeł was a steel tube like any other submarine. The deck was only a narrow platform attached along the top of the tube, with the sides of the tube sloping down on either side. There was no way that Tom could now jump to the deck. He would land on the side of the curved tube. With nothing to hold onto and no way to grip the steel side, he would simply slip down into the water. The waiting seamen had to make a human ladder over the side of this tube to catch Tom as he leaped across.

Another gunshot rang out from the guard at the office. This time he was aiming at Tom. The guard fired again.

"Sir?" I showed the Estonian guard's rifle to Grudziński. "I can easily hit the guard from here."

Grudziński looked at the rifle, before giving me a stern look. "No," he said, "that guard can't hit Tom from that distance, and if these ships open fire there is nothing you can do. So stand down, Blackie."

"Aye, sir."

As Tom neared the quay he jumped and landed just above the water line, on the Orzeł's pressure hull, at the bottom of the human ladder.

Grudziński slammed the engine telegraph to 'Full Forward' and ordered the helmsman to steer full starboard.

With Orzeł's starboard side against the quay, her stern moved slowly away from the quay, while our bow pushed slowly into the quay. We began our slow turn.

"Vlad," Grudziński said, "you're our pilot now, keep us off that sandbank."

"Yes, sir!"

As the Orzeł turned, Grudziński used the engine telegraph to change to 'Ahead Slow', the better to control the turn.

Tom was being pulled up the side of the hull. He was flat on his stomach, being pulled by his arms, which made me think he was dead. After a while of the human ladder pulling itself and Tom up the ship, Tom eventually stood on the deck.

"Thank God, he's alright," I said.

"Get below!" Grudziński shouted to the crew on the foredeck. "Now!"

As Grudziński watched the men clamber down the hatch, Vlad said from behind, "Sir, we're drifting toward the sandbank."

"Helm, keep full starboard rudder," Grudziński ordered, but at that moment we could feel the stern dragging on the sand and mud behind us. We came to a shuddering halt as our stern became stuck in the mud.

As we braced ourselves against the stop, Grudziński said, "Vlad, I thought you sounded the channel out. What the hell happened?"

"Don't know sir." Vlad looked puzzled.

"It could be the wash of our boat, sir," the helmsman said. "Maybe we created a mini current as we turned."

Grudziński turned the engine telegraph to 'Full Ahead', and we could see the propeller kick up a murky wash at Orzeł's stern.

"Can you move the rudder?" Grudziński asked.

"No sir, it's stuck in the mud and the weight of the Orzeł is probably leaning on it. So I can't move it. Don't worry though, it's turned to full starboard, so it's aiming the right way for the engines."

The Orzeł vibrated violently as the engines struggled against the mud.

"Sir," Vlad said, "I think our bow is heading towards the mud bank."

"What else could go wrong?" I asked.

"Don't worry," Grudziński said. "As our mid-ship hits the mud bank, the Orzeł should act like a lever and pull our stern off the mud.

As Grudziński predicted, the turn of the Orzeł did pull our stern from the mud.

"Rudder is free sir."

"Good, hard to port!"

Our engines were at full so we started to accelerate forward, while our stern began to creep back towards the mud bank.

"Helm ahead straight," Grudziński ordered.

As the helmsman corrected, we were now heading dead towards the Estonian gunboat that had escorted us into the harbor.

"Sir? Should I turn?"

"No, hold her steady."

As we approached the gunboat with increasing speed, the crew on deck began to panic and scatter. They were expecting a collision. I even saw some men running down the gangplank to the safety of the quayside.

"Steer forty degrees to starboard," Grudziński ordered.

As we turned our bow away from the gunboat, we sailed past her so close I could have spat on her. Our wake made the gunboat rock wildly.

"Vlad, where's the sandbank?"

"About twenty meters to our starboard, sir. Head straight for the Thalatta, and we'll be safe in the channel."

I could hear pings and sometimes a 'rat, tat, tat' around us. "What's that noise?" I asked.

"Small arms fire," said Grudziński, "Keep your heads down. It's probably coming from the destroyer behind us, but it won't hurt the Orzeł."

We all kept our heads low to avoid stray bullets, but Grudziński stood straight, keeping his eyes fixed on our course and looking out for any hazards.

"Vlad, what course do I follow to stay in the channel?"

Vlad poked his head up. "OK, run parallel to the Thalatta. When we get alongside, turn towards that light on the breakwater. That gap to the east of the light is where we entered the harbor. After that, we will be in the open bay."

"Helm, fifteen degrees to starboard."

"Aye, sir."

A moment later we were alongside the Thalatta, the German tanker that everyone seemed so protective about. I stood on the podium and poked my head above slightly to get one last look at her. That's when I saw our aft deck hatch open, and out came Freckles. He carried a sack tied with a rope, and standing on the deck, he swung it like the hammer of a Norse God. He let it fly with a scream, "We'll see you on the bottom!" His package landed on the side of Thallata's bridge. The stunned Germans, thinking it was a bomb, scattered. Many jumped into the water to swim away. Freckles gave them the 'fist' before diving back into the hatch.

"OK, helm, dead ahead," Grudziński said.

We straightened out and sailed swiftly through the gap in the breakwater that Vlad had mentioned. I was relieved when we finally reached open water.

"Don't worry men, the fun isn't over yet," Grudziński said. "The Estonians have good coastal defense batteries. They'll open fire on us when they learn we're making a run for it."

Whatever happened next, I was glad that Tallinn was behind us.

"Helm, steer north."

"Aye, sir."

"Vlad, thank you for your help. Now get below."

"Aye, aye, sir."

"Blackie, get back to the engine room, we'll be diving soon and I'm sure Foterek needs you."

"Yes, sir."

"And send Piasecki up here, I need to talk with him."

The Orzeł headed away from Tallinn on the surface, diesel engines pounding away, driving the sub at full speed. The helmsman on the bridge kept his eyes ahead, while Grudziński kept his binoculars to his eyes, scanning the coastline to the aft and the flanks. Searchlights from the destroyer were trying to pinpoint the Orzeł, but the submarine was increasing its distance, making those lights ineffective.

Lieutenant Piasecki climbed into the bridge. "You wanted to see me, sir?" he asked.

Grudziński stood on the podium, observing the view behind. "Yes," he said.

Just then three distant flashes appeared almost simultaneously at three separate locations on the distant shore. "Just a moment," Grudziński said, looking at his watch.

Piasecki stepped up onto the podium. "Is the destroyer following us?"

A moment later, three bangs from the shore guns could be heard in quick succession, followed by the sound of projectiles flying.

"No, their ships were slow to start, but when they get going they could soon catch up. Those are the shore batteries firing at us," said Grudziński.

The whistling projectiles became louder and crashed in a wide range, about three hundred meters off the Orzeł's port side. Their explosive splashes rose high into the night sky.

"They're not very good shots," Piasecki said.

"Ballistics," Grudziński said, keeping an eye on the shore batteries. "They are ranging us."

"Sir, should we dive now?" Piasecki asked.

"Not yet, we need speed to make as much distance as possible."

"But if they are ranging us?"

"First shot is to range the target, the second shot is to correct the accuracy, the third shot will sink us."

Just then there was a fourth flash from a different location on the shore.

"That's the one we have to worry about," Grudziński said.

"Sir?"

"The first three fired at about the same time, but from different locations and angles. Their shells landed at about the same time, so they are confused about their range."

The sound of the fourth gun reached their ears, with the distant whoosh of a flying projectile. The first three guns repeated, with three new flashes on the shore.

"That fourth gun," Grudziński continued, "fired at a different time from the first three, so he will be able to range us, and accurately target us much more quickly."

"Should we take evasive action?"

"I'm waiting for the second shot from that fourth cannon."

There was a whoosh and an explosive splash 250 meters off Orzeł's starboard bow.

"Helm, turn twenty degrees to starboard!" Grudziński ordered.

Three other shells made their splashes, three to four hundred meters off Orzeł's stern. A few moments later the second shot rang out from the fourth shore gun.

"Here comes his second shot," Piasecki said.

"Helmsman, get below and take the helm in the control room," ordered Grudziński, as he sounded the dive alarm. Grudziński paused, scanning the dark sky.

"Sir, should we get below?" asked Piasecki.

"I want to see where that shell hits."

Soon enough a whoosh was followed by an explosive splash about 200 meters off the port bow.

"Get below, let's dive!" ordered Grudziński.

———

As they dropped down into the control room, preparations to dive were already well underway.

"Sir, all indicators are green, all hatches are closed," the boson said.

"Sir, air pressure is steady, the boat is sealed," the midshipman said.

"What's our sea depth?" Grudziński asked.

"Eighty meters, sir," replied the helmsman, "current heading is thirty degrees."

"Dive to sixty meters, steer to port, heading 350 degrees, speed five knots," ordered Grudziński. "I saw a deep-sea anchorage as we came into port, we'll head underneath it to avoid detection."

"Sir," Piasecki said, "I suggest we continue north to the Finnish coast. We could hide in the Aland Islands. From there we could intercept the German freighters carrying iron ore to Germany from northern Sweden."

"That's probably a good idea, but I suspect the Estonians are also thinking that will be our best option to escape."

"So what is your plan, Captain?"

"As we pass the Paljassaare headland, we head west. There is a deep, wide channel south of Naissaar Island. We move through there quietly into the Baltic. It's longer but they won't expect us to do that."

———

After we sailed free from Estonian waters, our new Captain Grudziński announced over the ship's tannoy: "This is your commander speaking."

I noticed that he didn't say 'captain'. He seemed reluctant to speak that word.

"As you all know we have escaped internment in Tallinn, and our captain has been left behind in the hospital. I, Jan Grudziński, am now in command of this ship. I intend to attack all German vessels that we encounter, but we will do so according to international law and according to our instructions from the commander of the Polish naval fleet. We have limited resources but we do have enough to engage the enemy, and we will seek out any enemy ships and destroy them according to our rules of engagement. Commander out."

Well that was fighting talk, I thought. With five torpedoes, we could sink five ships.

11 Marinestation der Ostsee

Admiral Rolf Carls, Kriegsmarine Commander of the Baltic region, sat at his large oak desk. His office in the Marinestation der Ostsee, in the city of Kiel, was arranged with strict military formality. His desk was central to a semi-circle of eight ornate wooden chairs, better suited to a dining room. His officers would use these when they attended meetings. To the admiral's left as a simple office chair and school-style desk, where his secretary sat during meetings to take shorthand notes. To the admiral's right stood an ornate wooden chair, reserved for visiting dignitaries.

The large, ornate windows opposite welcomed the morning sun as it flickered on the estuary in the distance. The flocked wallpaper held paintings of four ships. The SMS Fürst Bismarck and SMS Breslau were two ships the admiral had proudly served on as a young officer in World War I. The U-124 and SMS Hessen were vessels he had commanded. There was also a large map of the Baltic Sea on the wall. This was the area that Admiral Carls commanded over.

The wall behind the admiral's desk held two portraits: Grand Admiral Erich Raeder, head of Naval Command, and the Führer und Reichskanzler, Adolf Hitler.

Admiral Rolf Carls held his fountain pen still above the paper he was writing. With his other hand, he smoothed his mustache and goatee as he contemplated his weekly report to Grand Admiral Erich Raeder. One section needed completion, but he would not have the necessary information until after 09:00. With his experience of command, he knew the answer that he would write, but he must first impress the urgency upon his subordinates.

At precisely 08:59 there was a gentle knock on the admiral's door. He waited until he returned his fountain pen to its holder, rolling the blotting paper over his last written entry.

"Come in," he finally said, admiring his neatly written page.

The door opened quietly, and his secretary entered. She stood politely by the door, with hands gently clasped in front of her. The admiral admired how - dressed in her crisp uniform with short-layered hair - she always looked like a young naval cadet.

"Sir, Commander Friedrich Oskar Ruge is here to see you."

"Very good," Admiral Carls said, without looking back down at his page. "Send him in."

His secretary gestured politely for Commander Ruge to enter, while she held the door open. The commander walked smartly into the room and the secretary exited, quietly closing the door behind her. Ruge had been here only once, before the invasion of Poland. On that day he was one of many officers in the meeting, who all received secret orders in preparation for the attack. Today was very different. He was alone, and the summons for this meeting did not indicate any reason. There had been no spectacular naval victories, so this could not be a commendation. Perhaps the lack of spectacle would be a reason for chastisement?

As he approached, he stopped at the center of the semi-circle of chairs. Previously he had sat to the side, with higher officers to the center. Now he was unsure where to sit. Clicking his heels, he stood to attention, raised his arm in salute, and said, "Heil Hitler." His arm remained in salute until acknowledged by the admiral.

"Heil Hitler," Carls responded almost casually as he looked up. The admiral observed Ruge with an emotionless stare before saying, "Please, take a seat," indicating the center of the semi-circle.

Commander Ruge removed his dress cap and seated himself in the middle.

Admiral Carls clasped his hands together, resting them lightly on the desk in front of him. "Commander, your flotilla of minesweepers have been very successful in the Polish campaign. I congratulate you on your successes."

"Thank you, admiral. Coming from you I take that as the highest of compliments."

"Your flotilla has even engaged with the Polish submarines. Am I correct?"

"Yes sir, we have inflicted some damage, but no kills to date. They have all fled. Three have escaped to Sweden and have been interned there."

"Yes, but there was one Polish submarine that has escaped to England to join the British fleet." Admiral Carls paused and looked at his report. "It is called 'The Wilk'."

"That is correct, sir, I understand that the name of that submarine translates as 'The Wolf'. However, it has fled to England with its tail between its legs."

The admiral smiled falsely. "Your observation that it has fled is quite correct." His eyes then narrowed. "However, Grand Admiral Raeder is very concerned that it has added strength to the already powerful British Navy."

There was a slight pause in the conversation. *So that's what this is about*, Commander Ruge thought to himself. *As commander of minesweepers and torpedo boats, this would be seen as my responsibility.* Ruge swallowed hard, as he imagined the worst was coming.

"Commander, I assume you are aware of a fifth Polish submarine?"

"Yes, sir, I am. The ORP Orzeł, or as her name translates, 'The Eagle'. She was interned in Tallinn, but she slipped her moorings on September 17th, and has now escaped."

Admiral Carls nodded. "When our embassy in Estonia learned that the Orzeł had entered the port of Tallinn, they easily persuaded the Estonians to have her interned."

"I see." Ruge wondered why he needed to know of political issues.

"Further to that," the admiral continued, "the Estonians agreed with our embassy to hand over the Orzeł to the Kriegsmarine. Sadly, that cannot happen now."

Ruge's eyes widened in surprise. "Sir, I was not aware of this. I agree that was indeed a missed opportunity."

"The Orzeł would have been a welcome prize!" The admiral now smiled. "She would have boosted our U-Boat fleet, and would have provided valuable proof of our military superiority."

"Sir, at least she is now heading for Sweden."

The admiral shook his head negatively as he explained, "Our intelligence suggests she is not heading to Sweden. If she were, she would be there by now.

"Sir, I can assure you, my torpedo boats will pursue her."

"She retains some torpedoes, and as such continues to be a threat to our shipping in the Baltic. You see, commander, this issue of the Orzeł has reached the highest levels in Berlin."

Commander Ruge felt a cold shiver shoot up his spine. His neck involuntarily pulled his head up straight. He realized that the attention of Berlin could only mean one thing.

Admiral Carls continued, "One submarine making its way to England is bad enough, but to allow this prize to escape and continue as a threat has enraged the Führer."

The admiral allowed a pause in the conversation. Commander Ruge dared not speak.

Carls then continued, "The Führer has declared that the Polish Orzeł must be sunk at all costs."

The admiral's stern gaze, coupled with the mention of the Führer, reinforced Commander Ruge's fear. "Admiral, as always, I am at your disposal. I only ask, what support can I provide with my flotilla of minesweepers and torpedo boats?"

"That is exactly why I have asked you here, Commander. There is a very important operation that I want you to lead. Before I tell you what you need to do, let me remind you that this plan has been handed down from the Führer himself."

Commander Ruge straightened his back, as he listened intently for the words of the Führer.

"Our Führer has decreed that we engage in Unternehmen Seeadler. Since you like your translations of terms into other languages, you may call this 'Operation Sea Eagle'. I find this a very inspirational name from the Führer," Carls nodded in admiration. "You see, the Sea Eagle is an ocean-going bird that hunts for fish, and it relies heavily on its eyes to find its prey. The Führer has ordered more eyes to patrol the Baltic to search for the Orzeł."

"Sir, I also find this an apt operational name, our Führer is truly gifted."

"Ah, but I have not yet explained your role in this operation."

"I await your orders, sir."

"The Führer has ordered more aircraft to patrol the Baltic, but we also need more ships. The Führer is aware that we are short of surface vessels. We simply do not currently have enough ships in this area to keep effective patrols."

Ruge now looked quizzical. "Sir, are you saying I should move all my boats off their current duties, and assign them to search for this Polish Orzeł instead?"

"There will be some non-essential patrols that you may reassign to be used in the search operations. Also, you have a good number of torpedo boats. These also can be used to search and destroy our target."

"But, sir," Commander Ruge pleaded, "most of my flotilla is engaged in clearing the Prussian coast and clearing the ports of Danzig and Gdynia of Polish mines. How can I reassign these resources?"

Admiral Carls sighed. "Commander, any delay in opening those ports is perfectly acceptable. Our Wehrmacht armies have all but won the war in Poland. This new assignment is much more important. What you must understand is that this Polish submarine has become an insult to the Kriegsmarine and the Third Reich itself."

The Admiral paused to allow the gravity of his statement to sink in. "This is why our Führer has ordered us to destroy this Orzeł. The Grand Admiral, Erich Raeder, is fully behind the Führer's decision. So we must ensure the destruction of that rogue Polish submarine."

Commander Ruge nodded. "Admiral, I fully understand, and I will reassign my flotilla immediately. My boats are relatively fast and can relocate quickly."

"I am glad you understand the need for our success. I will pass on all the relevant intelligence information I have to help you intercept the Orzeł." The admiral then opened a side drawer on his desk and pulled out a large manila envelope. "There is one other important item in Operation Seeadler that I need to discuss with you."

Commander Ruge eyed the envelope inquisitively.

The admiral held the envelope aloft in his right hand. "This contains a full transcript of the decree, but it also contains orders signed by the Führer himself, allowing you to commandeer civilian vessels for use by the Kriegsmarine."

Ruge held back from taking the envelope. "Forgive me for being puzzled, admiral, but for what purpose would I need to commandeer civilian vessels? They may be suitable for transport but not for combat."

"You are quite right to ask that question, commander. As for transport, the Reich always has the right to commandeer vessels when needed. So, allow me to clarify that this decree allows using civilian vessels for search and observation. Large commercial ships are not suited to this task, but smaller craft such as fishing boats can serve this purpose perfectly as they can move without suspicion."

"Sir, do you want my crews to be trained in operating fishing boats? This could take some time."

"That is the beauty of this decree. You do not need to assign an entire crew, nor do you need to operate the boats. We will place one Kriegsmarine on a fishing boat, and he will have the authority to instruct the boat's regular captain what to do."

Commander Ruge's eyes widened in awe and a smirk appeared on his lips. "Admiral, that is a spectacular plan, and I understand now the value it will provide. However, I still have one question. Why use my crew, instead of, say, crews from destroyers?

"You are an astute man, Commander Ruge. I see you always ask the right questions. To find the Orzeł, I would like to use U-Boat or destroyer crews, but they have other more urgent priorities. My second choice is your men as they have experience aboard torpedo boats and minesweepers, all of which relate to submarines. As we expand Unternehmen Seeadler, we will use crews from other surface ships, but you will be spearheading the start of this operation."

"Sir, I am honored for this opportunity to serve the Reich." Commander Ruge shed the fear he had felt earlier and held himself proudly.

Admiral Carls stood up and walked to the front of his desk. As Commander Ruge stood up, the admiral handed the envelope over. "You will find all the operational instructions you need in here. We have high expectations but full confidence in you, commander."

As they shook hands, Commander Ruge said, "Thank you, sir. We will find that submarine." Ruge stepped back, and, standing at attention, raised his arm in salute. "Heil Hitler!"

Admiral Carls returned the salute. "Heil Hitler." Commander Ruge turned smartly and marched quietly out of the office.

The admiral briefly looked at his watch, before returning to his desk. Sitting himself down, he picked up his pen and thought, *I can now complete my report and have it dispatched to Berlin.*

12 Patrolling the Baltic

Ship's Log entered by: Lieutenant Jan Grudziński
Date: September 18, 1939
Location: Baltic Sea south of Åland Islands, east of Stockholm
Entry: Having escaped internment in Tallinn, Estonia, and avoided the Estonian pursuit vessels, we are preparing to head south to engage enemy ships.

"Officer Kotecki," Grudziński addressed the Kat, seated in his radio room.

"Aye, sir."

"It is nearly dark, so we will surface soon. When we do, I want you to send a message to Naval Command on Hel peninsula."

The Kat grabbed his notebook and pen. "Yes, sir, what message should I send?"

"We have escaped internment in Tallinn, where Captain Kłoczkowski remains in hospital. We have eluded all pursuit vessels, so will proceed to intercept enemy ships."

"But sir, I have no codebooks, they were destroyed."

"It doesn't matter, send this on an open channel. I want Naval Command to know that we are still active. If the Germans listen to this then they will also know that we are a threat to them."

"Aye, sir."

"During the night when we are on the surface, I want you to monitor open channels for a reply."

"Yes, sir, will do sir."

Both Alex and I were assigned to look after the Estonian guards. I thought it was ironic that we had to guard the guards that were previously holding us captive in Tallinn. We didn't have a strong room where we could lock them in. In fact, we didn't need one. After all, where would they go? What could they do? Even if they did get control of the Orzeł, they wouldn't know how to sail her.

Since they were not locked up or tied up, all we had to do was to keep them company. If Alex or I had some duties to attend to, then either of us would look after them. We even showed them around the boat, explaining the different parts and how things worked. They ate with us in the mess room, played cards with us, and drank with us when we were given our vodka rations. During the very short time they were on board, they become a welcome addition to our crew. They even acclimatized to the natural stink throughout the Orzeł.

What surprised me was their ability to recognize the time. When darkness settled in, and we surfaced, they always asked, "We can go upstairs now for fresh air, no?"

Captain Grudziński always gave us priority on the cigarette shift, which neither Alex nor I would complain about. The two Estonians would share their Russian cigarettes while we shared our Polish brands.

On the second night, we were sitting in the mess room, finishing our vodka ration, when one of the guards said, "You always listen to the Polish radio, can we listen to Estonian radio?"

"Sure!" I said, "Do you know what frequency to tune to?"

As we tuned to their channel, they listened to a popular jingle, tapping the mess room table in time. This was soon followed by the news, at which point they both looked puzzled. One of them said to me, "We are not dead."

"Excuse me?" I asked.

"The news says that we are dead, and we have been killed by you."

Since nobody on board spoke Estonian, we could not understand the broadcast ourselves.

"What do you mean?" I asked, "what is your news channel saying?"

"It says that you captured us and killed us."

Alex and I looked at each other with a questioning expression. "Why would anyone say that?" I asked.

"I don't know," Alex replied, "I think we need to tell the captain."

———————

I alerted Grudziński who came to the mess room. We listened to news reports from both Russia and Germany and they all said the same thing. That the two guards who were captured by the Polish submarine had been murdered, their bodies dumped into the sea.

Grudziński looked thoughtful and worried by these news reports.

"We are not dead," one Estonian said.

"Why would they say that?" I asked.

"It's propaganda," Grudziński said, "the Germans want everyone to think we killed them. They want everyone to believe that we killed them. Let me check with the Kat, I want to know if he has heard any news on the radio."

With that, Grudziński went forward through the control room to talk with the Kat, our radio operator, leaving us in the mess room. I had to follow our new captain so I could hear for myself.

"Any news?" Grudziński asked the Kat when he got to the radio room.

"No sir, there is no reply from Naval Command. I have another message though."

"Hm," Grudziński thought out loud, "Maybe the base on Hel Peninsula has been overrun. Is there any news from Germany about the Estonians?"

"Yes, sir, I have intercepted news from both Germany and Russia, they both say that we have killed the Estonians."

"Well, that confirms what others have heard in the mess room."

"But we haven't killed them, have we, sir?"

"Of course not, you can see that can't you?"

"Will we kill them?" the Kat asked with some concern.

"Of course not, we are not at war with Estonia, and even if we were, there are rules that define how we should treat prisoners. Murder is not one of those rules."

The Kat looked relived by Grudziński's statement. "That's good, they are good men."

"You said you have another message," Grudziński said.

"Yes, sir." The Kat pulled out a note from his small table and handed it to Grudziński. "I received this only a few minutes ago. It is from the Polish sub, Ryś."

"Ah, the Lynx, what is she up to?" Grudziński began reading the transcript.

"She is damaged and heading for Sweden, she is wanting to rendezvous with us and give us her sea charts," the Kat said.

I suddenly felt good about this. It seemed as if the Ryś was limping into a Swedish port but wanted to help us to continue the fight against the Nazis.

Grudziński looked up with a puzzled face. "What?" was all he could say.

"The Ryś wants to rendezvous with us and give us assistance," the Kat repeated. "Shall I give her our location?"

"Wait!" Grudziński raised his hand. "This transcript says they want to give us their charts."

"Yes, sir, they want to help us," Kat said.

"Officer Kotecki, how do they know?" Grudziński asked.

"How do they know what, sir?" the Kat asked.

"How do they know that we need charts?"

I suddenly realized that we had been had.

"Oh shit…" was all that Kat could say.

"Yes," said Grudziński. "That is not the Ryś! That is a German ship trying to lure us into a trap. Do not respond to this transmission. Do not send any messages on any channel, unless I explicitly tell you to."

"Yes, sir, of course, sir. I didn't think sir."

Grudziński turned to leave the radio room and seeing me behind him, he said, "Now we must decide what to do with those two Estonians."

"Ah, Lieutenant Mokrski," Captain Grudziński said as he passed through the wardroom.

The Kid was sitting at a table, pen in hand, scribbling on some papers.

"Yes, sir." The Kid sat upright, placing his pen to the edge of papers as if finishing an exam at school. Turning towards the captain, he nodded.

"Lieutenant," Grudziński said, "you mentioned you want to see me, that you have something that will help us all?"

The Kid stood up. "Yes Captain, I have it on the chart table in the control room. Can I show it to you now?"

"Yes, I'm intrigued. Could this have anything to do with what happened at the harbormaster's office?"

"Harbormaster, sir? I don't know what you mean," the Kid said, feigning ignorance.

"I heard that you may have something from the harbormaster's office. After they confiscated our navigation charts and equipment, you seem to have returned in a happy mood."

"Happy, sir? Leaving those things behind was not easy for me. My uncle gave me that brass compass when I was young."

"I'm sure, lieutenant." Putting his hand on the Kid's shoulder, Grudziński said, "I know those things meant a lot to you."

"Oh, no. You've got me wrong. Those things mean nothing to me. It's the thoughts behind them that count." The Kid was now standing proud, straight and tall. "I was sad to let these things go because they belong on this boat. Things can always be replaced if you know how to do it. For instance, I've asked Blackie to make me a sextant. I gave him all the details he needs on how to fabricate one. In fact, I think he finished it."

Grudziński broke from his regular stance and looked amazed. "What?"

"Even better than that," the Kid continued, "I have a chart of the Baltic Sea!"

"So you *did* steal something from the harbormaster's office? Is that what it was? A chart?"

"Oh, Lord, no sir. I couldn't fit one of those big charts in my tunic. I made the chart myself, but I had to use something that I borrowed from the harbormaster."

"You borrowed something?"

"Well, sir, it was only a small booklet, and I think they have plenty of others, so they won't miss this one." The kid gestured towards the control room. "Sir, let me show you the chart so you will know what I mean."

The Kid then led the captain to the chart desk in the control room. There he unrolled a sheet of paper and spread it out on the table. "Here is the chart I drew," the Kid revealed proudly.

Grudziński's interest turned to puzzlement, even disappointment. "Kid, this is a hand-drawn, half scribbled sketch of the Baltic Sea, how is this supposed to help us navigate?"

"Ah, but sir, I understand your puzzlement, but this is not just any chart, this is my chart!"

"Lieutenant Mokrski, I cannot ensure the safety of this vessel on some half-baked sketch, I need something better to navigate through the Baltic."

"Sir, you asked me before about dead reckoning."

"Yes, we all understand dead reckoning," Grudziński folded his arms.

"Well, with a known starting point, we can sail on a given heading at a given speed for a given time."

"Yes, and then we can calculate where we end up," Grudziński concluded.

"Of course but taking into account any drift due to currents or weather, this method can never be perfectly accurate."

"Isn't that why you use the sextant, to correct any estimates in our position?"

"Yes I can, but what if there's bad weather and I can't see the sun or the stars? What if we are submerged?" The Kid then reached into his chart cupboard, once full of papers and charts, it now contained only one simple booklet. "This is what I stole – I mean borrowed – from the harbormaster."

The Kid proudly waved a copy of Leuchtfeuer und Signalstellen, published by the German Kriegsmarine. "This simple booklet contains all the lighthouses on the Baltic Sea."

"I don't see how that will help us."

"Sir, I have marked some of the more important ones on the chart," the Kid indicated. "Here, here, and here. Each one of these is entered into the booklet. Each beacon flashes in a unique way, so with this booklet, I can identify it visually. The booklet tells me the exact longitude and latitude, so I can get an accurate location."

Grudziński looked thoughtfully at the chart. The Kid offered him the booklet and Grudziński began thumbing his way through it, looking at the detailed entries.

"This lists all beacons and lighthouses?"

"Yes, sir."

"So harbor approaches and hazards?"

"Yes, sir. I know your next question – how to avoid the hazards."

"Yes, how do we avoid the hazards?

"If the beacon is signaling a hazard such as rocks, it is listed in the booklet. It also tells you how far the beacon is visible at sea level so you can figure out how near or how far you are from the hazard. We will have to avoid sailing near the shore, but we can use these beacons to correct our dead reckoning."

Grudziński looked thoughtful, "OK, I think you have something here, but I have a test for you."

"Yes, sir, what is it?"

"Plot a course for Visby."

"Visby in Gotland? Do you want to enter that port?"

"No, we will not enter the port, we can't risk internment again. We need to stand off the coast and safely drop off the two Estonians. Can you get us there?"

"Aye, aye, Sir!"

The Orzeł sailed on the surface through the night, following a southwesterly course towards Gotland. A cold, northerly wind helped to push her on her way as she plowed through the waves.

Grudziński checked his watch and saw it was nearly time to reach the first waypoint. Taking his binoculars, he climbed up through the conning tower to the bridge. "How is our progress, helmsman?"

Glancing over his shoulder, the helmsman replied, "We're on course, sir, but I don't see anything yet."

"Stay on course, we should be there soon." Grudziński stepped onto the podium and scanned the horizon in all directions. The lookouts on the cigarette deck were focused on their task of scanning the gloom for either danger or prey. *It is good that this night is quiet, so we can concentrate on testing our new way of navigation*, the captain thought.

Time passed as Grudziński kept his lookout from the podium. At first, he kept watch for the lighthouse, but it was his nature to scan the horizon and sky for danger. After some time, the helmsman called out, "Light ho, sir!" A moment later, the forward lookouts also called out, "Beacon light ahead, sir!"

Grudziński turned his attention southwards, and there it was! A light, blinking with a steady rhythm. Jumping down from the podium, standing beside the helmsman, he said, "Mark the time."

"23:50, sir."

"23:50," Grudziński confirmed. Calling down through the voice pipe, he commanded the duty officer, "Send Lieutenant Mokrski to the bridge, on the double."

Moments later, the Kid climbed up into the bridge. "Where are we?" he asked, looking around in the darkness.

"Look ahead, is that your lighthouse?" Grudziński said, handing his binoculars to the Kid.

Peering ahead, the Kid watched the light and counted the blinks, tapping his foot in time to the rhythmic cycle. Waiting for three full cycles to complete, he said, "There she is, Fårö lighthouse, dead ahead. How long ago since you spotted her?"

"Just a minute or two ago," replied the helmsman.

"Then we are about twelve miles offshore from her. What's our heading and speed?

"Two, two, zero degrees and fifteen knots."

"So what course do you suggest Mokrski?" Grudziński asked.

The Kid thought for a moment, gazing at the light, his expression blank as his brain made some calculations. "Steer two, five, zero degrees, we should then be off Hallshuk Point in about eighty minutes. Then we steer two, two, five degrees, and follow the coast. We should then arrive at Visby," he took another pause as he checked his calculations in his head, "at about four AM."

The helmsman whistled in awe.

"Can you be sure of all this?" Grudziński asked.

"Sir, Kłoczkowski had us patrolling this area a few days ago. During that time I became very familiar with the local charts. Of course I'm sure. There are no major obstacles or shallows to avoid, so as long as we maintain a safe distance from shore, we will be fine."

Grudziński nodded. "OK, helmsman, steer two, five, zero degrees, maintain speed, and keep a lookout for more lights as we approach… what point was that again, Mokrski?"

"Hallshuk Point, sir."

"Aye, sir, steering two, five, zero," the helmsman confirmed as the Orzeł turned slightly to the starboard. The Fårö lighthouse kept its steady rhythm as the Orzeł sailed on through the night.

I was sitting on the lower bunk with Alex, playing cards. The two Estonians were on the upper bunks sleeping.

"This is the first time the Estonians have slept so soundly," Alex said.

"It takes some getting used to the noise of the diesel engines, so I'm not surprised. Those poor guys must be exhausted," I said.

"Blackie, you're beginning to sound like a mother to those two guys. I'm surprised you don't sing them a lullaby."

With that the engines began to slow. "What time is it?" I asked.

"Ten minutes past four," said Alex.

"It's almost dawn, maybe we're getting ready to dive. They may need me in the engine room soon but if we're lucky there's time for another hand. Will you deal?"

As Alex dealt the cards, Piasecki came in. "Blackie, Alex, rouse the Estonians and report to the control room on the double. It's time for them to leave."

I slapped the cards on the bunk. "Shit, this was going to be my winning hand!"

"This isn't your lucky night," Alex said, "you wake the babies, and I'll put the cards away."

I led the two sleepy Estonians with Alex following behind. As we passed through the mess room, Freckles appeared from the galley with a small duffle bag. "Hey Blackie, I don't speak Russian, so you'll have to tell the two Estonians that this is for them."

"What's in there?" I asked.

"Some food, some water, and two bottles of vodka. Orders from the captain."

I turned to the Estonians, and smiling, I said in Russian, "Here are some gifts to keep you happy on your trip home."

They both shrugged and looked puzzled, but they attempted to say 'thank you' in Polish.

When we got to the control room, Piasecki was waiting. "OK, men, do you have everything? Did you get the supplies from Freckles?"

"Aye, sir."

Shaking the hands of the Estonians, Piasecki said in Russian, "I hope you enjoy your trip home and don't forget to tell the Germans how dangerous we are."

"You've been good to us," they replied. "We'd like to thank you."

"Thank us by getting back safe. Blackie, Alex, take them up to the aft deck. The captain is up there with some men, and they've prepared the launch. Keep things quiet, and no lights. We are close to shore, and Grudziński doesn't want to alert the Swedes."

The engines were idling as they stood on the aft deck. It was still dark, and we had no running lights or flags. The launch had already been prepared and was held alongside the Orzeł by two seamen. Grudziński stood beside a rope ladder to allow the Estonians to climb into the launch.

As we approached, Grudziński handed them an envelope. "Here is some money. You both may need some when you get ashore."

"Money?" they both said with surprise.

"Yes, courtesy of the Polish Navy. Now get into the boat and head towards the lights over there."

"You're not taking us?"

"No, this is as far as we dare to go."

"What is that place?" They asked.

"That's Visby, the main port on Gotland. This is Sweden. The Swedes should look after you there. Now hurry."

"But this is your lifeboat!" they both exclaimed.

"We're Polish!" I said, "we don't need any lifeboats. We only have them in case other people need them." Seeing that Grudziński wanted them to get moving, I led them towards the rope ladder. "You should have plenty of food, but don't drink any vodka until you get to shore. If you keep a steady pace, you should reach Visby harbor by sunrise."

"And keep your jackets buttoned, because there's a chilly breeze," Alex added, in a motherly tone.

As the Estonians sat in the launch and readied themselves with the oars, Grudziński gave the order, "Cast off."

They started to row and we watched as they began to head towards the distant lights of Visby.

"What about us, sir? Are we safe here?" I asked.

"No, we are not," Grudziński said. "We are within Swedish territorial waters without permission. If they spot us they could act aggressively."

"Shouldn't we leave?" I asked, scanning the horizon for any ships.

"We'll give those boys a minute to make sure they get underway. In this darkness, and with the Orzeł's low profile, any observers should think we are a fishing boat. But we need to be out of here before dawn."

13 Warsaw

Ship's Log entered by: Lieutenant Jan Grudziński
Date: September 29, 1939
Location: Mid Baltic, south of Gotland
Entry: Our patrols in the Baltic seem fruitless, the situation in Poland seems hopeless. I'm beginning to wonder if we should have resigned ourselves to internment in Estonia. We may have to retreat to a Swedish port for internment.

We sailed silently through the Baltic on the surface under cover of night. I was off duty and getting ready to hit my bunk. I wasn't ready for sleep yet, so I was hanging out in the mess room. Normally when on the surface, the captain would allow us to listen to the Polish radio while we ate or played games. We could only do this while on the surface as the radio cannot receive transmissions when underwater. This evening was different because we had difficulty finding the news from Poland.

"Hey Blackie," Stephan said, "I can't find the Polish station, can you get this radio to work?"

"I'm an engineer, not a radio operator. Why don't you ask Henry Kotecki to find the station? He's the radio operator."

Stephan had to go to the control room to ask Captain Grudziński's permission to let Henry tune our radio. While we were on the surface, Henry would be busy with his regular communications with Navy Headquarters, as well as listening for any other naval transmissions.

"What's wrong with the radio?" Grudziński asked.

"Sir, we can't find the Polish news," Stephan replied.

"Isn't it always tuned to the same station?"

"Yes, but something's different, maybe someone changed the dial. It should only take a minute for Henry to find it."

"Let me check to see if he's busy."

A moment later, Henry Kotecki appeared in the mess room, followed by Grudziński. "Be quick," Grudziński said, "I need you to keep listening for other broadcasts."

"Aye, sir," Henry replied as he checked the settings on the radio. He could only get static when he tuned the dial to the Polish frequency.

"The connections are good because I can receive other broadcasts, but Poland isn't there." To prove the point, he tuned it to a foreign station.

"Go check on your rig," Grudziński said, "I want to see if Warsaw is broadcasting."

The radio room was just forward of the control room. Grudziński followed him there with Stephan and I close behind. Henry sat at his controls and put his headphones on. He moved the dials, adjusting them back and forth checking for the Polish frequency. He also checked a few other frequencies while listening intently.

"Sir, there is no Polish broadcast."

"What? Are you sure?" Grudziński asked.

"Yes sir, there is no Polish news. I can locate some other signals, but not our news stations."

We all looked at each other, wondering what had happened to the news.

"Maybe the station got bombed?" Stephan asked.

We all scoffed.

"That is a possibility," Grudziński said. "Can you get any other news?"

"I can get the BBC, but who of us can speak English?"

"Get the BBC, I can speak English," Grudziński said.

In a moment, Henry had tuned his rig to the BBC. He then handed his headphones to the captain.

Grudziński listened, staring intently at the wall, mouthing some of the words silently. After a few moments, his eyes widened. "Oh shit!" He exclaimed. "Henry, go tune to this channel in the mess room, quickly."

Henry took off and we all followed, leaving the captain listening through the headphones.

In the mess room, Henry quickly tuned our radio to the BBC news. We heard the pleasant English accent flowing from the speaker. We recognized a few words like *'Warsaw'* and *'Poland'*. This indicated that something was happening, but we couldn't tell what. Grudziński was still in the radio room listening. We had to wait for him to tell us anything.

After a few minutes, it seemed the news bulletin was finished as the announcer seemed to speak about something else. That's when Grudziński stepped into the mess room, with a serious look on his face.

"Men, the BBC has just reported some very shocking news."

We stood motionless.

"Warsaw has surrendered to the Germans. They will enter the city tomorrow."

We all voiced different objections.

"No, it can't be!"

"Are you sure?"

Grudziński remained very matter of fact. "Henry, get command on the radio and find out what's going on."

"Aye sir." Henry ran back to his radio room.

"Men, the BBC has reported the fall of Warsaw, which was announced by General Walerian Czuma earlier today."

We just stood and stared. We had all been following the news of Warsaw, but this latest report shocked us to the core. The Polish radio had kept us informed of the Nazi onslaught marching through Poland. Through it, we learned how the German Luftwaffe had bombed our beloved capital city. Before the first week was finished, German Panzers had arrived at the outskirts of Warsaw.

That is when General Walerian Czuma had taken up the defense of Warsaw, and he made a bold statement that rallied the Polish spirit. *'Here we have taken up a position from which there can be no steps back. The enemy can receive just one answer now: Enough! Not one step further.'* So both soldiers and volunteers had fought side by side to stop the invaders from entering our city. As the days passed, we had listened to many reports of our brave Warsaw defenders, and how they stopped the Germans in their tracks. Such news gave us hope that Poland would withstand the Nazis with pride and dignity, because when the British and French joined in our plight we would all give Hitler a humiliating lesson on how to behave in Europe.

As it turned out, Britain and France were too slow to mobilize their armies. Worse than that, they didn't seem to have the will to make a clear decision to attack Germany. So Poland stood alone against the onslaught of the Blitzkrieg, leaving Warsaw exposed to the full might of the German army.

The BBC had now informed us that the siege of Warsaw has ended in surrender. We had to ask Grudziński what had happened, why we had surrendered.

His answer was simple. "General Czuma has surrendered because he wanted to save the people of Warsaw from further suffering."

"But sir," Stephan objected, "I thought we were holding the Nazis off?"

"Yes," Grudziński agreed, "we were. But remember, the Nazis had the city under constant bombardment. Not only were there civilian casualties, but hospitals were bombed, the water supply was destroyed. They were surrounded and were cut off from food supplies."

"But surrender?" Stephan was almost stuttering.

"If it's any consolation, Czuma and his army wanted to continue the fight." Grudziński now looked solemn. "The reason they surrendered was to prevent more civilian deaths."

We all stood there in silence, contemplating what it must be like back in the city. In truth there was no hope, the city was cut off, the Russians were now also invading from the east. Isolated and alone, with no possible help in sight, the situation was hopeless. General Czuma found himself defending a dying city, which must have left him with no other choice.

We were discussing this atrocity and cursing the Nazis for their evil cruelty when Stephan asked, "Why would they bomb a city like that? Why do they have to make the common people suffer? What purpose does that serve?"

Commander Grudziński was standing in the watertight door between our mess room and the control room. He was interested in our discussion but remained silent.

So, Stephan asked, "What say you, Panienka?"

No crew member had used this nickname to Commander Grudziński's face. We had always kept it to ourselves. Kłoczkowski used it, but we all froze when Stephan said it.

Grudziński did not flinch. "This is modern warfare," he said. "In the old days, it would have been a castle, and the attackers would bombard it with catapults or, more recently, with cannons. Nowadays the city can be a place of defense, it is much bigger than a castle, but if the enemy can make a city inoperable, then the defenders will find it difficult to do their job."

All eyes turned towards Lieutenant Grudziński, our commander. All who were present, including Stephan, straightened their backs to attention. It was as if Commander Grudziński had now become our history teacher.

"Centuries ago, as Genghis Khan swept his way across Asia and Europe, he would catapult the heads of dead soldiers into the city that he was trying to capture, thus causing panic within the city, helping to break the spirit of the defenders."

I think my stomach turned, along with the stomachs of everyone else who was listening.

"But now we have air power and heavy artillery to do the same job. This is not just modern warfare, this is now total war. We can expect no quarter to be given in any field of combat. The enemy will hit us in any way they can, like animals. But we must remain human, we must fight with the rule of international law behind us."

That day we all received a very clear explanation of why our capital city had fallen.

Our hearts sank twice, once for the brave soldiers who defended our capital, and again for the poor, innocent souls who suffered needlessly.

Just then someone in the control room called for Grudziński.

"Excuse me, I have a submarine to manage," he said, as he returned to the control room.

"Stephan!" I hissed, "what the hell do you think you're doing calling him Panienka like that?"

"I don't know, it just slipped out."

"Your brains have slipped out. You show him the respect he deserves. He got us out of Tallinn, and he'll get us to England."

"I said sorry, I didn't mean it." After a pause, he said, "Do you think he noticed?"

"You knucklehead, your brains really have slipped out."

"Well, maybe he thought I was talking to you?"

"Now settle down boys!" Freckles called through the serving hatch. "It's time for your medicine." He then appeared around the corner carrying a tray full of cups. In his apron pocket was a bottle of vodka. "Well don't just sit there, take your cups. I'm not your mother."

"Oh, yes, right," we all said. I jumped up, grabbing cups from the tray, and passed them around.

Freckles uncorked the bottle. "There you go lads, line up and I'll pour."

We all smiled as we got our daily ration of vodka. This would be something to cheer us up after all the bad news. It was hot and sweaty in the sub, and our spirits were low. Maybe this could lift us up and help us to forget the heat.

Everyone in the mess room fell silent as they savored their ration. We were allowed a shot every day at dinner time. If Freckles was feeling generous, we would sometimes get two shots. Many of the crew's thoughts must have returned to the fall of Warsaw; I know mine certainly did.

Nazi troops would enter our capital of Warsaw the very next day and our beloved country would no longer be ours.

Stephan started humming our anthem, muttering a few of the lyrics.

'*Poland is not yet lost,*' we all sang together. '*What the foreign power has seized from us,*

We shall recapture with a sabre!'

With that we stood tall, raised our cups high, shouting "POLSKA!" in unison, before drinking down our vodka. With that, we sat down. We all retreated into our own silent thoughts.

Every man on board had a saint to pray to. Mine was St. Christopher – the protector. There was a picture of St. Christopher on the mess room wall. At that moment, he didn't seem to be doing a good job of protecting Poland, so I thought my prayer might remind him that we needed some help.

After some period of silence, Tom Przadka spoke up. "Come on Stephan, tell us all one of your silly stories and cheer us all up. We've had to leave two good bottles of vodka with those stupid Estonian guards that we left on Gotland. I'm beginning to wonder if I should have stayed with them on that decrepit island beach."

Stephan stood upright. No matter what the situation, he was always ready to tell a good tale.

"So, you all know I live in Gdańsk with my mother?"

"Yes, yes," we all said, waiting impatiently for a story.

"You know how mothers always seem to know everything that happens at a market?"

"Yes," we all replied in unison.

"Well," Stephan continued, "a few days before war broke out, my mother sent me to the market to get some lemons. Somehow, she knew they were available, don't ask me how, I just say it was my mother's intuition."

"Yes, go on…"

"So off I go, and I'm thinking I'll get the lemons but maybe I'll get myself a beer as well."

"Now we're talking!" We anticipated some excitement.

"So, I get the lemons and put them in my Mama's bag, along with an assortment of fruit that were in season, like apples and a few pears."

"You're making us hungry."

"As I go through the market, I can hear a German 'Oompah Band', which must have been playing nearby, around the corner of the market. So, I head off to see them and what they are playing, and I must say, I wasn't particularly impressed."

"Oh? Why not?"

"Well, you know, these Germans call my city Danzig, which is OK because they are Germans, and they have a different language. But also, they want all of us Poles to get out because they don't think we belong there, which is crazy. After all, we have lived there for a long time, just like they have. Strange as it may be, they don't even like us watching their oompah bands, especially when they have all those brown shirt fellows dangling their red swastikas all over the place."

"Yeah, those flaming daemons!"

"So, I decided to approach these folk and went right to the front of the audience of Germans who were watching. I was carrying my Mama's shopping and I ended up pretty much face to face with the oompah players, who of course all play brass instruments."

"And?"

"And as they played their German marching oompah tunes, I smiled and appeared to enjoy the musical commotion."

"Hurry up with the story, some of us have to be on duty soon."

"OK, so, I pulled one of the lemons out from my Mama's shopping bag, along with a sharp knife which I carried in my pocket. I then preceded to chop the lemon into quarters and stuff each quarter into my mouth one at a time. When I finished one of the lemon quarters, I shoved in another, and the lemon juice ran down my hands and wrist and dripped from my puckered mouth. I even put slices of the yellow lemon skin under my gums to make it look like I had false teeth and as I smiled at a band player, I would then bite into the lemon skin to make him feel the sourness in his own mouth."

"You stupid fool, you sucked on a lemon, are you insane? Is your head on straight?" one of our crew said.

"Oh, make no mistake, I suffered terribly – but you miss the point! I challenge anyone to observe someone who eats a lemon. Because while you are observing them, your very own lips will also pucker in sympathy. This automatic behavior of the lips seems to be an impasse for anyone who plays a brass instrument, because while they observe a lemon being eaten, they will struggle to play a single coherent note."

"Stephan are you serious? What did you do to this band?" We laughed.

"One by one each player slowly saw my sour expression and painful puckering, one by one they all fell foul with their sour notes. The conductor enthusiastically guided the flowing music, but as the music soured, he became increasingly annoyed. I almost became afraid for the band because of the conductor's growing rage. The audience of Germans was completely perplexed as I had my back to every one of them and no one had any suspicion that I was the culprit performing this devious act."

"You are such an anarchist!" We were in hysterics at this point.

"Indeed, my poor mama had very few lemons left that day. But I had a fantastic time."

"Did you get away?"

"No, I didn't."

We all guffawed! "Oh, do you have bruises to show us?"

"Not quite. You see, there was a Polish girl who was watching, and she saw everything that I did. She approached me and grabbed my hand and pulled me away from the crowd. She probably saved my life, because only she noticed my citrus attack. She swept me away through the crowd, with lemon juice dripping from my chin and not a single German noticed my predicament."

You scoundrel, I thought, laughing along.

"I thought that she was the most beautiful thing I had ever seen in my life. Bright blue eyes, a silky red smile on her face, flowing blonde hair, and a figure that any man would faint for."

"Who was she?" I asked.

"Her name was Marlena. Marlena," he said again quietly.

After a moment or two, he continued. "She lives in Warsaw with her parents. She was visiting her aunt and she had to go back that afternoon on the train. After a few brief moments together in a Polish café, we drank some tea and ate some cakes. After a while, I walked her to the train station where we said our goodbyes and promised to see each other again. That's when she let me kiss her."

Our eyes opened wide, while our jaws dropped low.

"Marlena," he whispered once more with his eyes towards the floor.

There was a long, silent pause.

"When we all get back home off this damned boat," Stephan added, "I swear, I will go to Warsaw to find her." He did not shed a tear. Instead, Stephan pulled a face that could have killed an entire Nazi regiment.

The rest of us coughed as we tried to hide our damp eyes. What we originally thought to be a funny story we realized, to our horror, was a story of loss and the grief that had befallen our beloved nation.

14 German Fishing Boats

In the damp, pre-dawn light, Petty Officers Otto Braun, Gustav Schneider, and Johan Beck of the Kriegsmarine, bounced along in the back of the military truck as they drove to the Cuxhaven port.

"I thought this was supposed to be an important mission?" Schneider asked.

"It is, we're on orders from Berlin," Braun said.

"So important that they put us in a truck," Beck added. "Why couldn't they send us in a staff car?"

"The war effort!" Braun answered. "Resources need to be saved to get us to victory." Petty Officer Otto Braun was short and slim, with a fashionable pencil mustache.

"You mean saved for the top brass officials!" Beck chided.

"We could get Iron Crosses if we play our cards right," Braun added.

"Are you kidding me?" Schneider laughed. "They've assigned us to fishing boats! We are Kriegsmarine officers, not fishermen!"

The truck braked hard as it bounced along the dockside. Honking the horn twice, the fat, burly driver announced, "We're here!"

The three officers disembarked from the back of the truck, stretching their limbs after the long drive. Clumsily dragging their kit bags, they assembled themselves alongside the truck.

Seagulls called to each, announcing the morning, while waves splashed rhythmically. Looking around there were three trawlers tied to the dockside. Fishing nets, baskets and tackle hung from masts.

"Jeezus, it stinks around here!" complained Schneider.

"Ha!" laughed Beck, "That must be the smell of victory in the morning!"

"You can laugh," chided Braun, "but when I get that Iron Cross, I'll be laughing at you."

Braun looked at the first trawler in front of them, "Hey that's mine!" he exclaimed, "The Sea Eagle! Don't you think that's destiny? It has the same name as our naval operation!"

Schneider shook his head as he walked off towards his trawler. "Happy hunting, Herr Destiny. I'm assigned to the Merry Maid, I wonder what I'll catch with her."

"I'm on the Sea Breeze," Beck said. "I better report to her captain."

The Sea Eagle! Braun thought to himself as he stepped towards the trawler.

"Ahoy there!" he shouted, "preparing to come aboard!"

A large, disheveled figure appeared from inside the darkened wheelhouse, clothed in oilskins and a woolen hat. His face was hidden behind a full beard. What looked like a bent Dublin pipe hung from his mouth. "Who are you?" the figure grumbled.

"I am Petty Officer Otto Braun, of the Kriegsmarine. I am on orders from Berlin to commandeer this vessel."

The figure looked at Braun. "Get on board. Leave your sack of shit on deck and climb up here to the wheelhouse."

Officer Braun scrambled aboard along a narrow plank. Leaving his kit bag on the deck as instructed, he then climbed up a ladder into the wheelhouse. As he entered, he saw the figure sitting by the ship's wheel. Raising his arm in salute, Braun said, "Heil Hitler! You must be the captain…"

"Just call me Schmidt!" the figure said.

"Ah, Herr Schmidt, I am…"

"I know who you are," Schmidt said. Removing the pipe from his lips, he knocked out the old ash against the ship's wheel and onto the floor.

"I have papers," Braun said.

"I've seen them," Schmidt said, as he reached into his pocket and extracted a clump of course tobacco, stuffing it gently into his pipe.

"I'm here to commandeer this vessel."

"No you're not," Schmidt said. A match magically appeared and ignited as Schmidt leveled it over the waiting tobacco. "I'll tell you why you're here," he said puffing smoke on the pipe, "you're here as an adviser, and a lookout for the enemy."

"I'm on orders from Berlin!"

"I don't care if you're on orders from God. On this boat, I'm in command, I'm the one who stands between us and the sea." A large aura of smoke now surrounded Schmidt.

"Well in the Kriegsmarine, we're used to keeping a much cleaner and tidier ship," Braun nodded towards the ash on the floor, "so perhaps you can get things more shipshape? I'm willing to help you get some of these nets and lines stowed away."

Schmidt removed the pipe from his mouth with a scoff and stood up to approach Braun. Pointing his pipe in his face, he growled, "I give Neptune permission to wash my decks with his waves, and he is thankful for it!" Schmidt spat from the side of his mouth before continuing. "Every line, basket, and piece of tackle on this boat is exactly where it should be!"

Schmidt now prodded his pipe into Braun's chest. "What's more, every member of my crew knows exactly where each item is! They know exactly where to find what they need, when they need it! So do not dare to move anything from its place." Pushing Braun out of the wheelhouse with his pipe, Schmidt then threatened, "If they can't find something during a life-threatening storm, I will hold you responsible! I will personally keel haul you, and send your broken, barnacled body back to Berlin in a box!"

Braun ended up leaning backward over the railing, outside the wheelhouse, struggling to control both his bladder and his bowels. The slobbered mouthpiece of Schmidt's pipe pressing hard into his sternum.

"Get below!" demanded Schmidt. "Karl is down there, he will tell you where you can put your bag of shit!" Turning back toward the ship's wheel, Schmidt grunted, "We leave within the hour."

15 Hunting in the Baltic

Ship's Log entered by: Lieutenant Jan Grudziński
Date: September 30, 1939
Location: Southern Baltic shipping lanes
Entry: Crew morale is at a low as Poland has surrendered.
We think of our families at home and all are considering
internment in Sweden. I am considering all options we have.

If you can describe nothing, then you can describe what it
feels like to be without a country. Everything we had known,
everyone we had loved, everywhere we lived, had been
forcibly taken from us. The emptiness within me didn't make
me feel sick, it made me feel like nothing. I saw this in the
faces of my shipmates, who all had vacant, empty gazes. We
continued with our duties but only because there was nothing
left to do. We stumbled around the boat like voodoo
zombies.

On the Orzeł, we were free but free to do what? Other
than the magic that the Kid could muster, we had no
navigation. We only had five torpedoes, and no working deck
gun, so what real harm could we do? The fresh food had long
since run out and we were reduced to whatever Freckles
could concoct from the canned rations.

Grudziński tried to focus our attention on our duties, but
the neutral country of Sweden was nearby. The possibility of
seeking internment there began to grow in our ragged hearts.
Why not go to Sweden where we could sit the war out in
relative comfort?

The night was dark and the cold wind reminded us of
the beginnings of winter. Stanley and I were smoking atop the
conning tower, leaning on the gunwale, not even talking. The

fact that Stanley wasn't speaking reflected the poor mood we were all in.

The dive alarm went off and ripped the night into shreds. Stanley and I both spat our cigarettes into the water below.

"Lookouts get below!" Grudziński shouted from the podium on the bridge. With that order we all scurried down the ladder, sealing the hatch as we went. Grudziński was the last one down from the conning tower. He ordered both me and Stanley to remain in the control room.

Piasecki asked, "What's going on?"

"Take her down to periscope depth," was all that Grudziński said to Piasecki.

Piasecki ran through the commands to submerge the Orzeł. "Bosun, report the Christmas tree status."

"Green lights, sir, all hatches are secure."

"Good, pressurize the boat," Piasecki ordered.

"Pressurizing, sir, the barometer is holding steady."

"Good, flood tanks, three, four, and five."

"Tanks, flooding, sir."

"Helm! Bow planes down twenty degrees."

"Aye, sir! Bow planes, twenty degrees down."

The Orzeł pushed her nose down and began to descend into the depths.

"Bosun, read me the depth as we go."

"Five meters, sir." The bosun paused. "Ten meters, sir." Then after another short pause, "Fifteen meters, sir."

"Helm, level the bow planes," Piasecki ordered.

"Aye, sir, leveling planes."

After a moment, the Bosun reported, "Twenty meters, sir."

"Up periscope," Grudziński ordered. When the periscope broke the surface and was ready for use, he stopped his watch, holding it at chest height for everyone to see.

"Lower the periscope." As the Bosun lowered the periscope, Grudziński also ordered, "Piasecki, cancel the alarm."

"Yes, sir, canceling alarms, but what is going on?"

"That was good, but not good enough," said Grudziński, slowly shaking his head. "If we are to remain a fighting force then we must perform better than that. So over the next day or two, we are going to run through a few exercises to sharpen our responses."

"Sir?" Piasecki, asked, "Is this necessary? Poland is now lost, the men on this boat are exhausted and demoralized, do we need to continue the fight?"

"Are we Polish?" Grudziński looked around the control room assessing everyone's mood and attention. He then repeated the question, a bit louder this time, "Are we Polish?"

"Yes, sir, of course, sir."

"It is our duty to continue the fight for Poland. Many Poles have fled to England and France to continue their fight against Germany. We have five torpedoes, and we can still hurt the Nazis and their vicious cause. The shipping lanes are nearby, they carry raw materials into Germany. If we can sink five German ships, then that may slow Germany down. If our actions save the lives of any Polish, British or French soldiers, then we are doing our duty."

No one spoke in the control room. Everyone was listening to the captain.

"In order to do our duty, we must be at our best performance."

"What do you want us to do?" Piasecki asked.

"Before we enter the shipping lanes, we will spend the next day practicing a few important maneuvers, such as diving and surfacing. We need to improve our timing."

"Yes, sir, the men will certainly work on that. Anything else?"

"Torpedo firing solutions!" Grudziński let that sink in for a moment. He then continued, "As well as the charts, the Estonians took all our tools to calculate firing angles. They have taken the Is-Was, the handheld slide rule. We must do all the calculations manually."

Grudziński's eyes narrowed, beginning to look like the devil in the red light of the control room.

"In order to strike our targets, we need to do these calculations at speed. Therefore, we need to practice this and make it perfect."

"Sir," Piasecki said, "the Kid is a natural calculator. Maybe we can use him to help get the firing solutions right?"

"Good thinking, Piasecki. Call him to the control room and we can start work on that right away." Grudziński then turned towards me and, placing his hand on my shoulder, said, "Blackie, Stanley, I want you both to return to your posts and tell your officer what I have just said. I'll be along soon to explain to Officer Foterek and Officer Stelmaszyk in more detail."

We both nodded.

"Now go, on the double. We begin exercises immediately."

"Aye, sir!" We both saluted. Stanley headed forward to the torpedo room, while I headed aft to the engine room, on the double.

———

I couldn't wait to tell Foterek the news. He was in the engine room sat next to the electrical panel. Looking up he asked, "So what's all the excitement about? Are we attacking or running away?"

"Neither, we are on exercises!"

"Well, that's better than hiding at the bottom of the sea. Does the captain think he's going to improve morale?"

"He wants to head into the shipping lanes and target German ships."

"I like his fighting talk!" Foterek stood up now that I had gained his attention.

"But he says we need to be sharper, so he timed our last dive and said it was too slow. We need to improve, so it looks like we'll be practicing some maneuvers. He also told me to tell you that the engines need to respond quickly at all times. He said that you would understand."

"We already work fast, so what exactly am I supposed to understand?" Foterek asked with hands on his hips.

"He said things like changing from diesel to electric when diving must be done quickly, things like that."

"Well Blackie, if I have to work faster, that means you work faster too."

"Aye, sir, I'm happy with that. All I want is to sink some Germans! Isn't that our job?"

Foterek scratched his chin in thought. "So we have five torpedoes. I wonder how many German ships we could sink with only five?"

"That's another thing he was talking about because the Estonians took all our tools to calculate the firing solutions."

"That's a major problem!" Foterek was aghast. "How the hell are they going to calculate the intercept point, and set the torpedo gyro? Do you realize how complex that is?"

"Yes of course I do, I did the basic training."

"Have you ever tried to hit something?"

"Well, no, not exactly."

Foterek now started pacing up and down. "The geometry is straight forward to understand," he now pointed at me like an annoyed teacher. "There are three trigonometric equations to work out just to get the intercept point."

"Yes, I know."

"So how can they calculate that with paper and pencil quickly enough to fire accurately?"

"I don't know sir, but they're going to get the Kid to help."

"The Kid?" Foterek now looked thoughtful. "Yes, the Kid, he could probably do it all in his head."

"Yes, sir, I think he probably can. He is smart."

"Listen, Blackie, if we're going to sneak up on those German ships, we must get this boat running smoothly. While we're submerged, I want you to clean those valves on the diesels. There's a huge buildup of grease, clogging the intakes. When we're on the surface, I want you to keep watch on the batteries. We need to maintain maximum charge."

"Aye, aye, sir!"

"I'm going to have another look at the compressor. We need to keep that working smoothly." Once again he pointed his finger. "And when the engine telegraph rings, we all jump! Got it?"

"Got it, sir!"

———————

The attitude of the whole crew had changed. After the fall of Warsaw, we had all been ready to head to Sweden and give ourselves up. We could stay there and wait for the end of the war and pray for a better future. Now, everything had changed: We had spirit. We weren't going to wait for a better future, we were going to fight for a better future.

Everyone was busy working at their stations. Even when off duty or resting, the conversations were about the Orzeł and how she was performing. When the alarms sounded for the exercises, everyone jumped to their station swiftly and quietly, ready for battle.

Grudziński would make us practice day and night. He even made us practice on Swedish ships and fishing boats. Of course, we didn't fire torpedoes at them, but the control room and torpedo room had a lot to practice. For instance, the target's course could only be estimated by looking at the AOB or the Angle Of Bow. That would tell us the relative course to the Orzeł. There is no way to calculate this, it is up to the skilled eye of the observer looking through the periscope.

The Kid was now probably the busiest man on the Orzeł. He was essential in every practice torpedo run. In parallel, the torpedo crew had to work hard, loading and unloading the torpedoes. Despite their hard work, every time I saw the Kid or any of the torpedo crew, they always had a sparkle in their eyes.

———————

The general alarm sounded throughout the ship making a Godawful racket. "Here comes another drill!" Foterek shouted above the noise of the diesel engines. The engine telegraph rang but was barely audible above the noise. "Full speed ahead!" he shouted as he responded to the signal. "Blackie! Open all throttles!"

We raced around the diesels, squeezing every ounce of speed from them. When we were happy with the main engines, I checked the alternators to see what charge we were getting to the batteries. "Batteries charging at maximum, sir!" I shouted to Foterek.

He came over to double-check, patting me on the back. He said loudly into my ear, "We must be practicing an attack. If we were running, they would be more likely to submerge and hide."

I nodded in agreement. "I can't wait until we do it for real!" I replied.

When we changed to electric motors, we heard an announcement through the tannoy: "This is not a drill".

Oh, crap! This is a real one, I thought. Looking around the engine room, I could see the same thought in everyone's eyes.

———

On the bridge, the helmsman said, "Sir, our speed is now nineteen knots."

"Good," Grudziński said. "Maintain course just ahead of that freighter. We need to get closer to identify her."

Speaking into the voice pipe, Grudziński instructed the control room to send Lieutenant Mokrski to the bridge.

When Mokrski clambered up through the hatch, Grudziński continued to look through his binoculars. "What's our position?"

"We're about 120 degrees southwest of Long Jan lighthouse on Oland Island, sir."

"Distance?"

"About twenty miles, give or take."

"Give or take what?"

"At least twenty percent, sir."

Grudziński now looked at Mokrski with surprise. "What? Why so much?"

"Sir, during drill maneuvers I've only been able to use dead reckoning. Each of our drills involved course changes.

Even if those are only small changes it's difficult to track all of them, the errors were compounded. That's why I can't say with precision."

"OK, I get the picture. So we could be twenty-five miles or more out, which puts us at the edge of the shipping lane or even inside it. Do you agree?"

"Yes, that makes sense." Mokrski now peered into the distance where Grudziński was looking. "Are we after that ship?"

"Get below and prepare for a torpedo run," was Grudziński's answer. "And I want recommendations for a timed salvo versus an angled spread."

"Aye, sir."

"And send Piasecki up here with any ship identification books."

"Sir, the Estonians took all of those."

"If there is anything Piasecki has, tell him to bring it up, if I can't identify that ship, I can't torpedo it."

"Aye, sir!" The Kid almost jumped down the hatch.

As Piasecki clambered up into the bridge, he announced, "Sir, we have no identification documents," straightening his tunic and adjusting his cap against the night breeze. "Is that the ship in question?"

"Yes, have a look," Grudziński said, handing the binoculars to Piasecki. "We've been practicing mock attacks on small fry close to Sweden, so no identification was needed. I must identify any prey as German before we attack."

"We could get them to heel over, and board them?" Piasecki suggested.

"Yes, we must conform to maritime law," Grudziński confirmed. "However, there will be other ships around, and the radio traffic will be heard. The German coast is only eighty to a hundred miles away so aircraft could be on our heads before we can finish the job."

"So what do we do?" Piasecki asked.

"We sneak in close on the surface and identify her by her flag. If she's German, we hail her to heave to. If she stays silent, we board her and take their charts."

"What if she calls for air cover?"

"If that happens, we can easily run ahead of her and submerge at a safe distance."

"You're becoming quite a hunter, Captain." Piasecki saluted with an exaggerated snap of his hand.

"We will all be hunters from now on. She's about 110 degrees off our port bow, probably doing ten knots or less. Helmsman!"

"Aye, sir."

"Steer a course one six zero degrees and maintain speed. In about an hour, we will be in front of her. We can then just sit and wait for her to catch up."

While we were running exercises, we all had to stay at our stations, so I couldn't wander around the boat to find out what was going on. Even those who are not on watch had to keep the decks clear. Therefore, we had only two things to do: wonder what was happening on the surface and follow any orders that were given.

There is one other thing we did: we tried to make sense of the gossip passing through the boat. There must have been a dozen mouths and ears the news passed through and each one distorted or changed the message. All we could do was await orders and ignore the noise.

It was about an hour before the engine Telegraph gave us the order to change speed to 'Ahead Slow'.

On the bridge, Lieutenant Piasecki reported, "She is still coming up behind us, range is three kilometers and closing. I can see that she's fully laden, she's up to the Plimsoll line."

"Can you identify her?"

"Yes!" Piasecki said excitedly, "I see her flag! She's German!"

Grudziński called down to the control room through the voice pipe, "Get the Kat to hail the German ship to heave to, identify us as the ORP Orzeł." Then, turning to Piasecki, he said, "Use the lantern to signal them to heave to."

"Aye, sir."

"Helm, turn starboard and head towards the German freighter, increase speed to fifteen knots."

"Aye, sir, coming about, fifteen knots."

As the Orzeł headed towards our target, it wasn't long before the voice pipe on the bridge whistled. Grudziński answered the call, "Understood, but keep hailing the freighter."

"What did they say?" Piasecki asked.

"The Kat reports a coded message being transmitted, probably from the freighter."

Piasecki turned towards Grudziński and asked, "You mean they're calling for help?"

"I expected they would," Grudziński said. Pointing towards the freighter, he said, "Keep signaling them to heave to, if they don't stop, we will attack."

When the Orzeł closed to 1000 meters, Grudziński ordered, "Helm, turn to port, and run parallel to the freighter. I want to keep a good range for our torpedoes."

"Aye, sir."

The Orzeł easily outpaced the freighter. Keeping our distance, and running parallel, slightly to the freighters aft, Grudziński ordered the Orzeł to dive.

Inside the control room, when periscope depth was reached, Grudziński addressed the crew. "This is a live attack run on a German freighter that refuses to heave to. Are we ready?"

Everyone in the control room confirmed with a hearty, "Aye, aye, sir!"

Grudziński ordered, "Helm, maintain heading three, six, zero, speed seven knots."

"Aye, sir. Three, six, zero, seven knots."

"Stay on periscope Piasecki, you are our approach officer. Let's work out the firing solution. Piasecki, what's her angle of bow?"

As the periscope went up, Lieutenant Piasecki reported, "One, three, five, degrees, sir."

"Range?" Grudziński asked.

"1100 meters, sir."

"Helm, confirm our heading!

"Three, six, zero, sir."

"Lieutenant Mokrski, are you ready to do the calculations?"

"Aye, sir."

"What type of salvo do you recommend?"

"I think a time-delayed salvo would be best."

"Why?"

"Well, sir, given the range and angle, I think the course we calculate will be accurate, so she will cross the intercept point. That leaves her speed. We can compensate for speed errors with time delays. I suggest three torpedoes, ahead of time, on time, and behind time."

"Very good, Kid. I'll go with your suggestion, but I can only afford two torpedoes."

"Well, let me think about the exact timings when I do the solutions."

"OK, Kid."

Grudziński leaped over to the periscope and checked the target. Keeping his eyes firmly pressed on the periscope he issued the command, "Prepare torpedo tubes one and two!"

Warrant Officer Joseph Stelmaszyk grabbed the voice pipe in the forward torpedo room and listened to the command. He confirmed the order, shouting back into the pipe, "Aye, sir, tubes one and two!" Then he turned to his crew with excitement. "OK, boys, this is it! We have a live target! Tubes one and two. Load 'em up now!"

His torpedo crew jumped into action. Four men started by releasing two torpedoes from their storage constraints mounted on the sidewall. Steel straps were removed, allowing them to slide the torpedoes one by one onto their movable slings.

Stanley Uliczny was closest to the tube hatches. First, he checked they were empty, with no water inside, before he opened them to receive the torpedoes.

The crew extended the skids for torpedo one, pulling the deadly weapon from its hold. As they did so, the general alarm sounded, making their coordinated moves appear like a ballet, accompanied by unnerving music.

Stanley checked the tube for obstructions, announcing, "Tube ready!" He then attached the winch to the nose of the torpedo.

"Watch that guide pin!" Stelmaszyk said as they began to slide the torpedo into the tube. When it was fully inserted, Stelmaszyk said, "Close the breach and seal the tube!"

"Aye, sir, breach closed, and sealed," Stanley confirmed.

They then repeated the dance for the second torpedo, flooding both tubes with seawater, ready for firing. Stelmaszyk then confirmed through the voice pipe to the control room, "Tubes one and two ready, sir!"

———

With everyone at their stations, there was little room to move around, so Grudziński stood authoritatively in the center of the control room. "Helm, what's our heading?"

"Three, six, zero," was the reply.

"Piasecki, what's the target heading?"

"Three, six, zero, we are running parallel," he replied.

"OK, Kid, are you ready?" Grudziński asked, looking over his shoulder.

"I'm ready, sir."

"Piasecki, target range?"

After a moment checking with the Stadimeter, Piasecki replied, "1150 meters, sir!"

The Kid scribbled each value that Piasecki called out, ready for his calculations.

"Speed?"

"Ten knots!"

"Bearing?"

"Three, one, five degrees, sir!"

"Down periscope!" Grudziński ordered.

The Kid began calculating, with his head bent over the chart table. As he scribbled numbers on his paper, his lips moving in silent mumbles, and he nodded each time he finished a stage in the equations. When finished he called out the numbers.

Grudziński grabbed the voice pipe to pass the gyro setting and run depth to the torpedo room.

When the confirmation came back, Grudziński issued the order, "Fire one!"

The muffled sound of compressed air launching the torpedo was heard throughout the boat. There was also a slight judder as the torpedo shot ahead of the boat as though the boat were a blowpipe.

"What's our time interval, Kid?"

"Two ships' length, sir." The Kid counted the seconds on his stopwatch before saying, "Now!"

"Fire two!" Grudziński commanded into the voice pipe.

Again, everyone felt and heard the second torpedo as it was launched.

Now we waited. Nothing could be changed now. It was up to the torpedoes to complete their job.

When a torpedo leaves the tube, it travels in a straight line ahead of the submarine. This is a fixed distance, called the reach. At the end of the reach, the torpedo uses the gyro setting to turn towards the intercept point. After this turn, the torpedo will continue in a straight line to that point. This is the point that Lieutenant Mokrski has calculated the target would be, after so many seconds or minutes. On paper, the geometry is simple, but the calculations involve many variables such as the target's speed, distance, angles, as well as the torpedo's reach and turn radius. Without the slide-rule-like tool, the Is-Was, Lieutenant Mokrski had to perform the calculations on paper.

Now the lieutenant panted in the heat of the control room, leaning on his chart table with both hands, staring wide-eyed at his calculations, praying he was correct.

"Good work, Kid," Grudziński nodded towards the Kid. "We couldn't do this without you."

Seconds passed, slowly and silently as everyone listened for the explosion.

"Up periscope," Grudziński ordered.

Piasecki fixed his gaze on the target. He looked at his watch, returning his eyes to the periscope. "It should be about now," he said as he kept looking.

"Oh, shit!" Piasecki shouted.

Everyone turned towards Piasecki and the periscope, imagining the explosion that he was seeing. The sound would take longer to reach the Orzeł.

"Shit! She's turning!" Piasecki cried.

"Let me see," Grudziński stepped to the periscope. "Yes, she's turning hard. She's seen the torpedo trails, she's running evasive maneuvers. We missed, damn it!"

Jaws dropped. Our expressions changed from excitement to despair. Everyone mouthed or spat their strongest swear words and curses. The Kid slumped his head into both hands, almost crying. "No, no!"

"Damn it!" Grudziński repeated, stepping away from the periscope.

"What do we do?" Piasecki pleaded.

"Helm, turn to starboard, zero, nine, zero," Grudziński ordered.

"What? Oh, yes, sir," the helmsman stuttered, "turning zero, nine, zero."

"We break off," Grudziński announced.

"But sir," Piasecki pleaded, "she's still close, we still have a chance."

"We can't afford wasting more torpedoes on her. I'm not sure what else is out there. Air cover may arrive soon, so we wait for the next target." Looking around the control room, seeing the stress on everyone's face, he said, "Men that was good work! Lieutenant Mokrski, stand to attention."

The Kid pulled himself from his chart table, slowly standing erect. "Yes, sir," he said despondently.

"That was good work, lieutenant. None of us could have done those calculations in time. The fact that they are running scared is proof of that. Be proud of what you've done. That goes for all of you."

Turning towards Piasecki, he said, "Stand down from general quarters. Stay on our current westerly course for three kilometers. We can then surface to charge our batteries."

"Aye, sir."

Grudziński then turned as though to leave the control room.

"Sir, are you going to your quarters?" Piasecki asked.

"No, I'm going to the forward torpedo room to thank the men for their part."

"Aye, aye, Captain," cheered the men in the control room.

16 Decision to Head to UK

Ship's Log entered by: Lieutenant Jan Grudziński
Date: October 7, 1939
Location: Southern Baltic shipping lanes
Entry: Food, water and fuel are running low, we need to decide what to do. Head for a Swedish port? Or what?

The wardroom only had room to seat four officers at the table at any one time. Lieutenants Mokrski, Kaminski, Sosnowski, and Piasecki had finished their dinner of canned vegetables, canned pork, and noodles. They were now on the dessert: hot tea and canned peaches.

"So what are we going to do?" Lieutenant Kaminski asked, "when we run out of torpedoes?"

"Sweden," Lieutenant Mokrski said, as he shoveled the last of his peaches into his mouth.

"I hear that Stockholm is a beautiful city," Lieutenant Sosnowski said.

"I think we'll run out of peaches before we run out of torpedoes," Mokrski said, looking at his empty bowl.

"Kid, I don't understand how you eat so much and still are small," Piasecki said. "I don't think food touches the sides of your throat as it goes down."

"I think it's his brain cells," Sosnowski added. "They need a lot of energy to work."

The Kid just smiled as he wiped his mouth with his napkin.

Grudziński walked in, followed by Lieutenant Roszak and Warrant officer Foterek.

"Sir, would you like to sit down and eat? We're finished and can make room for you," Piasecki said. "That is if the Kid hasn't eaten everything."

"No thanks," Grudziński said. "But I do want to talk with all of you."

"Oh, all of us? What about?"

"Our next move," Grudziński said.

"Funny, but we were just discussing what we could do when the torpedoes run out," Piasecki said.

"Yes, we all know our food and water is running low, so after sinking some Germans, maybe a Swedish port is our best option," Sosnowski added.

"There is another option," Grudziński said.

"Oh? What could that be?" Piasecki asked as he started to gather the plates together.

"Great Britain."

Piasecki stopped, looking thoughtfully at the stack of plates he had gathered.

"You mean the Öresund straits?" Sosnowski looked surprised.

"Yes, the straits between Denmark and Sweden," Grudziński said. "Lieutenant Roszak and Foterek have given this some thought. I think they should explain."

All eyes turned towards Roszak and Foterek.

"Well," Roszak began, "we couldn't replenish our supplies in Tallinn. We also have limited fuel."

Everyone nodded. That was plainly understood.

"We can easily seek internship in Sweden, where we could be safe."

"And the Swedes would not hand over our submarine to the Germans," Grudziński added.

"So Sweden is the safe option, so why are we talking about Britain?" Piasecki asked.

"Fuel," Foterek stated.

"That's right," Roszak confirmed. "You see, we only have so much fuel. We have calculated that we have enough fuel to get to Britain. In a day or two, we won't have enough to cross the North Sea."

"So we need to make a decision now," Grudziński said.

"Aren't the Germans blockading those straits?" Sosnowski asked.

"Never mind the blockades," Piasecki said, "without charts, can we navigate those narrow passages?"

Everyone looked at the Kid, who silently burped having eaten too fast.

"Well?" Grudziński asked.

"My lighthouse book covers these straits," Lieutenant Mokrski said. "That gives us all the positional data we need. I also know enough about the depths and shallows in those passages to guide us through."

"Thanks to the Kid, navigation will not be a problem," Grudziński stated proudly. "Our real danger is the blockade and German patrols. If we could somehow sneak through and join the British fleet, we could continue our fight against the Nazis. We have already done enough, but there is always more that we can do."

Grudziński waited for that to settle into the minds of his officers before saying, "What I want is full support from all of you. Make no mistake, the Germans will be patrolling those straits, so we may have to fight our way through. As acting captain, I can order us to proceed, but I want your support. If any one of you has any doubt or dissent, I want to know now."

Grudziński's lieutenants thought about these options.

Eventually, Sosnowski broke the silence. "We've done enough, but we could do more."

"I always wanted to see England," the Kid said.

Kaminski clenched his fist. "The British need to know the fighting spirit of Poland!"

"What about German patrols?" Piasecki asked.

"That's the difficult part," Grudziński admitted. There will be many German patrols in that area, but I think they will be there to stop any British or French from entering the Baltic. The German patrols will be looking the other way, we should be able to sneak past behind them. We can also do a few tricks to hide our passage through the straits."

"Like what?"

"We can shadow neutral ships as they pass through. That will help to hide our propeller noise."

"What about minefields?"

"We have no information on minefields. We can only hope the Germans have not mined the straits. There is no doubt that this would be a big risk," Grudziński affirmed. "Following the neutral ships through the channels will help us to avoid minefields."

"Well I didn't expect an easy life when I joined this boat," Piasecki said. "So I say we head for Britain."

"Me too!" added Sosnowski. "We could teach the British how to give the Germans a run for their money."

"How about you, Kaminski?"

"I wouldn't miss this trip for the world," he replied. "Anyway, I have to look after you fellows."

"You can count on my engineers!" Foterek added. I think we'd all like to help the British."

The Kid stood up to leave. "I'll go and prepare a chart to guide us through."

"Excellent, we're all agreed," Grudziński said with a smile. "Let's start preparing and tell the crew."

We were running silently under the waves. Stanley and Alex were playing checkers in the wardroom. Alex looked in deep concentration trying to figure out his next move. I was playing cards with Jan and Paul.

"Have you heard the latest news about us?" Paul asked.

"You mean how we sank that Russian ship?" I asked, dealing the cards.

Jan slapped the table. "That is such a lie! How can the Russians tell such lies to the world?"

Stanley smiled. "Maybe when we missed that German freighter, my torpedoes just carried on up the Baltic to Russia."

"Your torpedoes are as dumb as my cards," Paul said, looking at his hand.

"You know, it's all propaganda against us," Alex said. "They are saying we are killers, and we have to be stopped." With that, Alex made his move on the checkerboard. Stanley responded immediately by jumping over two of Alex's pieces, landing on the end of the board to crown his piece.

Alex swore loudly. I thought he was going to throw the board across the room.

Foterek and Lieutenant Roszak then walked through the mess room. Foterek acknowledged me by waving his hand.

"Sir, should I go back to the engine room?"

"It's OK, Blackie, things are fine back there. I'm going to the wardroom with Roszak."

After they passed, Jan asked, "So what's happening in the wardroom?"

Freckles came out of the galley, carrying some glasses and a half-filled bottle of vodka. "All the brass buttons are in there, I think they're having a meeting."

"What about?" I asked.

"How should I know?" Freckles shrugged. "I wasn't invited."

"They must be discussing what to do next," Alex said, turning away from the checkerboard.

"What would you do?" I asked.

"Maybe hide in Sweden," Stanley said.

"No, Grudziński's after something big," Jan suggested. "I think we should go back to Gdańsk and sink that Nazi battleship."

"Hey, wouldn't that be a prize!" Paul nodded. "The defeated Polish sink the powerful Nazi battleship Schleswig-Holstein. What a kick in the head that would be for Mr. Hitler!"

"I have three torpedoes that can rip her fat belly wide open!" Stanley added.

"If we miss, Freckles can use his empty bottles as torpedoes," I stated. "He can even add some of his special mixture as he did to that German tanker in Tallinn! Good old Freckles, the Polish secret weapon!"

"So what do you have for us, Freckles?" Jan asked.

"I have some good news and some bad news," he stated.

"What's the good news?" I asked.

"I have your daily vodka ration," he said waving the bottle in front of us.

"That's the best news I've heard all day," I said. "A quick drink before we surface, smoke a cigarette on deck, and then find a soft bunk to sleep!"

"What's the bad news?" Alex asked. "Will the brass buttons put us through another drill?"

"Worse than that," Freckles said. "This is the last of the vodka."

"WHAT?" we all exclaimed.

"It's true," he said. "We're running low on everything."

"What about fuel?" Paul asked. "Can we get back to Gdańsk to sink that bastard?"

"Yes, I went over the fuel levels with Foterek," I said. "We can get to Gdańsk and sail up to Stockholm with plenty to spare."

"Jeez, no vodka…" Jan shook his head in despair.

Foterek suddenly appeared, standing tall and proud with his hands on his hips. "Gentlemen!" he announced loudly, "Enjoy your drink because we have some work to do. The captain has given us new orders!"

We all looked at each other, wondering if we should bet over whether or not our new orders were to hunt the battleship.

"We are going to Britain!" Foterek announced.

"Britain? Stanley asked.

"Yes, Great Britain!"

We must have looked very disappointed, because Foterek asked, "What's the matter with you all? Don't you want to join the Royal Navy?"

17 Escaping the Baltic

Ship's Log entered by: Lieutenant Jan Grudziński
Date: October 7, 1939
Location: 12 miles due east of Sandhammaren Lighthouse
Entry: Preparing to enter the Öresund Strait to leave the
Baltic Sea. The danger begins here.

In the red light of the control room, Grudziński and
Lieutenant Mokrski huddled around the chart table,
examining the lieutenant's hand-drawn charts. Grudziński
had asked his officers to meet him in the control room, and
they stood shoulder to shoulder with crewmen who manned
their stations. Everyone awaited orders.

"You've done well so far, Kid," Grudziński said.

"Thank you, sir."

Looking around at his officers, Grudziński continued,
"We'll soon be at the mouth of the Öresund Strait. We need
to approach carefully at night. We have to stay out of sight. If
any patrols spot us, they'll swarm around us like flies. So we
can only be on the surface during darkness."

Everyone nodded in agreement.

"Warrant Officer Stelmaszyk."

"Aye, sir."

"We need to be ready with torpedoes, in case we have to
fight our way through."

"Sir, we can keep all three torpedoes ready and loaded,
which would help with our reaction times."

"Good. And keep your men on full alert the whole
time."

"Aye, sir. I can swap shifts with the rear torpedo crew."

"Warrant Officer Foterek."

"Aye, sir.".

"The engine room must also be on full alert at all times,
are your men up to it?"

"Don't worry about us sir, we're ready to go."

"We must also be very careful with our batteries. We can only charge them at night when we are on the surface. I want you to keep me informed so we can run submerged as much as possible."

"Aye, sir. We'll watch the batteries for sure."

"Does anyone else have any suggestions or ideas?"

There was a thoughtful pause before Lieutenant Sosnowski spoke up. "Sir, you're saying we need to sneak through the straits and avoid being seen. However, if someone does see us, our name is displayed on our conning tower. Can we hide that?"

"Sir," Foterek spoke, "we don't need to hide it. We can easily remove it."

"How so Foterek?"

"We can detach them and store them for safekeeping. I can get one of my engineers to do it. That leaves our number designation. We can paint over that if you wish?"

"OK, paint over it with black. Get onto it right away, before we submerge."

"Aye, sir."

Piasecki's eyes lit up. "Foterek, do you have blue and yellow paint?"

"Yes, the paint is oil-based for metal pipes and such. Why?"

"Do you have enough to make a flag?"

"I think so. Why?"

"I suggest we make a Swedish flag. We can hoist it to help disguise ourselves."

Grudziński laughed. "Well, the Germans would think twice before they shoot us. God knows what the Swedes would think! We will need two flags, one Swedish as Piasecki suggests, but we also need a Danish flag when we are in Danish waters. OK, Foterek, make us a Swedish and Danish flag."

"Aye, sir. Two flags coming up!"

"That leaves you, Kid. What's our next waypoint?"

"We are currently heading two, two, zero degrees. As soon as we are due south of Sandhammaren Lighthouse then we need to head due west past Ystad. The next lighthouse is on the Smygehuk headland. At ten knots, we should get there in about three hours." The Kid looked down at his map. "Four to five hours to get to the Falsterbo Peninsula, that's the entrance to the strait."

"That should be a good run to charge our batteries," Piasecki said, "and to get the conning tower painted. We could then rest on the bottom until the following night to slip through the straits."

Grudziński nodded in agreement. "That's just what we'll do. We'll see how many patrols there are before we enter the strait and try to follow traffic through. So we all have our jobs to do, let's get on and do them."

"Aye, sir." Everyone saluted.

"I'll be on the bridge. We'll need extra eyes up there."

Lieutenant Piasecki climbed up the ladder into the bridge. "Coming on deck, sir," he announced.

The helmsman turned to look at Piasecki as he scrambled up.

Grudziński was standing on the podium, scanning the area for ships and planes. "Come on up, extra eyes are always welcome up here." Looking down at Piasecki, he continued, "I thought we would never get past Ystad with all those patrols. We had to submerge three times to avoid detection."

Piasecki climbed up onto the podium to join Grudziński. "At least the crew is making good times for diving, we're averaging thirty seconds."

"Yes, that is good, but has Foterek reported on the batteries?"

"He told me we're at 80%."

"That's what worries me, the more time we spend submerged, hiding from patrols, the less time we have to charge. It's nearly dawn now and we haven't reached Falsterbo Peninsula yet."

Piasecki looked around the dark sky. "Yes, it's nearly four a.m. now, we have nearly two hours until daylight. I think we could get a full charge by dawn. It is also overcast so the dawn should be pretty grey. We should be able to dive with a full charge as we go around the Falsterbo Peninsula."

"Yes, you are right, but only if there are no more patrols. Anyway, how are those flags? Have Foterek's men finished yet?"

"Yes, but it's oil paint, and I think it's still drying."

"Good, tell them to bring it up here, we'll dry it in the wind. Tell them to bring more black paint as well. A lot of it washed off when we were submerged, exposing the ship's number."

"Aye, sir. Anything else?"

"Get Lieutenant Mokrski up here, we must be getting close to the Kid's next waypoint."

Piasecki stepped down from the podium, and as he climbed back down into the control room, he called back, "I'll check with Foterek on the batteries as well."

Let me tell you, it is not easy to carry a wet, painted flag through a submarine. A regular flag can be neatly folded and carried under your arm. The passageways in a submarine are narrow and cramped. The paint was mostly dry but sticky, especially the Swedish flag. The two of us had to carry them like open sheets, not letting them touch anything. If we folded them, they would have stuck together. If we held them too wide, we would have smudged paint on everything we passed. We had to be careful.

"What do you have there, Blackie? Is that your mother's bedsheet?"

"Hey Blackie, are you and Alex changing your country?"

These were some of the comments Alex and I had to listen to, as we made our way through the boat.

"Come on Blackie, can't you move faster?" Alex said, "this paint stinks!"

"I'm walking backward, so I'm going as fast as I can."

Did I say carrying wet painted flags through a submarine was difficult? I won't tell you how difficult it was to carry them up the ladders to the top of the conning tower! When we got up there Alex and I had to hoist that wet mess into the top flagpole.

"Good work, men," Grudziński said, "they look almost genuine."

"Thank you, sir," I said, "it should finish drying in this fresh air."

"I want you both to stay handy, in case we need to submerge."

"Aye, sir." Alex and I replied.

As it was the driest, we tied the Danish flag between stanchions on the aft deck. The Swedish flag fluttered above us on the main flagpole. The yellow cross had nice straight lines, making it look quite convincing. I felt quite proud of the job I had done.

The Orzeł cruised along a westerly course, constantly watching for any patrols. Following a safe distance from the Swedish coast, she slowly approached the Smygehuk headland, the most southerly tip of Sweden. Lieutenant Mokrski stood on the starboard side of the bridge, scanning the horizon for the next lighthouse. The helmsman peered into the darkness ahead, periodically checking the compass by his side to keep on course.

Behind and slightly above them, Captain Grudziński and Lieutenant Piasecki stood on the bridge podium allowing them a raised vista into the dark, early morning hours.

"We should be safe from German patrols this close to Swedish waters," Piasecki stated.

"That's true, but I don't trust the swedes," Grudziński frowned. "They may want to use us as a bargaining chip with the Germans. These are uncertain times. I don't know who to trust."

"You can trust me and you can trust your whole crew, we are all behind you."

"Thank you, Piasecki, I appreciate that." Grudziński lowered his binoculars. "As well as our duty and this mission, I have to consider the crew's safety."

"Hey, Panienka," Piasecki nudged Grudziński's arm.

Grudziński turned towards Piasecki with a quizzical look.

"You know, that's what they used to call you, Panienka, or 'the damsel', if you want. That has now changed, what everyone calls you now is captain."

Piasecki stood and assessed Grudziński's reaction, who was slightly taken aback and continued his quizzical look.

"Kłoczkowski would never give you full control of our boat because I think he saw you as a young, inexperienced academic. Running a submarine takes skill and daring. The day you explained how and why Kłoczkowski avoided that bombing run by German aircraft, I realized that you understood how to drive a submarine. When you started those drills and prepared the men for action, I understood that you know how to drive the crew."

Grudziński began to blush, but it was not visible to Piasecki in the darkness.

"Now, you are leading us on a mission to join the British and continue the war against Germany. You are the captain of the Orzeł and captain of this crew. You are leading us, and we are following you. There isn't a single man on this boat who is not thankful that you are here."

Grudziński turned towards his lieutenant with worried eyes, but before he could speak…

"Sir," a quiet voice called up towards the podium. "Sir," the Kid quietly repeated, "I see the Smygehuk Lighthouse."

"Ah, yes, well-done, Kid," Grudziński said, looking back down towards the Kid. "What's the bearing?"

"About 300 degrees sir."

Less than an hour later, the Orzeł sailed past the headland at a distance of about eight kilometers.

"She looks like a searchlight," Piasecki said.

In the hazy gloom, the rotating light looked as if it was searching for the Orzeł. The main light would scan the

horizon like an evil eye. The rotating shields appeared to
wink, as if to acknowledge the lighthouse's discovery of the
Orzeł.

"Sir?" Piasecki asked, "perhaps we are too close? Will
that light illuminate us to other ships?"

"I don't think so, sir," the Kid said, "there is the port of
Trelleborg coming up, and traffic will be ahead in about
fifteen minutes."

"I agree," said Grudziński, "there is nothing near, and if
we are seen at this point, they could easily mistake us for a
fishing boat." Grudziński scanned the horizon. "We may
have to dive under the next shipping channel coming out of
Trelleborg. Piasecki, get below and prepare the boat."

"Aye, sir."

"And send Blackie and Alex back up here, we need to
stow their flag before we dive."

"Aye, sir."

————————

Whenever we were on full alert, all the watertight doors
had to be kept shut. Everyone had to remain at their station
and follow the orders transmitted to them. Most of our
orders in the engine room came through the engine telegraph.
They would tell us how fast or how slow we should go. I
didn't mind being closed up in the engine room, it made me
feel like I was part of the engine. The Orzeł's brain was in the
control room, her muscles were in the engine room. I was
just part of the nervous system, telling the muscles what the
brain wanted to do.

Foterek on the other hand felt frustrated. I knew he
wasn't claustrophobic, no one on a submarine can be
claustrophobic. He was frustrated because he didn't have the
information he needed. We knew what Grudziński had
planned, but had to figure out for ourselves what was
happening. Since we controlled the engines, we knew how
fast we were going. We also had our compass, so we knew
when we were turning. Using that information, we could
make a good guess for how far into the plan we were.

We were submerged and running on the quieter electric motors. Foterek then used this time to ask me, "So tell me again what Grudziński said he was planning?"

I rolled my eyes. "I told you already, after we pass around the Falsterbo Peninsula, we'll head northeast and follow the Swedish coast to the north end of the sound. From there we'll enter the open waters of the Skagerrak."

Foterek looked at his watch, then at his compass. "Well, we're still heading north, we should have turned northeast by now."

"You worry too much. There have been many speed changes, we're probably following a slow ship. We'll probably turn any time now."

"I think there's something wrong, I can feel it in my bones."

Foterek did have a feel for things, but the way he said that I began to worry as well.

———

"Sonar, how's the sound of that freighter?"

"It's holding steady, Captain. I estimate we are still 800 meters off her stern."

"What else can you hear out there?"

"Traffic behind us is still the same, but I hear increasing amounts of traffic to the northeast."

"What sort of traffic?"

"Large and small, sir. The large ones are too fast and too clean for freighters, I suspect they are destroyers."

"I think you need to take a look, Piasecki, up periscope."

"Aye, sir." As the periscope rose, Piasecki caught the handles in both hands. He then quickly spun around once, looking for immediate threats, then slower to examine what was out there.

Angling the scope forward, Piasecki said, "Yes, I also estimate 800 meters to the freighter, we are following almost exactly in her wake." Turning slightly to port, he then said, "I can see the Drogden Lighthouse, bearing ten degrees."

Looking aft, Piasecki reported, "We seem to have passed the rain, it's still hazy but visibility is increasing."

"What is to the northeast?" Grudziński asked.

Piasecki turned and scanned in that direction. He changed magnification a few times and scanned from left to right.

"There's a lot of activity there. I see at least three destroyers, but I can't identify them in the hazy darkness. There are also many fast patrol boats. They seem to be holding a picket line between Saltholm Island and the Swedish headland. Sir, would you like to have a look?"

Grudziński stepped forward, grasping the handles and slowly scanned the area northeast. "Yes, it looks like they are holding a picket line, checking all traffic going towards Malmö and the Swedish coast." He then scanned forward. "I don't see any immediate threats north of us, so we'll continue to follow this freighter."

'Sir, should I check the Drogden Lighthouse?"

"Down periscope," Grudziński ordered. "There's no need, Kid. There's only one lighthouse looking like the Drogden, and we have bigger worries to think about. I don't want the periscope up more than we need."

"Heading north will take us between Saltholm and Amager Islands. We'll have to sail past Copenhagen, is that wise sir?" Piasecki asked.

"It's the lesser of two evils. We can turn east when we pass Saltholm Island."

The Kid then spoke up. "Sir, there are shallows north of Saltholm. We must pass around Flakfortet Island."

"What if there are more pickets around Copenhagen?" Piasecki asked.

"I'm sure there will be, but they will be Danish, guarding their city. If there are any Germans, they will be looking north to stop an incursion by the British Navy. We should be able to sneak out from behind them. It's either this picket to the northeast who are probably looking for us, or any other pickets around Copenhagen who are probably looking for something else."

"Helm, what's our heading?"

"Zero degrees, Captain. Heading north."

"What's our sea depth?"

"Eleven meters, sir. We're about to scrape on the bottom."

"OK, prepare to surface. Call for Alex and Blackie to hoist their Swedish flag. We must bluff our way north past Copenhagen. Lieutenant Mokrski, I want you on the bridge when we surface, I'll need advice on the channel."

"Aye, sir."

"Helm, steer three, one, five degrees," Grudziński ordered.

"Aye, sir. Three, one five."

"Why are you heading towards the shallows?" Piasecki asked.

"We need to circle past the lighthouse. I don't want anyone there to identify us. We'll lose the freighter we are following, but we can find another when we get past that point."

Piasecki nodded.

The Orzeł surfaced and carefully steered its path around the Drogden Lighthouse. When he was satisfied that the Orzeł was past the lighthouse, Grudziński started to climb the ladder into the conning tower. Turning towards Piasecki he said, "We need to be careful in this channel. We'll stay on the surface as long as we dare. It is too shallow for us to dive but we can run awash, with only our conning tower visible, which should keep us at a low profile."

"Good plan, sir," Piasecki said.

"I'll be up on the bridge."

———

This time, Alex and I hoisted our Danish flag. The channel was Danish water, between Saltholm Island and Amager Island, with Copenhagen at the north end. The channel was about five kilometers wide, and we could see the lights on either shore. Grudziński kept us on either side of the bridge as extra lookouts. The helmsman stood at the wheel, steering us north through the channel. Lieutenant Mokrski stood watching the channel ahead. At one point, the Kid froze in terror. "There's a freighter heading south in the channel, it's going to pass right by us!"

"What will the captain do now?" Alex asked.

"I don't know, he was saying we would sail awash, which will make us look smaller."

"He must see it," the helmsman said, "but he's not ordering us to sail awash."

"Sir," Alex called to Grudziński who stood on the podium, "freighter approaching from the north."

"I see it," Grudziński acknowledged.

As we passed the freighter, Grudziński saluted the passing vessel. He also ordered the lookouts on the cigarette deck to salute.

"Jeez!" exclaimed Alex. "Do you see what he's doing?"

"Ha!" laughed the Kid, "he's pretending to be Danish!"

I smiled. "That must be what he meant when he said we have to bluff our way through!"

As we continued north, we soon began to see the lights of Copenhagen, blurred in the drizzly, dark hours before dawn. In the murky distance, we could see ships sailing into and out of the busy harbor.

Grudziński stepped down from the podium. "We're getting close to Copenhagen. What do you think the channel conditions are around here, Kid?"

"I can't say exactly, but I do remember it gets deeper when we get level with the port. There are two islands with lighthouses ahead, Nordre Rose and Flakfortet. Most of the traffic approaches the port between those islands. You can see the lights up ahead." The Kid pointed towards the rotating lights in the distance. "The gap between them is about five kilometers, and it will be deep enough to dive. The water is shallow on either side of them."

Grudziński looked ahead, pondering our next move. "Now we have to perform our next trick of deception."

Grudziński ordered the ballast tanks to be partially flooded, making the Orzeł sink low into the water. Her buoyancy was such that her fore and aft deck remained awash. Only her conning tower was fully out of the water. We slowed to seven knots. This slow speed, coupled with her low profile, made the Orzeł appear to be a small, slow boat, of no threat.

I felt as if our boat was sinking, but it wasn't, we sailed on. We were now moving slowly, but I have never seen the Orzeł sail this way. It was as if the conning tower was the only part of the boat. We sailed like this for about thirty minutes, by which time the dawn began to break through the gloom. We were ordered to take down the Danish flag and stow it below. Once everyone was safely inside, we dove down to periscope depth. I wondered if anyone on the nearby shore watched as a small vessel, the size of a fishing boat, disappeared below the waves.

———

Many of the men on the Orzeł found some solace in sitting on the bottom of the Öresund Strait. The blanket of water around them seemed a shelter to them, offering respite from the last few hours and previous days of running. Now we were quietly hiding.

The control room was quiet, bathed in its usual red light. Grudziński stood by the chart desk, staring down at the maps and sketches drawn by Lieutenant Mokrski. Deep in meditation, he touched nothing, his hands held in a prayer-like fashion, with his fingers pressed to his lips.

Piasecki stepped through the watertight hatch into the control room. Seeing Grudziński deep in thought, he announced, "Coming on deck, sir."

Grudziński did not acknowledge him.

Lieutenant Mokrski, the Kid, followed Piasecki into the control room. "You wanted to see me, sir?"

"Ah, lieutenant, Yes." Grudziński turned towards the Kid and smiled, "I need to discuss our route for tonight."

Both men stepped forward to join Grudziński at the chart desk.

"You said the deep water is between these two islands, Middlegrundsfortet and Flakfortet?" Grudziński pointed to two small circles on the sketched chart. "Between them is where most of the shipping traffic from Copenhagen travels."

"Yes, sir."

"And there is shallow water between Flakfortet and Saltholm, which we have now passed?"

"Yes, sir. I think we can sail between Flakfortet and Saltholm but because it is shallow, I think we can only sail on the surface."

"I see." Grudziński nodded. "So what is north of Middlegrundsfortet?"

"Sir, I don't know."

"It is open water, do you know the depth?"

"No, sir. I don't know what is north of Middlegrundsfortet, all I know is the deep water is on the Swedish side of this strait. I think there is a channel north of Middlegrundsfortet, but if you want to follow it, you will have to find the marker buoys."

"So how should we reach the deep water?" Piasecki asked.

"I think we can go around Flakfortet Island and head east towards Sweden. Then we can follow the coast, north into the Kattegat," The Kid said.

"That makes sense to me," Piasecki said.

"Yes, it makes sense to me too," Grudziński agreed. "It would make sense to any rabbit trying to run away." Grudziński scratched his chin, thinking deeply. "The Orzeł is a hunter," he eventually said, "but sometimes we must play the game of cat and mouse."

"Sir?" The Kid looked puzzled.

"I expect that is exactly where all the Nazi patrols will be concentrating. They will be watching the entrance to Copenhagen and the channels south, between Saltholm and Sweden. Maybe we can sneak right underneath them."

"Do you think we can do it?" Piasecki asked.

Grudziński looked at them both, smiling widely and almost laughing. "Gentlemen, I need you both to get some sleep. I will need you to be at your sharpest tonight when we set off. I will be in my quarters trying to sleep." Stepping aside, Grudziński nodded and exited towards his cabin. As he left he said, "Sleep, that's an order."

———

This wasn't like sitting on the bottom of the bay of Gdańsk.

I sat in the mess room with my cards laid out on my table. Nobody wanted to play with me, everyone seemed to be resting. So I played solitaire, playing against the deck itself. I enjoyed the deck, the cards were familiar to me, and sometimes the cards liked me, sometimes they didn't. Some people would call that luck. I called it knowing when to play and knowing when to quit.

Freckles leaned on the serving hatch, watching me intently. "This is like sitting on the bottom of the bay of Gdańsk with Captain Kłoczkowski."

"This is nothing like those times," I said, without looking up.

"What I meant is, it's as boring."

"It's not even that, this is the Captain anticipating our next move." I dealt the next card to myself. I was able to play it and move two other cards onto the ace.

Before Freckles could reply I looked up and said, "Be quiet. Can you hear it?"

"Hear what?"

"It's another ship coming by, I think this one is heading out of Copenhagen, it seems to be fast. They always enter the harbor slowly but leave quickly."

The rhythmic drumming of the passing ship's propeller became audible, before receding. Our eyes followed the faint sound as it seemed to move across the mess room.

"Jeez, Blackie, I thought you'd be deaf from working in the engine room. Maybe you should change to the sonar?"

"We are just so close to the shipping lanes going into Copenhagen, I can't help but hear them." I was losing against the deck, so I scooped up my cards. Standing up I announced, "I need to get some sleep, I have a feeling that we'll be busy tonight when we surface."

The air was stale, from sitting on the bottom all day. The close confines of the control room seemed to amplify the stuffy heat. The crew stood at their stations while Piasecki stood firmly in the center. "Men, are we all ready?"

"Aye, sir," came the chorused reply.

Grudziński looked at his watch. "It is 1830 hours, and the sun will set in about ten minutes. We will use the dusk light to assess the situation on the surface. I expect there to be many patrols. If we engage them, we will only attract more attention. Therefore we must play a game of cat and mouse, and we are the mouse."

Grudziński looked around as his crew nodded in agreement. "Sonar, what do you hear?"

"Regular traffic around the port, sir. Possible fast patrol crafts, but very distant, sir."

"Bosun, what's our battery reading?"

"Eighty-three percent, sir."

"OK, Piasecki, take her up to periscope depth. Head north, zero degrees at three knots."

"Aye, sir. Bosun, blow all tanks."

"Blowing all tanks, sir."

The Orzeł rocked slightly as she rose from the muddy bottom. Piasecki then cranked the engine telegraph to signal 'Ahead Slow'. "Helm, steer zero degrees."

"Steering zero degrees, sir."

"Dive planes up, fifteen degrees."

"Dive planes up, fifteen degrees, sir."

In the shallow channel, the Orzeł quickly leveled off, heading slowly north at periscope depth.

Grudziński ordered, "Up periscope." Catching the handles as they came up, he danced around, scanning the sea and sky for any threats. Moments later, he stated, "All clear. Down periscope." The Orzeł could continue unseen.

Looking towards Lieutenant Mokrski, Grudziński said, "OK, Kid, you're next. You need to get our bearing from those lighthouses and give me a course towards Sweden."

"Aye, sir." The Kid stepped forward, ready at the periscope. As the periscope rose, he looked for the lighthouses. "Flakfortet, bearing ninety degrees." Then, turning the periscope around, he said, "Middlegrundsfortet bearing, three, one zero degrees."

As the periscope went down, the Kid stepped back to his chart table. Triangulating on his sketches he marked the Orzeł's position.

"Good," Grudziński said. "We continue north another fifteen minutes and then head towards Sweden. Sonar keep listening for traffic."

"Aye, sir."

Those minutes passed slowly, but without incident. One more time, the Kid used the periscope to check the Orzeł's position before Grudziński ordered the change in course.

"Helm, steer, seven, zero degrees."

"Steering, seven, zero degrees, sir."

At that slow speed, the change was barely perceptible. Sonar continued to listen, using his stopwatch, and noting numbers on paper.

After some minutes of slow sailing, Grudziński called out, "Sonar, report."

"I detect two destroyers. One is at one, four, zero degrees, about fifteen kilometers, and the second is at four, three degrees, about seven kilometers. Both are accompanied by three small craft traveling fast, probably German torpedo boats. I also hear pings at timed intervals."

"Standard search tactic, they are looking for us. What's the timing?"

"Pings are every three minutes exactly, sir."

"German precision, I like it." Grudziński smiled. "We'll continue on course."

"Sir?" Piasecki asked, "doesn't that bring us between them?"

"Pretty much, I want to see how alert they are. Sonar, listen very carefully to those patrols, I want to know of any change in their movements. Alert me on every ping."

"Aye, sir."

"Sir," Piasecki spoke, "in open water, they will be able to detect us using those pings."

"We can't sit on the bottom forever, we have to move away from the port," Grudziński replied. "We need to reach open water to maneuver."

At that moment, sonar announced, "I hear a ping, sir."

Grudziński cranked the engine telegraph to 'Ahead Full'.

As the electric motors revved up to speed, sonar made another announcement, "Sir, the destroyers are coming about, sounds like they're heading this way!"

Piasecki looked worried. "Sir, when we are submerged, our best speed is only seven knots. You can't race under them at this speed."

"Helm, hold our course," Grudziński ordered.

"Holding course, sir."

"Sonar, tell me when we get the next ping."

"Aye, sir."

The minutes passed. Eyes looked from side to side, each man silently questioning the next crewman.

"All vessels heading directly towards us, sir," Sonar said.

Grudziński stood firm with his wrist raised to chest height, his eyes fixed firmly on his watch.

"Sir! There's the next ping!"

Grudziński shouted, "Helm! Turn hard to port! Heading three, zero, zero degrees!"

The helmsman spun his wheel around to the left. "Turning three, zero, zero degrees, sir!"

This time the turn could be felt. Loose items shifted and rolled to the right. The men had to adjust their balance as the Orzeł turned hard to port.

As the turn completed, Piasecki asked, "So now we run?"

"No," Grudziński said, as he continued to look at his watch. "The mouse cannot outrun the cat, what we do now is hide in our hole." A moment later, Grudziński cranked the engine telegraph to 'Ahead Slow'.

"What hole is that?" Piasecki asked.

"Piasecki, haven't you learned anything from Captain Kłoczkowski? Now, flood all tanks," Grudziński ordered.

"Aye, sir, flooding tanks." Piasecki looked puzzled.

As the Orzeł began to descend towards the bottom, Grudziński first cranked the engine telegraph to 'All Stop', before ordering, "Helm, dive planes up ten degrees."

"Dive planes, ten degrees up, sir."

Piasecki was perplexed. "We're diving with dive planes up?"

"We still have forward motion, and it is relatively shallow here. I want our bow tilted up so we don't get our bow stuck in the mud." Grudziński then moved to the tannoy and announced through the Orzeł's speakers, "Everyone, brace for landing on the seabed."

Seconds later the Orzeł made a bumpy landing on the muddy floor of the Öresund Strait.

"There's another ping, sir."

"You see Piasecki, sleight of hand."

"Yes, you're full of tricks, but I don't get it."

"There were two pings when we traveled in a straight line at seven knots."

"Yes," Piasecki agreed while all eyes in the control room were fixed on Grudziński for his explanation.

"Sonar, correct me if I'm wrong: The Germans can use the pings to echolocate us, and are then able to triangulate our position and therefore our speed?"

"Yes, sir, that is correct. On the first ping, they saw us and started to turn towards us. The second ping they would see we have moved forward, so they can calculate our speed and hence predict our forward path."

"So, gentlemen," Grudziński said proudly, "the Germans think we're over there, but we are not. We are safe and sound here in our mouse hole."

"Very clever, but what do we do now?"

"We do what all clever mice do, we wait, and listen."

"Sir?" the Kid asked, "can they locate us here sitting on the bottom?"

"No, they can track floating and moving objects. We are just a lump on the seabed."

"Sir, I detect splashes!"

"Where? How far?" Grudziński asked as everyone turned towards the sonar.

"Just a minute…" Kozowy said, listening intently through his headphones while scribbling numbers on paper. He then said, "Bearing, about sixty degrees, distance…" he paused, continuing to scribble, "about nine kilometers."

The muffled booms of the distant depth charges then arrived.

"As you said, Captain," Piasecki smiled, "they think we're over there, but we're not, we are right here."

Strange popping sounds began to pass through the Orzeł, followed by more muffled booms.

"What the hell was that?" the Kid asked.

"I think they are echoes of the depth charges," replied sonar, "bouncing off the Swedish coast."

"As well as the echoes," Grudziński said, "they will be firing a standard spread of depth charges in the areas they think we sailed into."

"You mean they lost us?' the Kid asked.

"Yes, but they are trying to find us," Grudziński replied. "They have tricks of their own to find little mice."

"Sir, pings have increased to every sixty seconds."

"They are in active search mode," Grudziński said.

"What do we do when they come looking over here?" Piasecki asked.

"They will do, sooner or later, make no mistake about that. I'm hoping we have time to lift off the bottom and go northwest to hide in shallows before they check this sector."

'When do we lift off the bottom?" Piasecki asked.

"As soon as they go back into standard search, we will know when they ping every three minutes." Although it was lowered, Grudziński leaned against the periscope column. "I expect the Swedes and the Danes will be calling their German Embassies to complain about the explosions in the shipping channels."

"Will that make them stop?" asked the Kid.

"No, of course not," Piasecki scoffed.

"We hope for the best, just like the little mouse does." Grudziński winked.

As the hours passed, the pings continued every minute. This meant the Germans knew something was out there, and they were eager to find it. They ruthlessly depth charged the area they calculated the Orzeł to be in. After some time, this stopped, as the German patrols began to regroup and consider their strategy.

"Sir?" Piasecki asked, "they seem to have stopped, this could be a good opportunity to rise and make a run to the northwest."

Grudziński was at the chart desk looking at the Kid's sketches. He raised his head. "Sonar, what's the ping frequency?"

"It is still every minute."

"There's your answer Piasecki, they are still looking for us."

"So we sit here and wait?" Piasecki asked.

"Yes, until we have a clear chance of leaving without being detected." Grudziński then walked over to the sonar operator. "Do you have any updates on traffic? Can you hear what they are doing up there?"

"Yes, sir. The freighters have steered clear of the current patrol area of the Germans. The smaller craft seems to be circling, as if following a search pattern. One destroyer has moved south and seems to be holding position east of

Copenhagen. The other destroyer has moved off the Swedish coast and is just south of that island, I don't know the name."

"That will be Ven Island," said the Kid. "There are deep channels to the east and shallow channels to the west."

"Sounds like those destroyers are trying to hem us in," Grudziński said aloud to himself. "They know we are here, somewhere."

"So what do we do? Run or hide?" Piasecki asked with open hands.

"We stay here and hide," Grudziński stated firmly. "The Germans are on full alert. If we move, they will see us and run us down. We have to sit tight and wait."

The night passed slowly while the heat inside the Orzeł seemed to rise quicker than usual.

"Is there an update on the German positions?" Grudziński asked.

"The destroyers are still holding their positions," sonar reported. "One is still north by Ven Island, the other is still east of Saltholm. The smaller craft seem to be moving away from their position."

Grudziński looked at his watch. "It's nine p.m., more German precision."

"I hear them spreading out, sir. They are dispersing in different directions."

"They stopped dropping depth charges an hour ago, maybe they're going home?" Piasecki suggested.

"I don't think so, they are still pinging at one-minute intervals. I think they're just widening their search area."

Checking his watch, Piasecki said, "We've been submerged now for eighteen hours, we'll have to come up for air sometime."

"We can easily last for thirty hours," Grudziński said. "More if we have to."

A moment later there came the sound of a distant, muffled explosion.

"What was that?" Piasecki questioned.

"Sir that was a depth charge, bearing one, one, six degrees. Probably about fifteen kilometers."

"Anymore?"

Listening carefully, sonar waited before saying, "Nothing, sir."

"What are they doing?" Piasecki asked. "Do they think they found us?"

"I don't know." Grudziński shook his head. "Maybe we should make a move?"

"You could be right, Captain."

"Sonar, I need an update on anything you hear."

"Sir, the ping has not changed, it is still every minute. The small vessels have spread out, moving in different directions."

"That means they're still looking for us," Piasecki said.

"It seems that way. What about the destroyers?"

"The destroyer to the south seems to be holding position. The one to the north seems to be sailing north, to the west side of Ven Island."

"Maybe he's heading for the narrows at Helsingborg?" Piasecki suggested.

"He could be," Grudziński agreed. "That gets him away from us for now, but he will be a problem when we go through those narrows."

Just then there was another sound of a distant, muffled explosion.

"Another depth charge?" Piasecki asked.

"Yes, sir, this one is bearing zero, three, zero degrees."

"What the hell are they doing?" Piasecki asked.

"I think it's random targeting," Grudziński said. "They're trying to scare us off the bottom. What is their range?"

"Various ranges, sir. They are crisscrossing all over the place."

"They are probably following a search pattern."

"I think you're right. Sonar, how long before they get here?"

"Difficult to say, Captain, but I think they will cover this area."

"So what does your mouse do when the cat comes by?" Piasecki asked.

"We have to sit here quietly until it goes away."

Even though the engines weren't running, it must have been the hottest room on the Orzeł. I suppose there was a lot of heat still in those big diesel engines which kept us hot. While we were hiding on the bottom, there wasn't anything to do except try to avoid the heat. Sitting still was the only thing we could do.

I think I had the most comfortable spot. It was away from the engine, but best of all I was able to rest my back against the hull of the Orzeł. I was hoping to get some coolness from the water outside. I even fell asleep. I dreamt I was in a park on a hot, sunny day. Suddenly there was a sharp clap of thunder, as a lightning bolt struck my head.

I woke up on the floor, with a Godawful pain in my head. I was more embarrassed about being on the floor, thinking I had banged my head on something. That's when I saw Foterek coming towards me, he was clutching his head and looked angry. "I'm sorry," I said weakly, "I must have had a bad dream."

"Get up!" was all he said as he stepped over me. I then noticed where he was going, the electrician, Henry Rebizant was on his hands and knees, retching heavily. There wasn't a puddle, but the mess went through the floor grates into the crawl space below.

"What's going on?" I struggled to ask.

"Depth charge!" was all Foterek said, as he handed a rag to Henry.

"Are we sunk?" I asked.

"Why did it make me sick?" Henry asked.

"The Orzeł is a long tube," Foterek stated. "The pressure wave from the explosion travels along the tube. We are at the end where the pressure is the worst. Now get up, we must check everything, and I mean everything."

"Jeez! That was close!" Piasecki exclaimed. "My ears are ringing."

"Never mind your ears," Grudziński turned towards Julian at the sonar desk. "Are you OK? Is the sonar damaged?"

"I'm checking now sir. When I heard the splash and shouted out the warning, I took my headphones off. I thought I had made a mistake because nothing happened for so long."

"Yes, it was timed to go off deep, it may even have been on the bottom. The deeper they explode, the stronger the pressure wave becomes." Grudziński then turned towards the intercom. "Damn it, this isn't working, I can't contact the engine room or the forward torpedo room. Piasecki!"

"Aye, sir."

"Go to the forward compartments, I need a damage report and to know whether there are any injuries. Mokrski!"

"Yes, sir."

"Likewise, go aft and report back if there is any damage or injuries."

When Lieutenant Mokrski came to check on us, there wasn't much to report. We first looked for breaches in the hull, inspecting the bilge to see if any extra water was flooding in from outside. There were some burst pipes but those were internal and so not a major problem. We had to switch off some equipment before we could do the repairs.

A lot of circuit breakers had tripped, causing some equipment to shut off. It didn't take long to reset the breakers and replace blown fuses. We had to make sure everything started up in its proper sequence.

As for injuries, we had bumps, bruises, and headaches. If anyone made a mess, like Henry, then they cleaned it up themselves. That is normal on any submarine, you always have to clean up after yourself. There was no doctor on board the Orzeł, so if someone was badly injured, there was little anyone could do, other than dispensing first aid and kind words.

Foterek went to inspect the other parts of the Orzeł. When he came back to the engine room, he gave me the order. "Blackie, go to the forward torpedo room, they need you there."

"What's the problem?"

"Inspect and maintain the torpedo tubes, take your toolkit."

"Aye, sir."

Going through the Orzeł, it was plain to see everyone was busy fixing and cleaning. Everyone's eyes held the look of shock. They showed the fear of being blown up and the relief they have survived.

As I passed through the control room, I announced, "Coming on deck, sir."

Piasecki patted me on the back. "Good work, Blackie."

"Thank you, sir."

I don't know what he was thanking me for, but that simple gesture made me feel much better.

In the torpedo room, all the crew was busy huddled around the tubes.

"Ah, Blackie," Warrant Officer Stelmaszyk, greeted me, "Foterek said you would help us."

"What's the problem?" I asked.

"After inspecting for leaks, I got the crew to check the readiness of the torpedo tubes. Stanley, how are we doing there?"

"Tube one is almost ready, sir. The outer door is open and the tube is flooded." Stanley then opened the bleed valve, showing that some seawater dripped into the cabin. "We made sure these tubes were cleaned and open, this is how we test to see if the tube is full of water. If we open the breach while the outer door is open, we'll flood the boat."

I knew the basic mechanics of the torpedo room, and I agreed that was an important test.

"So all the bleed valves are clear?"

"Yes, Blackie, at least on tubes one, two, and three, which is all we need at the moment." Stanley then stepped back from the breach. "We're about to test flushing tube one."

"OK, let's proceed," Stelmaszyk said. He stepped back to make sure the watertight door was closed. This sealed us off from the rest of the Orzeł. Next, he gave the order. "Close the outer door."

Stanley, and Able Seaman Nowak, suddenly changed from their slow, shell-shocked manner, and sprang to life. Their training made them crank the outer door shut fast. Within seconds, they were finished. Stepping back, they both relaxed. Stanley said, "Outer door shut, sir."

Stelmaszyk gave the next order. "Flush tube one."

Stanley pulled the lever, allowing compressed air to force the seawater out of the tube.

"Check tube is clear," Stelmaszyk ordered.

Stanley quickly opened the bleed valve. A burp of compressed air sprayed water onto the floor grates. There was no flowing water, indicating the tube was drained.

"Open breach," came the final order.

Nowak then turned the wheel on the breech and opened it wide, revealing the fins and propeller of the torpedo waiting inside. If the bleed valve was clogged or failed for any reason, if the tube was open to the sea, then we would not be able to close the breach against the inrush of seawater. If that happened, we would all perish instantly. Everyone understood this fact, but no one flinched in the execution of their orders. We all knew our jobs and trusted each other to complete their tasks safely. That is why Stelmaszyk made sure the watertight door sealed this compartment from the rest of the boat. If such a disaster did happen, at least the rest of the crew would have a chance to survive – maybe they could reach the surface. If they didn't, no one would even know where our graves were. We would simply be lost at sea.

"Shall we test tube two?" Nowak asked.

"I wouldn't," I said.

"Blackie is quite right," Stelmaszyk said. "We need to conserve compressed air. We can test the other tubes when we surface."

That simple sentence sent a shiver down my spine. I think everyone else knew the risk too. We were having some issues with the compressor and if that failed for any reason we would be stuck there on the bottom. In the meantime, we didn't even think about it. We knew there was compressed air, and we would prove it worked when the time came.

––––––––––

"Sir." Foterek saluted Grudziński as he reported to the control room. "I'm happy to report the electrics are back in working order, it was mostly circuit breakers and fuses. Even your intercom should now work."

"Good work, Foterek."

"When you have a chance, you can thank Henry Rebizant, he's my electrician."

"I will do it. In the meantime, I have another job for you."

"Aye, sir, what is it?"

"I want the soda-lime packs opened and put in all the ventilators. CO2 levels are getting very high. It's almost daylight, so we must survive down here until this evening."

"Aye, sir, we can all feel it. I'll do it right away." Foterek turned to leave as Grudziński thanked him once more.

"Midshipman."

"Aye, sir," Edmund Brocki acknowledged.

"Run all ventilators at medium. We need to circulate the air, but I don't want to stress the batteries."

"Yes, sir."

"And release one tank of oxygen into the ventilation, we'll save the other until later. I don't want to raise the fire risk."

"Yes, sir."

"Piasecki, is there anything else we need to cover?"

"All the repairs are complete, sir. As you know, the air down here is getting worse, but we can't surface now."

Just then another depth charge exploded in the middle distance, making a sound like a clap of thunder.

"They like to remind everyone that they are still looking for us."

"Sonar. Distance and bearing?"

"Six kilometers, bearing three, four, zero," Bosun Kozowy replied. "Pings are still at one-minute intervals."

"It's midday," Grudziński said, looking at his watch. "The sun should be high in the sky now."

"I wonder what the weather is like up there," Mokrski said.

"Maybe it's still raining," Piasecki said, looking up towards the ceiling. "That would be nice and refreshing. There haven't been any depth charges since 0800 hours, the Germans seem quiet. Maybe we should have a look and see what's happening up there?"

Grudziński wiped the sweat from his brow. "We can't be hasty, if we make one false move, the Germans will find us."

Piasecki clenched his fist and nearly spat. "I'd rather fight them to the death than sit here and suffocate!" With wide eyes, he glared at his captain. "Look what they have done to our homes! Our land! Our freedom!"

Grudziński held up a calming hand. "If we fight and die here, we lose! If we want to win, we must survive! To survive, we must get to England."

"So what is our plan?"

"We make our move at sunset. We need the darkness for cover. In the meantime, we must wait."

"I hope our air holds out until then."

"It will hold out, we have another tank of oxygen we can release later." Everyone gulped before Grudziński continued. "We won't last long sitting down here, but we have to make it until this evening. We have no choice other than to rise at sunset. By then the Germans will think we have escaped or sank. One thing is sure, they will be as tired and frustrated as we are."

"At least they can breathe," Mokrski said.

"Wind and rain can also affect a man's concentration. For now, we all need to rest. When we do rise, we have to be ready to run, fight, or both."

Let me tell you, that was the longest and the worst afternoon any of us had ever had. Breathing everybody else's bad air and smelling everyone's rancid sweat. The captain had released oxygen into the boat, and the soda-lime packs helped to absorb the CO_2, but the air continued to get worse. We tried to rest as best we could, lying in bunks, sitting on boxes. Some were even sitting and lying in gangways.

Breathing was hard for everyone, as though you wanted to fill your lungs but couldn't. I wasn't sleepy, but I kept yawning. I noticed other men were yawning as well. That seemed to be the only way we could take a deep breath.

The officers tried to reassure us. They would say things like, "Well done," and "good work." The irony was, no one was working or doing anything. All we had to do was breathe. The repetitive praise for doing nothing became annoying.

Henry Rebizant and I squatted in the gangway, sweating, breathing, and waiting. My clothes were so soaked with sweat that even my pockets were wet. My cigarettes were becoming damp and I was worried whether I would ever be able to light them. My biggest concern at that time was my deck of cards. I couldn't be bothered to play, not even solitaire, but I kept pulling the pack out of my tunic pocket. The cardboard pack they were in was beginning to get moist with damp, making the paper soft.

Henry saw me toying with my deck. "No, I can't be bothered to play," was all he could say.

"I don't want to play either, but my deck is getting wet with sweat."

"Leave them by the engine, they'll soon dry."

I was appalled by his suggestion, leave my cards by the engine? I couldn't bear the separation. Instead, I loosened my tunic, making sure the pocket was off my sweaty body. That way I could keep them as dry as possible while keeping them close to me still.

Just then Foterek walked by, carefully stepping over us. He was silent as he passed. He was probably heading to the control room.

After he passed through the watertight door, Henry nudged my arm.

Glancing over, I didn't even bother asking what he wanted.

"Good work," he said, "well done."

I just rolled my eyes and yawned.

———

"Coming on deck."

"Ah, Foterek," Grudziński welcomed him into the control room with a nod, "we are preparing to move and I want to check that everything is ready."

"Aye, sir. We are ready."

"How are your men?"

"Last time I looked, they were still breathing, sir."

Grudziński smiled. "What about the batteries?"

"We're only running lights and ventilators, but we are now below one third. The batteries are warm so there may be more charge. I would have to get my electrician to confirm the exact reading."

"Good work, Foterek." Grudziński patted Foterek's shoulder. "When we move, we will need the electric motors while we scan the surface. When we do surface, you will need to charge as much as possible. We will need to pass through the Helsingborg narrows submerged. So we must be careful with the batteries."

"Understood, sir."

"After that is open water in the Kattegat, but as we approach Helsingborg, you need to keep me informed. Batteries are critical at this stage."

"Yes, sir, we'll get out and push if we have to."

"It won't come to that," Grudziński laughed.

No one else laughed as Foterek went back to the engine room.

————————

"OK, men, this is it, prepare to surface." Grudziński looked at his men crowding the control room. "I plan to rise slowly and quietly to periscope depth and head northwest towards the Danish coast."

The eager men listened and nodded.

"We need to vent and charge batteries. To do this we must avoid any contact. I'm thinking the shallows to the west will help to hide us as we sneak towards the narrows at Helsingborg. From there, we have open water and freedom."

A sense of anticipation and pride stiffened everyone's backs as we thought of the path ahead.

"Foterek, get your boys ready with the Danish flag. I expect to run close to the coast. Stelmaszyk, get forward and be ready with torpedoes. If we must fight our way out, we'll give them hell!"

The crew cheered. 'Aye, aye, Captain!"

"That includes you, Mokrski, I need you to give me headings, but in a fight, I will need accurate firing solutions."

"Yes, sir! I'm ready!"

"To your stations everyone, I need everyone alert."

'Aye, aye, sir!" Everyone scurried to their positions, those already in place stood erect and ready.

"Sonar, what do you hear?"

"Usual traffic from Copenhagen, sir, heading northeast. The patrol vessels seem to be shadowing them."

"They're watching the shipping lanes, but we're not going there. What about the destroyers?"

"I can't hear the one in the south, and the one to the north must have stayed in the Kattegat. Both seem to be gone, sir."

"What about pings?"

"Times are now irregular, every four or five minutes. The last one was over six minutes ago."

"It seems they have broken off their search and are on standard watch. This is our chance to make a move."

Grudziński looked around at the tired and weathered faces of his crew. "Let's make ready to blow tanks and surface."

Everyone breathed deep breaths.

"Piasecki."

"Aye, sir."

"Take us up to periscope depth."

"Aye, sir." Piasecki cranked the engine telegraph to standby. He then began to issue his orders. "Midshipman, blow tanks one, two, five, and six."

"Aye. Sir, blowing tanks one, two, five, and six."

The air compressor came to life. The sound of air flooding the tanks was heard throughout the boat. This in itself was enough to raise spirits. Everyone had the same thought, *the compressor works, we are going to surface!*

As the water was displaced through the bottom vents of the ballast tanks, we could hear the mud and rocks being pushed aside from the bottom of our hull. All eyes in the control room were fixed on the depth gauge, waiting for it to change.

Soon the compressors stopped, along with the turbulent noise of rocks and mud beneath our feet. Grudziński placed his hand on the periscope column in readiness. Piasecki gestured his arms in an uplifting motion. Nothing happened. The Orzeł fell silent.

Piasecki slowly turned his head towards Grudziński with a questioning face.

"No movement, sir," the helmsman reported.

"Are we stuck?" the Kid asked.

Another silent moment passed.

"Captain, we can blow tanks three and four," Piasecki said. "That should get us off the bottom."

"Wait…" Grudziński looked worried. "That will bring us up too fast. We won't stabilize at periscope depth. Instead, we'll break the surface."

More silent moments passed. Should we force our rise to the surface and risk detection?

"Maybe we could use the engines?" Piasecki asked. "We could slowly rock the Orzeł forward and back to break the suction that's holding us down."

Grudziński's eyes lit up. "That's not a bad idea!"

Just then, creaking and rattling sounds were heard beneath our feet. Rocks in the mud below were grinding against the hull. The Orzeł began to shudder as it slowly forced its way out of the mud like a boot stuck in a muddy hole. The stern rose first, leaving the bow in the mud. Everyone leaned back to adjust their balance. What we heard sounded like an eerie scream, as the bow pulled free, scraping along rocks and mud.

The depth gauge now showed the Orzeł was rising.

"We're free!" Piasecki shouted, followed by loud cheers from everyone. The feeling of relief echoed throughout the Orzeł.

The Orzeł rose in an oscillating manner, as the stern and bow tried to compete who would be first to the surface.

"Let's stabilize!" Grudziński announced. "Engines, ahead slow! Three knots!"

'Aye, sir!" Piasecki cranked the engine telegraph.

As the Orzeł nudged forward, it continued to rock slowly, like a see-saw.

"Helm, nose planes down five degrees," Grudziński ordered.

"Aye, sir. Nose planes down five degrees."

"We have to keep her off the bottom, so now level off the nose planes."

"Aye, sir. Nose planes level."

The Orzeł still see-sawed as it moved forward.

"Now, helm, bow planes five degrees up."

"Aye, sir. Nose planes up five degrees."

"Helm, do you feel it?" Grudziński asked.

"Yes, sir! Compensate for the oscillation. When the nose goes down, I pull up. When the nose goes up, I pull her down."

"Exactly, the Orzeł will follow her nose. I'll let you stabilize her. Set her at thirty meters. Maintain course, three, zero, zero, degrees. Speed, three knots."

"Aye, sir. Heading three, zero, zero degrees, speed three knots."

"Sonar, any ping activity?"

"Still the same sir."

"Has anything changed? Speed? Or course?"

"Nothing has changed sir."

"Good, the cat is still sleeping."

It didn't take long for the helmsman to settle the Orzeł at periscope depth. "Up periscope," Grudziński ordered. As the periscope rose, he caught the handles and said, "It's time for the mouse to have a look."

Grudziński did the usual dance as he checked the area for danger. He then rotated slowly, changing magnification as he went. "I see a small freighter heading north, bearing three, one zero. About nine kilometers or more." As he continued to scan the area, he said, "The closest vessels are three small fishing boats heading south, bearing, one, three, five. About six kilometers."

"Sir? Are you sure they are fishing boats?" Boson Kozowy asked.

"Yes, I can see their rigging, they are trawlers, but they are not working their nets. Why do you ask?"

"I can hear them now on sonar, and I have been listening to them for a while. They sound like trawlers, are slow like trawlers, but they act like patrol boats."

"What do you mean they act like patrol boats?" Piasecki asked.

Grudziński continued to look at the trawlers, changing magnification.

"I've heard a few groups like them. They seem to travel in pairs or threes, sailing back and forth as if they are looking for something. Fishing boats go to a location and then circle slowly as they look for fish. These guys are not looking for fish.

"I can see their flag," Grudziński said, as he indicated for Piasecki to have a look. "They are German trawlers. It looks like we now have to be afraid of fishing boats."

"They are probably acting as extra lookouts," Piasecki said. "I don't see any weapons on them and they can't be fast enough to pursue anything."

"They probably have a naval observer on board who can call in firepower from the gunboats. In the future, we must keep our distance."

"OK Lieutenant Mokrski, do you need to look to get your bearings? We need a course along the west side of the sound.

"Well, sir, I don't think the Kronborg Lighthouse at Helsingborg will be visible yet." The Kid stayed by his chart table and indicated points on the map. "We need to pass midway between Ven Island and the Danish mainland. We can keep the Kronborg Lighthouse directly to our north until we get near the narrows."

"Piasecki, where are the fishing boats now?"

"Still moving away from us, heading south, now bearing, one, three seven. I estimate seven kilometers."

"OK, let's hope their attention is on something else because we need to surface. Down periscope."

The Orzeł continued on its northwesterly course while the crew prepared to surface.

"Captain, you don't seem in a hurry to surface."

"That's right Piasecki, I want to put some distance between us and those fishing boats. Even if they don't see us as a threat, they are likely to report us to our German pursuers. The closer we get to the Danish coast, the less likelihood of us being spotted."

As we prepared to rise, the control room was crowded. Grudziński was to be first up the ladder into the bridge, Alex and I were to follow close behind with our Danish flag. Four lookouts were to follow close behind. The rest waited below to breathe the fresh air as it wafted down through the hatch.

When we surfaced and rushed up the conning tower, I thought it would be refreshing to get back into the air. Instead, it was cold, damp, and windy. We were wearing our navy-issue duffle coats. Despite these warm, wooly coats, our clothes were so damp with sweat, both Alex and I began to shiver as we raised the flag. I hadn't noticed before, but I realized my fingers resembled prunes from being so damp for so long.

"You men get back down below," Grudziński ordered, "and send Lieutenant Mokrski up here. Make sure he has his duffle coat."

"Aye, sir," Alex confirmed.

We both descended the conning tower as if we were drunk. The cold air and fresh oxygen must have rushed to our brains. I was the first to stumble back into the control room. I was surrounded by men gulping down the cool air as it blew down through the hatch.

"Hey, Blackie, what's it like up there?" someone asked.

"Cold and windy!" I exclaimed. After I stood upright, I said, "But it's good!"

As Alex came down he said, "Hey, Lieutenant Mokrski, the captain wants you up top. Make sure you wear your duffle coat."

I thought that Alex sounded like a mother telling the Lieutenant to wear his coat, but Alex was a bit drunk on fresh air. I stood as long as I could by the open hatch, enjoying the air as it came down in short gusts.

"Blackie," Piasecki said, "you need to go back to the engine room, make sure the batteries are charging."

"Aye, sir," I said with some sadness, as I wanted to stay by the hatch longer. "Can we open the rear hatches?"

"Yes, I've assigned a guard on each hatch to keep it open. Also, to close it in case we need to dive in a hurry. We will be running the vents at maximum. But remember, no one is allowed on deck unless the captain orders it."

When I got back to the engine room, the diesel engines were running at full throttle. This made everything hot and noisy. Even with the vents running and the hatches open, it still felt as if we were stuck on the bottom running out of air, the only difference being it was now noisy.

———————

In the northeasterly wind, the heavily painted Danish flag made a strong flapping sound as it waved above the Orzeł's conning tower. Below it, Grudziński and Piasecki stood on the bridge podium, scanning the horizon around them for threats.

"We are level with Ven Island," Piasecki said. "I can see the white cliffs on its western side."

"Yes, at this speed we should be at the narrows in less than an hour."

"Do you think the cliffs of Dover look as white as that?"

"The cliffs of Dover are much whiter and much bigger than that." Grudziński patted Piasecki on the shoulder. "We'll all be seeing those Dover cliffs soon enough."

Grudziński turned his attention to the north, where the Kronborg Lighthouse blinked slowly in the distance. "We have a way to go," he said almost to himself. "It's those narrows I need to focus on."

"I think Tycho Brahe, the Danish astronomer, used to live on that island," Piasecki said, keeping his eyes fixed on the white cliffs.

"Maybe so," Grudziński replied. "My science hero was Copernicus."

"What's that?" Piasecki asked.

"What do you mean? He was the Polish astronomer, of course." Grudziński turned and then realized Piasecki's gaze was fixed on something else. "What do you see?"

"South of Ven Island, there's a ship coming into view. She's sailing south, but I can't see her fully yet, the island is eclipsing her."

"Yes, I see her! She's a warship, there's a gun on her bow."

The lookouts behind began alerting to the new sighting, but no one could identify her yet.

"Shall we dive?"

"No," Grudziński said, "she doesn't fully see us yet. If we make a suspicious move, the freighter ahead could send out an alert. We have to hold steady for now."

"I hope you're right, that could be the German destroyer we saw the other day. You know, the one that headed north."

"You're right, it could be coming back. If we were both moving at the same speed, she would remain eclipsed by the island. Unfortunately, she's faster than we are, so she will soon clear the island. If she does spot us, she will try to hail us for identification. Get below and check with Petty Officer Kotecki, see if there are any messages on the open channels."

"Aye, sir." Piasecki dived below to check with the radio officer, Henry Kotecki, the Kat.

By the time Piasecki returned to the bridge, the distant ship in question was fully visible. It was continuing on its southerly course, southeast of Ven Island.

Behind Piasecki, the Kat climbed up into the bridge.

"Is there anything to report?" Grudziński asked.

"Bad news, I'm afraid," Piasecki said.

"Sir," Henry began, as he filled his lungs with fresh, cool air. "Since we surfaced, I have been testing the radio and I am not able to send or receive any messages."

"Shit! If anyone tries to hail us, then we have an immediate problem." Grudziński looked towards the distant destroyer. "Worse still, how can we contact the British? What happened to the radio?"

"Sir, I think my radio was damaged during the depth charge attack. There were some electrical surges, most circuits were off but some were on. Anything that was on would have blown something."

"Can it be fixed?"

"I don't know yet, I have to take it apart first. Maybe I can use parts from the crew radio in the mess room?"

"Well, get onto it right away. If you need anything, Lieutenant Piasecki will help you. We need that radio back in order as soon as possible."

"Aye, sir."

"Sir, do you have any other orders?" Piasecki asked.

"Yes, I need a sonar report, send Bosun Kozowy up here, I need to keep an eye on that destroyer."

"Aye, sir."

Moments later, Bosun Julian Kozowy stepped up onto the bridge podium. He followed the Captain's gaze into the distance. He then asked, "Is that the ship you want to ask me about?"

"Yes."

"Well sir, we are in shallow water, so the sound doesn't travel too well here. It tends to bounce between the water surface and the seafloor, so I get lots of echoes and I find it impossible to get direction."

"So we are pretty much deaf, but can they hear us?" Grudziński asked.

"They have the same problem. Our sound is bouncing around these shallow waters, coming out into the open water at different places and at different times. So if they do hear us, they won't be able to get a direction on us."

"What about their pings?"

"Don't worry about those, sir, they are erratic; about every five minutes. In the shallows there are too many echoes, there is no way they can track us here."

"OK, Bosun, get back below and keep listening."

"Aye, sir."

Moments later a cry came from one of the lookouts. "Destroyer turning to starboard!"

Grudziński leveled his binoculars at the destroyer. *Damn it!* he thought, *they've spotted us and are coming to investigate.*

"Sir, what should I do?" the helmsman asked.

Grudziński was silent as he watched the destroyer slowly turn. "Wait, she's not turning towards us. I think she's heading towards Copenhagen. We stay on course for now."

"Helm, steer one, four, zero," Grudziński ordered.

As Boson Dabrowski changed course, he asked, "Sir, I thought we were heading towards the narrows, this heading takes up back around Ven Island?"

"That's right, I want the freighter to think we are patrolling this area and not heading through the narrows. When we submerge, we'll head back north."

As the Orzeł sailed southeast, our distance from the freighter widened.

"Lookouts," Grudziński ordered, "take the Danish flag down and get below." As they scurried below, he also ordered helmsman Bosun Dabrowski below, before sounding the dive alarm. Grudziński secured the hatches as he descended into the control room.

"Piasecki, take her down to periscope depth."

"Aye, sir." As Piasecki issued orders to dive, he gave a concerned look towards Grudziński. "Sir, you ordered us to head southeast, are we avoiding something?"

"No, we are fine. I just wanted any ships in view to think we're heading away from the narrows."

When the Orzeł settled at Periscope depth, Grudziński addressed the crowded control room. "Now we are submerged, we will turn north and head through the narrows. The Kattegat beyond these straits got its name from the Norse word for 'cat's throat'."

"And we are the mouse!" Piasecki chuckled.

"Exactly, and we must pass through it. What lies ahead is very narrow, about four kilometers wide, but it is also busy. Any ship, or even people standing on the shore, could betray us and tell the Germans where we are." He looked closely at his crew crowding the control room. "We must remain submerged, and be cautious when using the periscope. We have to follow the shipping lane on the east side of the narrows, which is for all northbound traffic."

"What about the German sonar?" Piasecki asked.

Boson Kozowy spoke up. "With the Kattegat being so narrow, and shallow, that should create a lot of echoes. The busy traffic will also help to deafen the German sonar."

"However," Grudziński continued, "there is no guarantee of safety. Once we are in the Kattegat, Lieutenant Mokrski has advised that there are no depths in which to hide. We think the deepest is on the east side, so we will follow the Swedish coast north." Grudziński looked around, letting the information sink into his crew. "Are there any questions?" he asked.

"No, sir!" everyone chorused.

I had to be on station in the control room with my flags, just in case we had to surface. If we surfaced on the east, I had to raise the Swedish flag. If we surfaced on the west, I had to raise the Danish flag. I didn't mind so much because I thought I would get some fresh air.

It was funny to watch them dance around the periscope. Grudziński ordered it raised every five minutes. He checked his watch carefully and timed it exactly.

"Up periscope," he would order.

Lieutenant Piasecki would then do his dance, looking around and reporting the bearing for various ships and landmarks.

As we headed to join the northbound shipping lane, Piasecki announced, "Sir, there is a line of five fishing boats about one kilometer off the beach south of Helsingborg."

"What are they doing?" Grudziński asked.

"They are not fishing and they are not moving."

Grudziński rubbed his chin. "They are probably watching the northbound traffic as they approach the narrows."

At first, I thought Grudziński looked nervous, because he kept staring at random points, random instruments in the control room, or even at the floor. I soon realized that his world was on the surface, so he did not need his eyes at all. Our captain had a map in his head. Everything he saw was inside his head. He didn't look through the periscope once, relying only on what Piasecki told him.

Grudziński wanted to shadow some ships that were traveling northwards through the narrows. He wanted to follow a freighter, while keeping another second freighter behind us. To do this he listened to Piasecki's observations before calling out speed and course changes so we could squeeze into our little space between the two ships.

On occasion, Bosun Kozowy would announce a sonar ping. He would also announce the echoes as the pings bounced around the narrows. "Ping, source forward," he would say, then moments later, he would say, "echo east, three ten degrees," then "echo west, one fifteen degrees."

"There's something up ahead, sending out those pings," Grudziński said. "Can you identify any Germans ahead?"

"No, sir, I'm pretty much deafened by the traffic." Kozowy held one hand to his headphones. "I have a line of ships ahead of us and behind. There is also a line of ships along our port side heading south." He shook his head. "I'm sorry sir. I can't be more specific."

I wasn't watching the time because I was too busy watching everyone in the control room. It could have been forever, but I think it was only an hour that we took to get through the narrows.

"Sir," Lieutenant Mokrski spoke up. "Kullen Lighthouse should soon be visible to the north of us."

"Very good, we'll keep our heading along the coast."

"Sir, I hear three fast boats, bearing three, two zero degrees."

"What's their heading?"

"My best estimate is one, zero, four zero, sir. If that is their true heading, they will pass almost next to us."

"Distance?"

"I can't be sure, about seven to eight kilometers."

"Piasecki, all stop!"

"All stop, sir," Piasecki replied, as he cranked the engine telegraph to stop.

"Midshipman, flood all tanks."

"Flooding all tanks," came the reply.

"We sit and rest, while they pass," Grudziński whispered.

"Let's hope that Norse cat doesn't swallow," Piasecki whispered back.

"Sir, that's where the pings are coming from, they are German torpedo boats."

A moment later, I felt the Orzeł settle gently on the muddy bottom.

"Keep me informed if they change course."

"Aye, sir."

I knew the German boats couldn't use their sonar to hear us talking, but I didn't want to speak, just in case. What worried me was, did they hear us coming through the narrows? Did they hear us sitting down on the bottom?

"Sir, three boats are closing fast, now bearing three, zero, zero degrees."

"Distance?"

"They're getting loud, about five kilometers, and closing."

These German boats seemed to be coming to get us. I waited as Grudziński stared at the floor.

Piasecki watched Grudziński, waiting for a reaction. Piasecki nodded his head slowly as if counting moments.

"Midshipman, stand by to blow tanks, but not until I give the order."

"Aye, sir, standing by to blow tanks."

"Sir, boats now bearing two, eight, zero degrees."

"Distance?"

"About one kilometer, sir."

"Jeez, they're almost on top of us!" Mokrski said.

"Any moment now they could drop their depth charges!" Piasecki said.

"Wait, they're coming at an obscure angle," Grudziński said.

We waited in silence.

"Sir, boats now bearing two, six, zero degrees."

"Distance?"

"The same, sir. About one kilometer."

Grudziński smiled gently, "They're passing us."

"Yes, sir. Sounds like they're heading south, into the sound."

I watched as Piasecki stood proudly with his hands on his hips before he said, "Captain, I thought you were being over-cautious, but maybe your order to turn south just before we headed into the narrows is what did it."

"Did what?" I asked.

Piasecki looked at me and smiled before explaining. "Someone saw a sub, heading south, and they're going to investigate."

Grudziński brought his mind back from the surface and refocused on the control room. Looking around he said, "We'll sit here for five minutes to let them get further away from us. After that let's get the hell out of here!"

"Blackie," Grudziński said, "when we are on the surface, I need to keep the lookouts focused on their job, so I need you to remain here in the control room to handle the flags. We may have to change them quickly depending on what coast we sail along. I've told Foterek and he says you can stay here."

"Aye, sir."

Lieutenant Piasecki joked with me. "Blackie, you are now our official flag master. Keep your coat handy, the weather up there is cold and windy."

I didn't mind the new duty, but I missed the engine room and my shipmates. The good thing about my new job was I could go up the conning tower to set the flag. I then had to stay there and act as an extra lookout, looking out for ships, planes, and any other threats.

Our passage through the Kattegat was mostly on the surface, sailing close to the Swedish coast. We sailed on the surface quite swiftly and without any German encounters.

The lookouts had their shifts so the captain swapped them out every two hours, that way they stayed fresh and alert. I was an extra hand on the conning tower, so grew tired and lost track of time. It must have been five hours later that we approached the Swedish port of Gothenburg.

Lieutenant Mokrski spoke up. "Sir, there are a lot of small rocky islands on this part of the Swedish coast. We will need to steer west to avoid them."

"I agree," Grudziński said. "I also want to avoid the traffic around Gothenburg."

"The Island of Læsø should be due west. We can sail past that towards Denmark and hug the Danish coast until we reach the Skagen Peninsula. After that, we are in the open Skagerrak and the North Sea."

Grudziński ordered us to sail west across the Kattegat, which meant I had to change the flag from Swedish to Danish.

As we passed on the north side of Læsø, there was another port on the Danish side, which we had to avoid.

As we approached the north side of Læsø Island, Lieutenant Mokrski spoke up. "Captain, the Danish port of Frederikshavn is quite busy and you may want to avoid that as well."

"What course do you suggest?"

"Ahead off our port bow is the Norde Rønner Lighthouse, I suggest we turn north when we get level with it. At our current speed, we would then pass Skagen point and be in the Skagerrak in about one hour."

"That sounds like a good plan, Kid."

I watched the blinking of the Norde Rønner Lighthouse on Læsø Island as we passed. As we turned north, leaving the lighthouse behind us, I wondered at the searchlight as it scanned through the dark mist. I know I should have been more alert and watching for enemy ships, but I was so tired I nearly fell asleep standing up.

That's when Grudziński shouted, "Lookouts, get below. Blackie, take down the flag. We're preparing to dive."

"Aye, sir." Coming out of my daze, I wasn't sure if we were under attack. As the dive alarm sounded, I was back in the control room with my Danish flag.

"Piasecki, take her down to periscope depth."

"Aye, Captain."

"I want to stay submerged as we sail through the shipping lanes. From here on we stay under until we are in the Skagerrak."

Grudziński approached me with a sympathetic grin. "Blackie, I know you are tired, but I need you here a little longer. Once we reach the Skagerrak, I will relieve you."

"Thank you, sir, I'll be OK, but I am looking forward to some sleep."

As we sailed submerged, it took us longer than Lieutenant Mokrski estimated. The anticipation was immense as Lieutenant Piasecki kept calling out the distance and bearing to Skagen's Grey Lighthouse. This beacon signaled the entrance to the open water of Skagerrak. From there, we would turn west into the open sea, and head for England.

"Skagen Grey, bearing three, two, zero, range, eleven kilometers," Piasecki would call out as he looked through the periscope.

The periscope would then be lowered to keep us hidden, but it wasn't long before Grudziński ordered the periscope up again.

"Skagen Grey, bearing two, nine, eight, range, eight kilometers."

Everyone waited silently as the periscope went down. The minutes seem to tick by like hours.

"Up periscope," Grudziński ordered.

More moments passed as Piasecki first checked the area for threats. Finally, we watched as he focused on the lighthouse. "Skagen Grey, bearing two, six, nine, range, five kilometers. She's directly on our port side!"

"We are in the Skagerrak!" Grudziński announced.

We all cheered and clapping and cheering spread throughout the Orzeł. Every voice sang out in joy. At last, the Baltic was behind us and now England was ahead of us.

As the shouting died down Grudziński said, "What do you say men, shall we head for England?"

"Aye, Aye, sir!" came the raucous response from everyone.

"Helm, steer to your new heading of two, seven, zero."

"Aye, sir, heading two, seven, zero."

As we turned west, we all thought of the future that lay ahead.

When we settled into our new course, Grudziński said, "Sonar, give me a ping. I want to see if there are any shallows as we head around Skagen Point."

"Aye, sir."

As Kozowy sent the ping out, his face changed to an expression of horror. "Sir! Multiple echoes two hundred meters dead ahead!"

"Helm! Hard starboard, ninety degrees!" Grudziński leaped forward as he shouted his order, helping Dabrowski to turn the wheel faster.

As the turn completed, Grudziński ordered again, "Sonar, give me another ping."

"All echoes to the port side sir, we are clear."

"What the hell was that?" I asked.

"Minefield!" Piasecki said.

"We'll have to go around the minefield," Grudziński said. "We'll have to be very careful as we cross the North Sea."

18 The North Sea to UK

Ship's Log entered by: Lieutenant Jan Grudziński
Date: October 13, 1939
Location: 57⁰, 06', 14" North, 6⁰, 34', 03", East. Mid North Sea.
Entry: Preparing to approach England, need to have radio repaired to signal Royal Navy.

Piasecki knocked on Lieutenant Grudziński's cabin door. There was no response. He knocked again, this time a little louder. "Captain? Are you awake?" this time Piasecki heard movement, at the same time the door handle started to move. The distance between the bed and the door was so small that Grudziński used the door handle to steady himself as he stood out of his bed.

"Piasecki?" he said as he focused his eyes.

"Yes, I'm sorry to disturb you, sir. I know you haven't had much sleep, but you did say you wanted to be informed of any new developments. I brought you some fresh coffee, sir." Piasecki offered the mug of hot black coffee.

Grudziński looked at the mug with tired, sleepy eyes. He reached slowly and clasped the mug in both hands. Raising it slowly to his lips, he started to sip. "So what is happening?"

"Nothing serious, sir, but when you are ready, I think you should meet me in the radio room."

"OK, Piasecki, I'll be there in a minute."

"Aye, sir."

Grudziński left the door open, sitting back down on his bunk as he placed his coffee mug down. Grabbing his shoes to put back on his feet, he thought, *radio room... I wonder what nightmare the Kat wants to tell me?*

Lieutenant Piasecki had already nicknamed them 'the two Henry's'. Chief Petty Officer Henry Kotecki sat in his radio room, while Petty Officer Henry Rebizant, the Orzeł's electrician, stood to his side. Lieutenant Piasecki couldn't fit into the closet-sized room, so stood in the gangway, listening to their technical explanations.

Captain Grudziński strode along the gangway, wide awake with focused eyes. "So gentlemen, how is the radio?"

Piasecki, stepped back from the radio room doorway. "Sir, I think I can let the two Henry's explain."

"Ah, Captain." Petty Officer Rebizant stood upright and turned to face the captain, saluting.

Chief Petty Officer Kotecki, the Cat, stayed seated and focused on his radio. "You can see we've been busy fixing and testing my radio."

Wires were trailing everywhere around the tiny radio room. Components of all shapes and sizes were scattered on every available shelf or floor space. The whole radio room looked like it was some kind of electrical experiment.

"My God! What's going on here?" Grudziński asked.

"Sir," Rebizant said, "when that depth charge hit us close by, there were a lot of electrical surges throughout the boat. Luckily most of them were caught by the circuit breakers."

"Yeah, but not all," the Kat continued, "some surges hit my radio before the circuit breakers tripped."

"So, what is the damage?" Grudziński asked, "can you salvage the radio?"

"Well, we think we have," answered Rebizant.

"What is that supposed to mean?" Grudziński asked with a frown.

"Sir, let me clarify." The Kat now turned towards Captain Grudziński. "You see, the initial surge damaged some vacuum tubes. Luckily the circuit breakers protected the rest. Some tubes were completely blown, but we managed to replace those using parts from the radio in the mess room. Some other tubes we could not replace, but we think we have repaired them."

"These are vacuum tubes, even I know you can't repair them." Grudziński looked perplexed.

"Of course, sir, but there are some tricks that I know."

"Oh? Like what?"

"What I did with the help of Rebizant, is to build some circuits to do conductance testing. That's what all these wires and components are for. It's a little like a vacuum tube repair kit."

"That's right," added Rebizant enthusiastically. "We tested the bad ones and replaced them. Some of the broken ones we were able to repair."

"Yes," the Cat continued. "You see, there are three connectors to these tubes, one to charge the filament, one to input a current or signal, and a third is the bias, which acts as a control switch. Using the circuit that Henry made we would heat the filament for a couple of hours. I don't apply a signal voltage or the bias. After the conductance test, the valve usually works well."

"There is a small problem where the valve emission decreases over time," Rebizant said.

"What good is that?" Grudziński asked.

"Captain," the Cat tried to look hurt, "These were dead valves that we fixed, so anything is better than nothing."

"Do we have a working radio?" Grudziński clarified his question.

"Yes, we do," answered Rebizant.

The Kat clarified by adding, "The output signal levels on the valves we repaired will decrease over time, so our broadcasts will get weaker and our reception will also get weaker."

Rebizant looked at the Kat. The Kat raised his shoulders and hands in question, "Maybe three to five hours?"

"Is that the best you can do?" Grudziński asked.

"Well, we could switch the radio off and on to manage the time," Rebizant suggested.

"Yes, we could, but until we surface and test the radio this could all be a fanciful conversation," said Grudziński, looking at his watch. "We'll surface in thirty minutes, get ready."

————————

Telegraphist William Mackay sat back on his chair in front of the wireless set. Despite his slight build, his feet lay heavy on his desk. He was reading his book but wore his headphones to alert him to any wireless signals.

Warrant Officer Jeannie Boyce walked by on her way to her desk. "Sit up straight, Billy, didn't your mother ever tell you about posture?"

Billy put his feet back on the floor and shuffled upright. "Nothing is happening this morning, just like any morning. This is a phony war."

"Don't you say that young man, haven't you heard the news? The Royal Oak was sunk last night, right in Scapa Flow, by some underhanded German submarine. And put that book away this minute! You know what Officer Duncan thinks of you slacking off. If he sees you reading again, he'll have your hide for britches!"

Just then the radio came to life and a Morse code message started tapping out. William Mackay sprang to life. Tossing his book aside he grabbed his notebook and pencil and began jotting down the message.

Date: October 14, 1939
Time: 07:00
Operator: Telegraphist William Mackay
Location: Eyemouth Royal Navy shore wireless station
Message: Current position 56 12 10 North, 2 18 32 West. Request permission to enter harbor. Need pilot and escort. No chart. Radio damaged. Will send receive every hour ORP Orzeł.

It took several minutes to transcribe and check it as the message was repeated. When he completed the transcription, he looked over to Jeannie who was now at her desk.

"Hey, Jeannie. What's an Orzeł?"

"A what?"

"An Orzeł," he repeated.

Jeannie walked back to the wireless desk. "Let me have a look." She read through the message. "This is odd, it has no identification, are you sure you took the whole message?"

"Yes, it repeated the standard number of times, that's the full message."

"O, R, P, Orzeł," Jeannie read aloud. "They're going to send and receive every hour an ORP Orzeł, whatever that is."

Petty Officer James Duncan stepped out of his office, placing his cap firmly on his head. He walked over to the wireless desk where Billy Mackay was sitting. Duncan placed a folder onto Billy's desk. "These are the messages for transmission this morning." Noticing the book on Billy's desk, he scowled at him. "Have you been reading again, while on duty?"

"Uh, no sir. I left this here from yesterday, sir. I'll put it away, sir."

"Sir," Jeannie held out her hand, holding the radio transcript. "Billy just received this message, we can't make it out. Can you have a look?"

Officer Duncan took the sheet from Jeannie and started to read. "This is nonsense, it has a location but no identification. Are you sure you took the whole message?"

"Yes, sir. It repeated the standard number of times, that's the full message."

"Sir, look at the words 'ORP Orzeł'," Jeannie pointed to the transcript. "I think it's a code of some sort. Something about sending it every hour."

"Yes, Jeannie, you're quite right." Duncan handed the transcript back to Warrant Officer Boyce. "Send this over to signals in Rosyth immediately. They'll know what to do with it. It is not our job to decipher messages. Otherwise, keep it under our belt because it may be something secret."

"Aye, sir."

Duncan then turned to walk away. He paused and turned back to say, "Remember, loose lips sink ships."

———————

Lieutenant Edward Mack, Commander of the destroyer HMS Valorous, stood on his bridge overseeing the morning patrol. He thought about the Scapa Flow incident of the previous night. *How can one U-Boat sneak past defenses to sink a battleship at anchor?* He frowned at the thought. *Those bloody U-Boats, I'll be damned if they get the better of me while I'm in command.*

Bosun Phillips came on the bridge. "Sir, there's a message for you from Naval Command in Rosyth." He handed the transcript to Lieutenant Mack.

First officer Jenkins turned towards Mack. "What is it, Captain?"

After reading the message, Mack handed it to Jenkins. "We are to investigate a mysterious contact at that location."

Jenkins looked up from the transcript. "Sir, it also says it could be a German trap. Shall we request an air reconnaissance before we approach?"

Mack stepped forward and looked ahead out at sea. As he scanned the horizon he said, "Jenkins, I think that message tells us something."

"What sir?"

"We are the reconnaissance."

Mack then turned back to Bosun Phillips. "Thank you, Bosun, that'll be all." Then he turned towards his second officer. "Jenkins, set a course for that location. I want this ship on full alert, so double the watch, and have all crew at their stations."

"Aye, sir."

"Oh, and Jenkins? I want sonar to inform me if so much as a codfish breaks wind."

"Aye, aye, sir."

———————

"I could almost enjoy this morning," Grudziński said as he stood on Orzeł's conning tower. "Can you see that island to the west? It looks like a wall of rock guarding the Firth of Forth."

"Yes," agreed Piasecki. "It looks like an English castle, but let's not get too comfortable, who knows what's lurking out here."

"You're right, maybe the Germans followed us across the North Sea." Grudziński gazed back to the east. "They could be using us as bait."

Piasecki scoffed. "They wouldn't dare come this close to England. How does that song go? 'Britannia rules the waves!' I just hope the English have heard our radio signal."

"They haven't responded yet… they are suspiciously quiet."

"What are our options when those radio tubes stop working?" Piasecki asked.

"Approaching the port without guidance will be extremely dangerous, we don't know what minefields are out there. Also, shore batteries will undoubtedly open fire on us. Aircraft will also be called in to attack. Britannia doesn't rule the waves without defending herself."

"So close and yet so far," Piasecki said.

One of the lookouts called out, "Vessel approaching, bearing fifteen degrees!"

Grudziński and Piasecki immediately trained their binoculars on the target.

"Impossible to identify at this range, sir," Piasecki said.

"She's coming in fast though, look at her smoke trail," Grudziński said. He looked up at the Polish flag waving in the wind above their heads. "Get below Piasecki, tell the Kat to try and hail the vessel. Ask her for identification. Send out our identification. On the double!"

"Aye, sir."

19 In a Scottish Port

Ship's Log entered by: Lieutenant Jan Grudziński
Date: October 14, 1939
Location: Port of Dundee, Scotland
Entry: We have been escorted by HMS Valorous from the specified rendezvous point at the Isle of May to Dundee.

The engine telegraph signaled us to stop so we put the diesel engines into idle mode. As I checked the oil levels and pressures, I could feel the Orzeł bumping into something solid. Moments later, the engine telegraph signaled 'Finished with Engines'.

"Shut her down," Foterek called out, and we busied ourselves shutting the diesel engine down. The huge pistons in the engine casing beat slower until they finally stopped completely. The engine was now fully stopped, leaving us with a sudden silence. I looked around as Henry Rebizant the electrician switched the ventilation to run on batteries. Even this sound was but a whisper. We could now talk without shouting, but the change in sound told me that our journey was over. We were now in England. I watched Foterek as he walked around the diesels, wiping certain valves with his rag, and patting the engine with his hands. I felt as if he was putting his baby to sleep for the night. I realized that we were all watching him, waiting for instructions. He eventually turned towards us and smiled. He simply said, "We're here."

"What are we waiting for?" I asked, "Let's go have a look."

We all moved towards the hatch in the rear torpedo compartment. The compartment was empty as all the torpedo crew were already on deck. I climbed the ladder and as I raised my head above the deck, I was greeted with the sounds and smells of the dockside. Seagulls squawked as they flew above, as men and machines worked on the dockside. Fresh sea air blew on my face, ruffling my hair, while the afternoon sunshine warmed my cheeks.

"I thought you'd never come out." Stanley stood there on deck, hands on his hips, breathing in the fresh air. "It's a beautiful afternoon!"

As I pulled myself up the ladder and stepped onto the deck, I asked, "Where are we?"

'Welcome to Scotland!" Stanley said, as he grasped my hand and shook it vigorously. "We made it! We're here in the city of Dundee."

"Dundee?" I repeated mindlessly. I looked around at the proud British warships on the dockside, along with freighters unloading their cargo. In the distance, I could see the city with church spires towering above the rooftops. "We made it!" I cried out, turning to Stanley, I said it again, "We made it!"

"Hey, Blackie!" Foterek was on the dockside, waving for me to come down and join him.

"I have to go," I said.

"Yes, bosses always keep us busy."

Walking down the gangplank, I thought to myself 'Welcome to Scotland', as I stepped onto dry land. I walked over towards Foterek, who was standing with Captain Grudziński and a bunch of other British naval officers. As I joined the group, I saluted, followed by many handshakes and welcomes. The British officers then continued talking in English with Grudziński. Foterek didn't speak English, but he knew I was trying to learn. He said to me quietly, "You listen and tell me what they say."

Although I was trying to learn some English words from the radio, I couldn't understand a single sentence these men were saying. Eventually, Grudziński, who did speak some English, turned to us and said, "These officers welcome us all to Britain." Grudziński indicated one officer, "This is Lieutenant Commander Donald Fraser, and he will be helping us in the next few days."

"Hello gentlemen," Commander Fraser said in Polish, as we exchanged handshakes "and welcome to Scotland."

"Ah, you speak Polish very well," Foterek said.

"Yes, I acted as liaison officer for some time before the war."

"This is my engineer, Bosun Leo Wrona, he is learning to speak English."

I shook Fraser's hand and said in very broken English, "Hello, sir, I am pleased to meet you."

He complimented my English before saying to everyone, "We are all very surprised that you are here, we heard reports that you had been sunk by the Germans. So this is a very welcome surprise for us all."

"As you can see, we are all very alive," Grudziński said, "and we are keen to join the British fleet."

"I'm sure your crew deserves a good rest after your adventures. I will also assign one or two more liaison officers who speak Polish to work with your crew. Their main job will be to help with radio communications with the fleet.

"They will be welcomed by my crew, commander," Grudziński responded.

"One last thing, Captain, we will need to inspect your submarine tomorrow for any repairs. We need you to be shipshape before joining the fleet."

"Foterek is chief engineer, he can work with you tomorrow."

———

Early that evening we sat in the mess room when Lieutenant Piasecki introduced us to a new liaison officer. "This is Signaler Wilton Green, who will be joining our crew."

"All right mate? You can call me Wil," Signaler Green said to everyone in English as he shook their hands.

"Do you speak Polish?" Alex asked.

"Of course I do mate, that's why I'm here," Signaler Green replied in Polish.

"Do you speak other languages?" Alex continued questioning.

"Est-ce que tu parles français?" Signaler Green said with an exaggerated smile. "That always gets the birds going."

"The birds?" Alex looked puzzled.

"You know, the girls!"

"Where are you from?" I asked, "Your accent is very strange."

"I'm Cockney, mate."

"I thought you were English?"

"I am, but I'm Cockney. That's the East End of London. If you live near Bow Bells, you're Cockney."

I was getting dizzy with all the information he was giving us, the more questions we asked, the less we knew. I was determined to learn more about this curious man.

"So how come you know all these languages?"

"I've been around, 'aven't I? Ever since I was a little spadger, I worked on the docks. As soon as I was big enough, I started working on the ships. Now that we're at war, I'm in the navy." Looking around at us dumbfounded sailors he said, "Anyway, ain't you gonna offer a fellow sailor a little tipple? Don't you boys have anything hidden away?"

"We ran out of vodka some time ago," Freckles said with a frown.

"Tut, tut," Will said, "that is a poor do. I can see what you boys need is a drink, but don't worry about that, mate. There's a pub by the dock gate."

"What's a pub?" Freckles asked.

"A public house," Will replied, "a place where you can have a pint."

"A pint?"

"You know, beer," Wilton said, with a nod and a wink.

I was puzzled, so I asked, "In English, does the word pint also mean beer?"

"No, mate, you drink a pint of beer." Wilton held his hand as if drinking a glass of beer. "A pint of beer," he repeated.

We all livened up to the idea of drinking beer.

"Are we allowed to go?" Stanley asked.

"Of course, mate! You lot are heroes, no one will stop a hero from having a pint."

"So where is this pub?" I asked.

Before I knew it we had gathered a fair-sized group to visit this so-called pub. Will led us across the dockyard past the guards at the gate. On the other side of the street, he indicated the 'pub', an old, disheveled looking building. We walked to the oak door, above which hung a pitted sign depicting an angelic figure.

"Welcome to the Angel," he said as he opened the door, gesturing for us to enter.

I walked in first with a happy smile, anticipating the beer we would soon be drinking. The room was dark and smokey, the smell of alcohol, sweat, and dirt filling the room. What suddenly changed my mood was the sound of talking and laughing, which suddenly stopped as everyone in the pub turned to look at us. I stood still, wondering if we should enter, but the throng of my shipmates behind pushed me forward through the doorway.

I can't stop now, I thought to myself, and I slowly made my way towards the large oak bar. I felt as if I had walked into a German bier Keller in Gdańsk, where Polish men were not welcome.

"We're right behind you," Alex whispered from the rear.

I approached the bar slowly, when a man the size of a mountain, dressed in a dirty boiler suit stepped forward. He had unkempt red hair which stood out like firebrands and a red beard that covered a scarred face.

"Och, aye!" he bellowed. "What ye be wantin' in this place?"

I couldn't understand what was being said in English, but Will spoke from behind, saying, "These men are from the Polish submarine Orzeł, and they've come for some beer."

"Och, aye!" the mountain bellowed again. Faster than lightning, his fist, which was the size of a granite boulder, appeared inches away from my nose. I feared for my life, but I was prepared to go down fighting. Foterek stood firmly behind me, which helped to reinforce my bravery.

"This wee laddie!" he bellowed at everyone in the pub, "stuck it up Hitler's nose!"

His other hand then patted me on the shoulder so hard, it nearly broke my collar bone. A hearty cheer thundered around the room. I realized that we were not being threatened. Somehow, in fact, we were being recognized as heroes.

Slapping his fist down onto the bar, he bellowed at the barman. "Hey, you Jimmy! Whiskey!" He gestured toward me and my crewmates.

"Nay, lad," the barman replied, "whiskey is rationed."

"Get a fa! Ya basa!" the mountain bellowed. "Whiskey! Now!" and he thumped the bar hard.

More guttural grunts and moans came from the barman which I couldn't begin to understand, but he quickly assembled a line of glasses on the bar. Reaching down into a low cupboard, he pulled out a bottle of whiskey. Pulling the cork out with a pop, he filled each glass with a good dose of golden-colored liquid.

"Och, aye." The mountain said, soothingly. He picked up a glass and gently offered it to me. "A wee little dram for ye," he said with a smile. I accepted the glass and the mountain then passed other glasses around to my shipmates. With each glass he passed, he said in a soft, sing-song voice, "A wee little dram for ye." Finally, he picked up a glass for himself. Holding it to his nose, he heartily smelled the perfumed aroma and sighed like a baby. "Ah, Scotland."

His attention then returned to us, and he bellowed the command, "Drink!" He then held his glass up high and with a shout that could have sunk a battleship he yelled, "SCOTLAND!"

The crowd in the pub echoed his rallying cry. "SCOTLAND!" they all shouted.

Foterek raised his glass and shouted, "POLSKA!"

"Och, aye!" the mountain also shouted, "POLSKA!" indicating to the crowd to do the same. Everyone shouted

"POLSKA!" as they downed the golden liquid in a single gulp, followed by a fiery but satisfied collective sigh.

The mountain slammed his glass onto the bar. I was amazed it didn't shatter. He demanded more whiskey from the barman, saying that we should also have a pint of 'heavy'.

"I think you made a friend there!" Will said from behind.

"What's a pint of heavy?" I asked.

"Don't worry mate, he's getting us all a beer."

"How many words do you have for beer?" Before he could answer, I received a large pint glass of frothy beer in one hand and another glass of whiskey in the other.

"Drink up, laddie!" the mountain commanded, as he passed more glasses to my shipmates.

———

Foterek stood over me as I lay on my bunk. "Here's some coffee." He held the mug towards me, urging me to drink it. "We have to be on the dockside in half an hour."

I dragged myself upright, clasping the mug with two shaking hands. I looked at Foterek. "Are you wobbling, or am I cross-eyed?"

Foterek rubbed his bloodshot eyes. "Wee laddie," he said jokingly, "I'm not drinking with your friends anymore. I don't even remember how we got back to the Orzeł."

I heard Alex's sheepish voice from a nearby bunk. "Keep the noise down, my head hurts."

Slurping my coffee I said, "I thought us Poles were heavy drinkers, but those Scotsmen know how to put it away! What's happening on the dock this morning?"

Leaning on the bunk above my head, Foterek said, "If you remember, there will be some Royal Navy engineers to inspect our sub for damage. We have to be there to show them around the Orzeł."

"Well, they can start with my head, sir."

"Thirty minutes, Blackie."

"Aye, sir. I'll be there."

———

Walking down the gangplank I was welcomed by the sounds of the port, machines, and cranes working, men calling to each other, ships horns in the distance. I saw that the group of engineers had already gathered. Foterek was there with Lieutenant Piasecki, as they saluted and shook hands with the British engineers. The weather had changed from the bright afternoon of the previous day. It was now heavily overcast with a light spray of mist in the air, not quite rain and not mist. I later learned that this weather was called 'Scotch Mist'.

Signalman Wilton Green was with the crowd. He casually saluted me as I approached. "All right mate?" he said in English. Then in Polish, he said, "I'll be your translator as we go around the sub."

I liked the way he mixed English and Polish when he spoke. Not only did it help me learn new words, but it also taught me English mannerisms.

Commander Fraser spoke to us in Polish. He indicated a motor launch moored to the bow of the Orzeł. "Those are our divers," he said. "They've already inspected the hull and I have their report here."

Piasecki was surprised. "They've already completed their inspection?"

"Yes, the River Tay is a tidal estuary with very murky water. It doesn't matter what time of day or night, even with underwater lights, most of the inspection needs to be done by hand."

"So what have they found?" Grudziński asked.

"There are several problems they found, nothing critical, but they need to be fixed before the Orzeł can be operational. First, the keel ducts for the ballast tanks are damaged. They are not clogged, but the damage should slow the blowing of some tanks. Second, the lower two torpedo tube caps are damaged. I suspect they are not operational, but I'll have to speak with your torpedo officer."

"Yes, I can introduce you to Warrant Officer Stelmaszyk, our torpedo chief," Grudziński said.

"Finally," Fraser announced, "there is some propeller damage. The starboard propeller has dropped a blade."

"All this seems to be damage to the bottom of the Orzeł," Grudziński said. "We grounded several times, and did so quite hard at least twice while evading the Germans."

"Quite so," Fraser agreed, "these are common problems for submarines in wartime. However, these repairs will require time in the dry dock."

"How long?" Piasecki asked.

"Only a few days, our boys can work pretty fast. The problem is with scheduling the time. You see there are many ships that need repairs and I have to put this to my commanders. I do know there is already a list of ships waiting for dry dock, so it could be a couple of weeks before the Orzeł is scheduled. Until then, she will have to remain here in Dundee."

Foterek then asked, "Is that the end of the inspection?"

"Certainly not, my dear fellow," Fraser said. "There are many more things we need to inspect. Given the extended schedule due to dry dock, I don't need to look at everything today. However, we have three priorities which are all to do with your weapons systems."

"What priorities?" Grudziński asked.

"We need to make sure you can load and fire our torpedoes."

"We should be able to handle the Mark XIII, that model is already used in some of our destroyers."

"The deck gun and anti-aircraft gun both had their breeches removed. We can easily engineer replacement breeches, but I must know if the caliber matches our ammunition. If not, we may have to replace the guns."

"Lieutenant Sosnowski will be able to work with you on that," Grudziński said.

Commander Fraser then looked at Foterek. "Warrant Officer, Foterek."

"At your service sir," Foterek replied.

"Of course we will not replace your engines, but if there are any spare parts you need, then please let me know. Our machine shop here on base can soon have any parts ready for you. I do think that you and your men are best suited to tell us what you need."

"Very good sir! I'll have a list of parts I need by this afternoon," Foterek replied. I could see he was encouraged by Commander Fraser. Foterek knew that he himself was the best-qualified person to inspect his engines.

"I have a radio operator who will be assigned to the Orzeł. Lawrence Jones, who also speaks Polish, will join us tomorrow. He will work with your electrician and radio operator. We will need to upgrade your radio and code books to work with our communication systems."

"We look forward to his arrival," Grudziński smiled.

"Other than that, I think we can conclude for today." Grudziński looked at us. "Any questions?" he asked.

"No, sir," we all agreed.

"Ah, there is something I forgot," Commander Fraser admitted. "The ORP Wilk joined us a few weeks ago. They didn't have the same adventure as you, but they have joined the flotilla based in Rosyth. When your repairs are complete, the Orzeł will be assigned to the same flotilla."

"The fighting Wolf!" Foterek exclaimed. "She's here, and we'll fight the Germans alongside her!"

Our spirits now soared! Even Grudziński lit up and asked excitedly, "The three Polish destroyers, the Błyskawica, Burza, and Grom, they were part of the 'Peking Plan', to send ships to Britain. Did they arrive safely?"

"Oh, yes," Fraser said. "They arrived as planned and unharmed. They are now on active duty."

Poland was not finished if we had forces in Britain to fight back.

20 Medals

Ship's Log entered by: Lieutenant Jan Grudziński
Date: November 17, 1939
Location: Dundee, Scotland
Entry: Repairs to the Orzeł are nearly complete. The Royal Navy has arranged an awards ceremony, where many of my crew will receive medals.

I stepped out of the conning tower's door, onto the deck of the Orzeł. Foterek was standing there, fussing with his clothes.

"Hey Blackie, what do you think?" Foterek stood in front of me, smoothing down his clean tunic with the palm of his hands. "Do I look presentable?"

"Sir, you look great." I gave him the ok sign. "But why are you so nervous?"

"Grudziński said that I have to look my best."

"Yes, sir, we've all been told to look our best, but is there something special that's going to happen?"

Foterek pulled his tunic straight before answering. "I got word from Lieutenant Piasecki that there is going to be some sort of awards presentation."

"Sir, wait a minute, are you going to get a medal?" My question made Foterek even more nervous. He looked around, checked his pockets before brushing his tunic.

"I have no idea, he just said it was an award."

"Don't worry sir, you've got the best awards from us! You're the engine of this boat."

Piasecki blew his whistle to signal for us all to fall into rank and file on the dock. We all scuttled off the boat and arranged ourselves into three orderly lines, with officers standing to the side. He called us all to present to our left, so we all turned to face away from the Orzeł.

Grudziński walked alongside our ranks, checking that we were all smartly dressed. I couldn't help but think that this whole parade was not natural for us. We were submariners, we lived and breathed diesel fumes and oil. We are comfortable with the noise of loud engines, while we tolerated the sweat and stench of each other. Yet here we were trying our best to look clean and smart.

"Straighten your tunic," Grudziński would say to one. "Chin up, and chest out," he would say to another. "Remember, we represent Poland! We are a proud nation, and we fight for freedom."

"Have you noticed?" I whispered to Rebi. "He says that to everyone as he walks alongside our ranks."

Foterek overheard my comment. "No talking in the ranks," he said. "He is our captain and deserves our respect, so straighten up and look smart! Let's make our captain proud."

We had to march all the way around the harbor in uniform to get to the HMS Unicorn. Along the way, British sailors and dock workers stopped what they were doing to watch us pass. Occasionally a sailor would offer a quick salute.

As we marched towards the Unicorn, I noticed there were no masts, making the ship look ineffectual. We knew it was an old historical sailing ship, built just before the age of steam power, so the Unicorn never saw active duty. Strangely, the only mast was the bowsprit. Under that pole was a bright white figurehead, visible from across the dockyard.

"Hey, look at that figurehead!" Rebi said excitedly, "It's a white unicorn!"

"Wow, that's incredible," I said, "so white and bright, it seems to brighten this damp November morning. But why would they send a Unicorn into battle? I thought they were magic creatures from children's stories."

Stanley was a couple of rows ahead of us and heard our comments. He turned his head and answered me, "It is a British trick. The enemy would be so puzzled why a Unicorn is coming towards them, they would forget to shoot back." Nobody laughed, but we were all smiles as we walked past.

There was a small navy band waiting at the bottom of the gangway. Grudziński, who was leading our crew, saluted the bandleader as we approached. "Are they going to play us in?" I asked.

"It doesn't look like it," Rebi said. "They're just standing around waiting for something."

"Maybe they're having a tea break," Freckles joked. "You know what these English are like."

"No talking in the ranks!" Foterek repeated. "Come on men, single file up the gangway, we are supposed to assemble on the main deck."

We followed where Foterek pointed and walked up the covered gangway, to board the Unicorn. Although this was a sailing frigate from the 1800s, she was never completed. She was now used as navy offices and a meeting place for dignitaries. A tarpaulin roof stretched high above the decks, from bow to stern, giving shelter from wind and rain.

At the top of the gangway stood some British sailors, acting as doormen. They politely guided some men to go up the steps to the quarterdeck. They seemed to know who to select. "Please, sir, step this way," they'd say, and they would indicate to that person to climb up the stairs. Foterek was one who climbed confidently, but my friend Alex Kamecki was also guided towards the upper deck. He looked at us, shrugging his shoulders, not knowing why he was being separated. We looked back at him, also shrugging our shoulders, as the rest of us of our crew were guided to assemble on the main deck where we were arranged in nice, neat rows.

The quarterdeck was above us and in front, acting as a stage. A group of British naval officers was there to welcome Lieutenant Grudziński and his crew members.

"Look at them up there, all nice and friendly," Rebi said, "while we have to stand and wait down here. We do all the work and who shakes our hands?"

Just then, one of the British sailors standing to the side caught our attention. As we gazed over towards him, he signaled us with the two-fingered, forehead salute.

"Hey, did you see that?" I asked excitedly, "that's how we all saluted each other in Tallinn before we escaped!"

The British sailor then surprised us a second time by saying, "Witaj Polski."

"Mówisz po Polsku?" I asked.

"Sorry mate, I don't speak Polish, I only know how to say hello."

"I speak only a little English," I replied. "Hello to you!" I returned the two-fingered salute.

Another British sailor on the other side of our ranks also spoke. "Oui, Polski!" He held up two fingers in a 'V' sign and said, "Victory!" Other sailors who stood around then followed suit showing us the 'V' sign, saying things like, "Victory" and "Well done, Polski".

Those were the best awards we received, and they made us all stand straight and proud.

That's when the microphone crackled over the loudspeakers, while a large staff car pulled up on the dockside. A British officer stood at the microphone on the quarterdeck, welcoming us aboard the HMS Unicorn. As he spoke, another British liaison officer translated for him.

The speech was a bit boring, stiff upper lip British talk about winning wars. We were distracted by the staff car on the dock but couldn't see who had arrived. We could hear the new guests walking up the gangway. When they arrived on deck, a British sailor announced the arriving dignitaries with his deck whistle.

The dignitaries paused as they were welcomed on board by British officers.

"Oh, look," Rebi said, "it's the Polish Ambassador, Count Edward Raczyński. I guess, he'll be giving out the awards."

Behind Count Raczyński, another man stepped onto the deck. He was dressed in a sharp, clean Polish officer's uniform, unadorned by medallions. He stepped onto the deck as a commanding figure, tall, lean, proud, and maturely confident.

"Holy shit! Do you know who that is?" I exclaimed. "It's General Sikorski!"

"General Sikorski!" echoed around our crew, as we all stood to attention.

The British seamen also followed their protocols and stood to attention as the general was acknowledged and allowed to board the ship. The entire crew of the Orzeł was beyond emotion – it was as if our savior had arrived. This was General Władysław Sikorski, the hero of both WW1 and the Soviet War. He was now the Prime Minister of the Polish government in exile.

"Orzeł, salute!" Lieutenant Piasecki shouted the order.

"Ya!" we all shouted, stamping our right foot down.

"Ya!" we all emphasized our stiff stand at attention.

"Ya!" we snapped our right hand to salute and held it there.

Silence.

General Sikorski nodded towards us before silently climbing the steps to the quarterdeck while we remained proudly at salute. He strode towards the microphone and spoke slowly and precisely. "Captain Grudziński, officers, and crew of the Orzeł." With these last words, he held his gaze on us. I felt as if he was looking at me directly as he nodded and smiled gently. "I salute you." He then saluted us, but he held it for a long time before snapping his hand away from his forehead.

We all responded by releasing our salute. We did not need a Sergeant Major to lead us.

"Stand at ease men," Sikorski said gently.

"Ya!" We all stamped our right foot a measure to the side, while we clasped our hands smartly behind us. We were now at ease, but we remained stiffly attentive to whatever the general would say.

"Men, you have all done the impossible. You have escaped the jaws of the enemy, and you have returned to fight another day."

As he spoke my eyes began to water. I couldn't believe that General Sikorski was standing in front of us and speaking to us. I couldn't wait until I told my mother about this, knowing she would be so proud of me.

"And now I would like to present some medals." The general then signaled to the count, who placed a tray of medals on a small table near the microphone.

The general held up a medal, showing it to us all. "This is the Krzyż Walecznych or the Cross of Valor. It is only awarded to the bravest or most determined soldier.

Ambassador Raczyński then read off the names, one by one, of officers and crew to receive the medal. These were the men selected to join the officers on the quarterdeck. This list included my boss, Wacław Foterek, and my friend Alex Kamecki. As they stepped forward, General Sikorski would greet them, shake their hand, and exchange a few words. After that brief moment of conversation, the general would pin the medal on their chest, before shaking their hand once more.

As they walked back to their places, the ambassador would then hand them each a large envelope, containing the official letters and papers that signified the award.

Rebi and I patted each other on the back as Foterek received his medal. This made us feel that the whole engine room was given the Cross of Valor.

Alex Kamecki was awarded the Cross of Valor for quietly overpowering the Estonian guard on the Bridge. If that guard had sounded the alarm, we would not have escaped. Alex was the man who everyone thought was a weakling, but without him having skillfully silenced the guard, we would still be captives in Estonia.

When General Sikorski had finished giving out the medals, he paused as we all reflected in the silence. He waited,

almost like a priest after a Sunday sermon, with his hands
clasped in front of him.

Ambassador Raczyński looked on expectantly.

"There is one more medal I wish to present," Sikorski
announced. "This is the highest military award that Poland
can offer. I will give this to one man, but this is deserving to
all of his comrades."

The general then looked to the left of the quarterdeck
where officers and crew waited. "Lieutenant Jan Grudziński,
please step forward."

Our captain then slowly approached the general and
ambassador.

"Lieutenant Grudziński, you have gallantly led this
submarine and its crew to a place of safety, where they can
continue to fight against the enemy. You have shown to the
world that Poland is not yet finished, you have shown that we
will continue to fight, for our homes and our loved ones."

The general then reached for the last medal which
Ambassador Raczyński held religiously.

"I present to you the Silver Cross better known as the
Virtuti Militari." The General held the medal, ready to pin it
onto Grudziński's chest. "In Latin, this title means 'For
Military Virtue', and you have earned this title, along with
your crew. So it is with great pride that I bestow this award
upon you."

General Sikorski then bent forward to pin the medal
onto Lieutenant Grudziński's tunic. When it was attached, the
general stood back and saluted Grudziński.

Grudziński looked down at his chest where the medal
hung. He stammered and breathed, before looking back at
the general. "My men deserve this, more than I," he
whispered.

The general then turned towards us on the main deck.
"Let's hear it for your captain, hip, hip!"

"Hooray!" we all shouted.

"Hip, hip!"

"Hooray!"

"Hip, hip!"

"Hooray!"

The applause that followed was tremendous, taking many minutes to subside.

"Can you believe it?" I shouted above the clamor, "the Virtuti Militari! Given by Sikorski himself! This is the most amazing day of our lives!"

"Whoa," Rebi said, "slow down. Have you seen the car that just pulled up on the dock?"

"No," I said, "why?"

"Because it's a Rolls Royce, the best car in the world! I think someone important has come."

"Important? What do you mean? Isn't Sikorski important? Who is it? Can you see?"

"No, the deck rails and tarpaulin are in the way, all I saw was a top hat."

The band on the dockside then began playing a song. As the music drifted over the Unicorn, the noise of conversations began to quieten.

"What are they playing?" I asked

"I think it's the British national anthem," Rebi replied.

"Holy shit!" I exclaimed, "Is that Winston Churchill coming on board?"

"Winston Churchill?" Echoes started around our ranks.

As the anthem played, the British sailors standing to our sides stood to attention with their chests out, facing forwards.

Once again, the British sailor blew his deck whistle to announce the arrival of a dignitary. This time was different because when he finished his reverie, he stood to firm attention with his chest out and nose high.

The band stopped playing the moment the gentleman stepped aboard. No one questioned his arrival, he did not need permission to come aboard the Unicorn.

That doesn't look like Winston Churchill, I thought to myself.

"Oh, my God," Remi said breathlessly, "that's the King!"

"The King?" I asked stupidly.

"King George the VI."

"Should we bow?" I asked quietly.

"I don't know," Remi whispered back.

All the British sailors and officers stood firmly to attention facing the King. They all looked proud and honored to be in the royal's presence.

King George made elegant strides to mount the quarterdeck. Crossing the stage slowly, he nodded and acknowledged salutes from the officers. The King politely cleared his throat before standing at the microphone.

As he made his speech, Remi whispered a comment to me, "I like the way he speaks, very slow and deliberate. I can understand every word."

"I think that's called 'the King's English'," I whispered through the corner of my mouth.

"I wish they would all speak like that," Remi concluded.

The King awarded our captain the Distinguished Service Order. This isn't the highest medal the King could give, but it was pretty good. It allowed our Captain to change his name, he could now call himself Lieutenant Jan Grudziński, DSO.

21 Dancing

Ship's Log entered by: Lieutenant Jan Grudziński
Date: December 1, 1939
Location: Rosyth, Scotland
Entry: We have been transferred to Rosyth to join the second flotilla. I have granted shore leave to all crew.

Rosyth is very close to Dundee, we could have sailed there in a few hours. Instead, we spent the whole day at sea before we entered Rosyth. We spent a whole day at sea running trials that the British Navy had ordered. In addition to the three liaison officers that were assigned to us, four additional officers monitored the trials. They wanted us to test all the repairs, but I think they also wanted to test us, to see how we worked as a crew. They made notes of everything while their stopwatches timed everything we did.

We had to test our speed and maneuverability. We did at least half a dozen diving and surfacing trials. We were not carrying any torpedoes, these would be loaded in Rosyth, but the tubes had to be tested forward and aft. We even tested the new targeting methods for the torpedo runs. Captain Grudziński even took things a step further. I think he was trying to impress the observers. Our deck gun and anti-aircraft gun were still not operational, so not part of the trials. We have not yet received the new breeches, these were due to be fitted in Rosyth. Grudziński ordered Lieutenant Sosnowski's gunnery crews to ready the guns for firing. This additional performance was also timed by the observers.

We sailed into the naval dockyard exhausted, but full of pride. Grudziński ordered all non-essential sailors to man the rails as we sailed in. Groups of men would fall out to man the dock lines when ordered, while our captain deftly maneuvered the Orzeł into the dock like a royal swan.

Every day at Rosyth, we kept busy running some sort of drill. The British were very particular about their procedures, and it seemed like we had to learn all of them. There wasn't anything new, running a submarine is pretty much the same in any navy. We just had to do things their way.

———

On Friday, we went to the mess hall on the dock for fish and chips, a very British meal. Freckles always came with us to the mess hall. "I need to check the British food," he always said.

"What's that green stuff they put on our plates?" Alex asked.

"That's mushy peas," Freckles replied.

Alex poked at it with his fork. "Why do they mush it? Why can't they just give us peas?"

"It's a different kind of pea that goes mushy when you boil it," Stanley said, as he shoved a forkful into his mouth.

"Where's the lemon juice to squeeze onto our fish?" Alex asked.

"Use this," I said, passing a bottle of vinegar to Alex, "they use this instead of lemon."

After dinner, we sat on the dockside near the Orzeł, and smoked cigarettes. The sun had long since set, but there was still a glow in the sky making the Forth Bridge a silhouette across the estuary.

"Isn't that a spectacular view?" Alex asked everyone. "I think the Forth Bridge is the biggest thing I have ever seen."

"I want to know what happened to the first three…" Freckles said.

As we learned English, we always joked about the strange English names. The Firth of Forth had too many 'F's in its name, so we made fun of this. I always said, 'The Fifth of Forth.'

Stephan always said, "How do you know it's not more? Maybe it's the Sixth of Fourth?"

That's when Freckles said, "How many places have we been to in Scotland?"

Everyone looked at each other, dumbfounded. "Two," I suggested., "We were in Dundee, and now we are in Rosyth."

"No! This is the Forth!" He announced with glee.

No one laughed, we just gave him the 'stupid' eye.

———

On Saturday night, Signaler Wil Green gathered a bunch of us to go out. "We've got to take the bus into Dunfermline, I hear there's a lovely little band playing tonight."

"Where's Dunfermline?" I asked.

"It ain't far, it's only a short hop on the bus. But there will be birds there, and I hear they have a bar open."

"What should we wear?" Alex asked.

"Don't worry about that, mate, just wear your uniforms. The birds always go for foreign blokes like you, in uniforms. Just get yourselves all sweet and nice, we'll have a great time."

It was a cold winter night, and it was already dark. There was a stiff wind blowing off the estuary, so we had to wear our duffle coats. Thankfully, it was only a short wait at the bus stop. While we waited, I shared my cigarettes with everyone. I lit a match, cupping it in my hand to shield it against the wind. After I lit mine, I extended my lit match to Alex, who lit his cigarette. I then offered my protected match to Wil to lite his cigarette.

Wil blew out the match. "Never take the third light," he said.

"What?"

"It's bad luck, mate."

"Why? What do you mean?"

Wil looked at me with a serious expression. "They say in the trenches in World War One, the third light will kill you. You see, the first light will alert the sniper," he then looked around as if haunted, "the second light, he takes aim." Wil then raised his hand, pretending to hold a pistol aimed at my head. "The third light, he shoots." Wil stood back, lowering his hand. "Never accept the third light, it's bad for you."

Alex added, "I always thought of the saying, 'third time's the charm.'"

"Lucky for the German sniper, not for you! Never accept the third light." Wil waggled his finger at us like a scolding mother.

We looked at each other, spooked by this idea of a sniper aiming at us and shooting on the third light. We all cupped our cigarettes close in our hands to hide the tiny but revealing light.

When the bus arrived, Wil led us upstairs to the top deck, where passengers were allowed to smoke. We felt more at ease, there on the bus.

Wil sat on the very front seat, above the driver. "Oi! who's gonna sit here with me and pretend to drive the bus?"

I volunteered and sat next to him. Sitting there, we had a perfect view of where the bus was going. With the enforced blackout, so the German bombers couldn't identify ground targets, the world outside was dark. Even the headlights of the bus were subdued so we could only see what was immediately ahead.

"I can hardly see where we're going, and we're on the wrong side of the road!"

"In this country, we all drive on the left, you ain't in Poland now, so you have to get used to it."

The bus braked, slowing around a corner. In the gloom ahead, a bus stop appeared where more people waited. The bus came to a halt to let the new passengers on.

"I hope you saw that stop mate," Wil said, 'we can't miss any passengers, especially on a cold night."

As we rode into Dunfermline, Wil explained all the rules of the road for driving in Britain.

We soon arrived in Dunfermline, where we disembarked in the town center. It was a short walk to the dance hall, where we paid to enter, depositing our coats in the cloakroom.

Wil Green waited until we were all gathered inside, before moving us as a group to sit by the dance floor. We had a table but not enough chairs for all of us to sit. Half of us would have to stand, while the other half could sit.

"Don't worry mates!" he said above the music, parking us around the table. "If you're tired from dancing, then have a seat, otherwise, it's up periscope and have a lookout for the gorgeous birds!"

We all fumbled around the table, taken in by the music and the crowd of couples moving on the dance floor.

"Take your pick, mates!" Wil announced, "If you spot someone you fancy, go ahead and ask them for a dance! Who knows, you may get lucky!"

Alex went to the bar and returned with a tray full of beers. I sat at the table but was too enthralled by the spectacle of music and dancing to even care that I had a drink. I heard much of this music on the radio in Poland, but I had never seen it played live in a dance hall. I knew all of the dance steps but watching so many people dancing at the same time amazed me. I wanted to dance, and I listened to Wil's advice and looked for some girl I fancied.

Seated nearby, Stanley shouted over to me, "This place is great!" He was tapping his hand rhythmically on the table to the beat of the music. "Do you see anyone you fancy?" he asked.

I looked at him and smiled. Then he said, "I like that girl over there." He pointed. "Do you think I should ask her for a dance?"

"Go ahead, you may get lucky," I said.

Stanley stood up, straightened his tunic and his hair. Suddenly he sat down. "Maybe I'll have a bit of my beer first."

I chuckled to myself It sometimes takes a bit of courage to ask a girl to dance. Stanley and I both picked up our beer, clinked our glasses, and downed a good mouthful each.

Turning my head back to the crowd, that's when I saw her.

She sat at her table on the other side of the dance floor, surrounded by her girlfriends who were all laughing and joking. She looked like Marlene Dietrich, but with bright red hair, waved with long curls. She sat amongst her friends watching the band, her legs elegantly crossed with one foot tapping in the air. Her right arm rested on the table near her drink as her hand tapped gently to the rhythm.

Occasionally a man would approach her, offering his hand, I would assume to ask her for a dance.

Each time she was approached, she seemed to show reluctance, using her left hand to either waft the interloper away, or to hold her brow as if to feign some sort of distress.

"What are you looking at?" Stanley asked.

"I think I know who I want to dance with," I mumbled.

Suddenly I was surrounded by my shipmates all looking in the same direction as my transfixed gaze. Only Wil was missing as he was already on the floor, dancing with a nice-looking brunette.

"Do you see what I see?" Freckles asked, pointing towards my red-haired beauty.

"Why don't you go ask her for a dance?" Alex asked.

"She doesn't want to dance, I've seen her reject quite a few offers already."

"She wants something," Alex countered. "You should go and introduce yourself."

That gave me an idea. I waited for the song to end. When the dance floor stopped, and everyone began applauding the band, I stood and walked towards my red-haired beauty. When I arrived in front of her, she said, "The music has stopped, you're a bit late to ask for a dance."

"My lady," I said, "please excuse my approach." I then bowed slightly.

She appeared to take some quizzical interest in me.

"I am Polish, and in my country, we normally have to be formally introduced to a girl, before we can dance. So I have a big problem, I would very much like to dance with you, but I do not have anyone to introduce me."

Her girlfriends heard what I was saying and some started to giggle. My beautiful redhead just sat there, wide-eyed at my approach.

"So madam, I would be pleased if you would accept my introduction. My name is Leo Wrona, Boson on the ORP Orzeł." I bowed slightly once more. "I would be much honored and very pleased if you would tell me your name."

The giggles stopped and turned into gasps.

My red beauty looked at me as her eyes widened. I gazed into her emerald green eyes as they looked back at me. Bright red hair, ruby lipstick, and a clear white complexion. I had never seen anyone so beautiful in all my life.

"My name is Aila Baird."

"Aila Baird," I pronounced slowly and correctly, "it is my pleasure to meet you. If I may say, you have such a nice name." I bowed slightly one last time and clicked my heels gently, as European gentlemen often do. I couldn't remove my gaze from her exquisite green eyes.

After a moment, the bandleader announced the next song, 'Heart and Soul', by Larry Clinton. I didn't know the song, so I had no idea how to dance to it.

"I think I like this song," Aila said. "Can you foxtrot?"

"Of course," I replied.

Aila then uncrossed her legs, sat upright, and held her right hand off the table towards me, palm facing down.

I couldn't believe it! The most beautiful woman in the whole room was holding her hand towards me, inviting me to dance. I gently held her hand as she rose from her chair to stand before me. As the music began, we slowly assumed the gentle embrace of the foxtrot. My left hand held her right hand aloft and to the side, while my right hand gently held her waist. She mirrored this position and looked expectantly into my eyes as the music began.

This was my cue, as I then led her step by step onto the dance floor. The foxtrot sounds like a fancy dance, but it is easy and anyone can do it. The question is, can you do it well with your dance partner? At first, we slowly explored each other's abilities, carefully following the music of the band. As we both became more comfortable with each other, our two-step synchronized with the beat. Our bodies began to swing to the rhythm.

She seemed to glide into every step of the dance. I couldn't believe how graceful she was.

I wanted to impress her, but I felt that my dance steps were not as rhythmic as hers. I desperately wanted to hold her closer, but with her arm on my waist, she held me at the correct distance.

My outstretched right hand held her left hand, and we would sometimes move these hands, up, down, forward, or back. Sometimes, her fingers would move along mine, almost intertwining in a finger embrace. When she did so, her eyes would offer me a sideways glance, and I think I saw a gentle wink.

When the music stopped, we were both breathless.

"Thank you," I said. I moved my hand from her waist. I gently touched her cheek with the back of my fingers. Looking into those beautiful green eyes, I said, "That was the most exquisite dance I have ever had."

She looked at me and touched her fingertip to my nose. "We are not finished yet," she said, "the band will play another song, and we will dance some more." She moved closer, and I felt her next to me.

Looking into her beautiful green eyes, time was meaningless. When the next song began, we danced some more. Each song the band played we engaged with more passion.

———————

On the bus back to Rosyth, Wil once again led us up to the top deck. This time he made us sit at the back of the bus. "We should be driven back," he said, "let the driver do the work, while we sit back and enjoy the ride home."

I didn't care where I sat, my mind was not on the bus. All I could think of was Aila.

We all spread ourselves out, giving ourselves space to put our feet up. When we all got comfortable for the trip back to Rosyth, Will spoke up and said, "Alright then boys, let's have a little game. Who had the most dances? Let's start with you Stan, how many dances did you have?"

"I had two dances," he said between hiccups.

"Well done, mate. That's good going for a beginner. Do you remember their names?"

"Julie, and Agnes," Stanley replied.

"Well, I danced with seven birds," Wil bragged. "Can anyone do better than that?"

"I danced with only one," I stated, "all night long."

"Only one?" Alex scoffed, "Can't you do any better?"

I was still in my daydream, thinking of Aila. I was still thinking about how we danced together. Most of all I was thinking about how we embraced before we parted.

"We also kissed."

"What?" Wil asked.

"We kissed," I said again. "She had to leave early, so I walked her to the bus stop. As we went she talked about Scotland and I talked about Poland. We waited a little while for the bus. When it arrived, I asked her if we could meet again."

"Flippin' heck, mate! What did she say?"

"She said that I'll know where to find her. Just before she stepped onto the bus, she turned and kissed me on the cheek."

Will looked closely at my face., "Bloody hell lads, he's right! There's lipstick on his cheek!"

Suddenly I was the hero! Everyone was patting me on the back and congratulating me.

Wil hugged me with one arm and rubbed my hair with his other hand. "You're a right old Casanova, I take you to one dance and you score big time. Well done mate!"

All the way back to Rosyth I could only think of one thing: my beautiful Aila, with her bright green eyes and soft, flowing red hair. I was troubled by what she said, that I would know where to find her. The only place I could think of was the dance, but I would have to wait until next Saturday. How could I wait that long? In my daydreams, I began to think like a detective. I knew what bus she took home. If I rode that bus back and forth, maybe I could find her somewhere along the way.

22 Patrolling the North Sea

Ship's Log entered by: Lieutenant Commander Jan Grudziński
Date: April 3, 1940
Location: Rosyth, Scotland
Entry: The British are satisfied with our performance while on escort duty with convoys in the North Sea. The crew have adapted well to the new operating procedures. We do not yet have replacement breeches for our 105mm gun, or our 44mm AA gun. We have been ordered on our second independent patrol to intercept enemy ships.
The crew are in high spirits, we are now officially hunters!

"Hey Blackie, are you starting your shift?" Alex was reclining in the mess room, leaning with his back against the bulkhead. In his hand, he held a shot glass full of tawny liquid. "You can have a drink with us if you're not."

Alex, Stanley, and several others had finished their dinner and were enjoying their rum before they headed for their bunks.

It was Wednesday morning as I walked through the mess room towards the ladders leading to the conning tower. I had long since finished my breakfast and was now dressed in my duffle coat and cap. "I've been called up as a lookout, so I'll be up on the cigarette deck as we start our patrol."

"Oh, you poor man, I hear there's a bit of a storm this morning. But don't worry, we'll be sitting here warming ourselves with this British rum, while you brave the North Sea weather." Alex raised his glass in a mock salute.

"I hope you enjoy drinking that rum! I miss our vodka, I like my spirit pure, and perfume free," I said. "I think that rum is a drink for pirates."

Freckles was listening in the galley and shouted through the serving hatch, "Rum is standard issue in the British Navy, you have to like what you're given!"

"Well, it does taste like old raisins, but it keeps us warm. I forgot Blackie, you have to stay sober because you have a girlfriend," Alex winked. "Have you met her parents yet?"

"Sure I have, I went for Easter dinner last Sunday, just after our last patrol. Her father gave me a glass of sherry."

Alex put his feet on the floor and sat up straight. "You're kidding! You met her parents? What the hell is sherry?"

"He was out with her again last night," Stanley said.

"Last night?" Alex looked surprised. "Today is Wednesday, I thought you only went dancing with her on Fridays? There's no dancing on Tuesday nights."

"They went walking together," Stanley added.

"As we walk, we talk, and she helps me with my English," I explained.

"I bet she does," Alex said, as he stood up and placed his hand on my shoulder. "Blackie, I didn't realize this was so serious, you've met her parents, you get cherries from her father,"

"Sherry, it's a drink, like wine," Blackie corrected.

"Whatever," Alex continued, turned towards his comrades around the table, "and you go for walks together. Gentlemen, raise your glass to Blackie, it looks like he'll be the first of us to get married."

"Hurray!" They all shouted with laughter as they downed their shot of rum.

Lieutenant Piasecki stepped in from the control room and ordered, "Blackie, get up top, on the double, we're preparing to leave and you're on lookout."

"Aye, sir! On my way."

––––––––––

Normally when we set sail, I was always in the engine room. Today was different. I was transferred to be on lookout on the conning tower, as we sailed out of Rosyth. I was familiar with the estuary, as I had viewed it many times from the shore, but I had not seen it from the water. The

Firth of Forth Bridge was something we all knew, but as we approached the huge steel structure, I was transfixed. From a distance, it was magnificent, but approaching close to it on the water was a spectacle I will never forget.

I didn't notice Lieutenant Piasecki, as he climbed up onto the cigarette deck where I kept watch with three other lookouts. I was the forward lookout, but as we approached the Forth Bridge, my eyes were locked onto the enormous structure we were about to pass under.

"She's incredible, isn't she," Piasecki said, approaching to stand alongside me.

"I've never seen anything so huge," I said feebly. "We are about to pass under it."

"When we returned from our patrol last March, we sailed under while a train rode over," the lieutenant said with obvious awe. "We could hear the clickety-clack of the rails, and the puffing of the locomotive as she passed over our heads. It was probably heading into Edinburgh."

"We don't have anything like this in Poland," I said. "I'm always amazed at the engineering of the British."

"And the Germans," Piasecki added. "Look at what these empires can build. It makes me fearful of the horrific weapons they'll use against each other in the coming conflict."

"So you think there will be a big war?"

"I'm sure of it," Piasecki stared into the distance. "This has only just begun. It will make World War I look like a playground."

We stood in silence as we sailed out of the Firth of Forth, scanning the distance through our binoculars. I couldn't help but think about what Lieutenant Piasecki had said about the coming conflict. Up until now, I only thought about how Germany had acted like a criminal towards Poland. What could happen next?

Soon, we passed south of the Isle of May, beyond the mouth of the estuary. This was where we first rendezvoused with the British. Banks of cold rain blew across the sea, but I could see the island and its lighthouse.

As we sped on the surface, away from the British Isles, we sailed west into the North Sea. The cold rain pelted my face. Throughout my watch, we remained on the surface, battling the wind and waves. With my face into the wind, I kept a close eye on the seas ahead, frequently wiping my binoculars. My fingers and face became painful with the cold and wet. When the captain gave the order to dive, I could hardly grip the rungs of the ladder to climb below.

"OK, Blackie," Lieutenant Piasecki said, as I climbed down to the control room, "have a break and then report back to the engine room."

"Aye, sir."

As I passed through the mess room, Freckles gave me a hot mug of tea, which I carried aft, towards the engine room. When I got there, Foterek approached me. "Hey Blackie, you look a bit wet, have you been outside?"

"Yes, sir, I would have stayed longer, but Piasecki ordered me back here."

"Dry your coat and cap on the diesels, while they are still hot. We're running on electrics now."

Leaving my tea on a bench, I stripped my duffle coat off and laid it over a warm block to dry. While I did this, Foterek asked, "Have you got any news for me?"

"Sir, I was talking with Lieutenant Piasecki and he says this will turn into a big war."

Foterek just stood there silently, as the electric engines hummed. He slowly took his rag out of his back pocket, shook it out, and started to polish levers and dials. He eventually said, "The lieutenant is a very astute man."

Ship's Log (Supplemental): Lieutenant Commander Jan Grudziński
Date: April 8, 1940
Location: Skagerrak, southwest of Kristiansand, Norway.
Entry: Orders are to stop all enemy shipping and sink their fleets as necessary.

Lieutenant Grudziński entered the control room. "What's our status, Piasecki?"

Lieutenant Piasecki was examining charts with Lieutenant Mokrski. "Sir, we're about eight miles south of Mandal, the southern point of Norway. Our heading is zero, nine, zero degrees, our speed is fifteen knots. Batteries are at 100 percent. No enemy sightings to report, only light local shipping traffic."

"Very good Piasecki, it's 0800 hours." Grudziński looked at his watch. "I think it's time we submerged. Take her down to periscope depth and continue on an easterly course at five knots."

"Aye, sir." Lieutenant Piasecki shouted into the voice tube to the cigarette deck. "Lookouts, get below." He then shouted into the voice pipe to the bridge. "Bridge, get below, prepare to dive."

Next, he sounded the dive alarm.

The four lookouts dropped into the control room, followed by the helmsman and another lookout from the bridge. "Conning tower secure, sir," one said.

As everyone manned their stations ready for the dive, Piasecki ordered to pressurize the boat. With that order, the lights on the Christmas tree turned green one by one, showing that all vents and flood valves were closed.

"Barometer steady, sir," the midshipman called out.

"Blow ballast tanks 3 and 4," Grudziński ordered. "Dive planes 20 degrees." He kept his eye on the depth gauge and, just before the Orzeł reached periscope depth, he issued the order to level out.

"Dive planes level."

The boat glided into level sailing.

Piasecki then rang the engine order telegraph to 'Half Speed' and set the RPM indicator.

"Sir, we are at periscope depth. Maintaining course nine zero, speed five knots," Piasecki said.

"Very good, Piasecki, we need to scan the surface every ten minutes with the periscope. We must watch for enemy shipping and aircraft."

———

Grudziński was leaning on the chart table, talking at length with the Kid, both of them pointing out places on the charts. They discussed the shipping lanes, trying to figure out where to find German ships.

Piasecki maintained watch on the periscope. As time passed, he spotted several freighters, all of which were identified as Norwegian or Danish. It wasn't until we were south of Lillesand that Piasecki announced, "Sir, interesting vessel approaching from the southeast. I think you should take a look."

Grudziński moved from the chart table towards the periscope. Giving Piasecki a quizzical look he asked, "What's so interesting about it?"

"Take a look, sir, she's not flying a flag."

Grudziński pressed his eyes to the periscope, changing magnification several times. "You're right, I don't see a flag. I do see her name on the bow, she's called the Rio de Janeiro."

"Maybe she's South American, and doesn't realize there's a war on?" Piasecki suggested.

"Either way, we need to investigate. Lower the periscope," Grudziński ordered. "She's heading between us and the coast. We'll set an intercept course. Helm, heading zero, one, five degrees, slow our speed to three knots."

"Aye, sir, heading one, five degrees, speed three knots."

It was many minutes before the Rio caught up and steamed alongside the Orzeł.

"Raise the periscope," Grudziński ordered. He danced around checking for other threats before homing onto the

Rio's stern. "I want to see her port of registry." Changing focus and magnification on the periscope, Grudziński said, "It's painted over, but I can still make out the letters. She's from Hamburg! Down periscope!"

Piasecki flipped through the shipping reference and found the entry for the Rio de Janeiro, registered in Hamburg. "She's 6,800 tons, passenger liner operating in South America."

"So what's she doing way up here?" Grudziński mumbled to himself. He then started barking orders. "Piasecki, take us to the surface, Midshipman, alert the lookouts. I think we have a German prize!"

The Orzeł broke the surface on the port side of the Rio, about 1000 meters distant. Lookouts manned the conning tower.

On the bridge, Grudziński ordered, "Signal her to stop engines, and dispatch a boat with her captain and ship's papers to meet us."

Several minutes passed without a response from the Rio.

"It looks like she's increasing speed," Piasecki said.

"We have to get her to heave-to," Grudziński said. "Piasecki, get the gun crew to man the 105mm gun!"

"But sir, the gun is inoperable, we still don't have a breech, let alone ammunition!"

Grudziński leveled his gaze at his lieutenant. "Do they know that?"

Piasecki waggled his finger with a grin. "You're a sneaky one!"

"While you're at it, call the AA gun crew to man their station," Grudziński said. "We may as well exercise both gun crews."

As ordered, the gun crews rushed to their stations. The 40mm AA gun was quickly winched from its well, up into the cigarette deck behind the bridge. The crew for the 105mm opened the protective shell forward of the conning tower, revealing the cannon. When the gun crews were ready, their bosun shouted, "Gun ready, sir!"

"Good work, men!" Grudziński shouted to the gun crews. "Now, aim at the Rio!"

"Aye, sir!" the gun crews quickly cranked their weapons, to aim at the ship.

"Standing by, sir!" came the confirmation.

Many seconds passed before the signalman on the bridge reported, "Sir, they're returning a message saying, message understood, stopping engines."

"You see? All they needed was a little friendly persuasion." Grudziński smirked.

The Rio de Janeiro slowed to a gradual stop and remained silent in the water.

"Aircraft approaching!" one of the lookouts shouted. "Three, four, five degrees."

Grudziński and Piasecki both trained their binoculars in the alerted direction.

"She looks like a small seaplane with no armaments," Piasecki said.

"Yes," Grudziński confirmed. "It has Norwegian markings. She must be a spotter plane."

"They want to see what all the fun is about," Piasecki laughed. "AA Gunner, stay aimed at the Rio." Turning to his captain, he said, "We don't want to frighten them away."

The plane banked around the two ships, circling twice before heading back towards the coast.

"I guess it's too choppy for them to land on the sea out here," Piasecki said.

"He'll radio back that there are some fun and games involving a Polish submarine." Grudziński then turned his attention back to the Rio.

"Helm, keep us alongside the Rio, and maintain a distance of 1000 meters."

"Aye, Captain."

Helmsman Victor Dabrowski had a perfect 180-degree view through the portals on the bridge. He managed the rudder with the ship's wheel while controlling the Orzeł's speed with commands issued to the engine room using the engine telegraph.

The voice pipe whistled and Piasecki listened to the message as it was relayed from the control room below. "Sir, the radio room is reporting that the Rio is sending a coded message and is repeating it.

"It's probably a distress signal to their Nazi masters," Grudziński said. "I expect they are requesting air cover."

"But, sir, there is no activity on deck."

"I think they are wasting time." Grudziński shook his head. "It's a long flight time to get air cover from Germany, but we don't have all morning."

Both the captain and Lieutenant Piasecki kept a watchful eye through their binoculars on the Rio de Janeiro.

Some minutes passed before Lieutenant Piasecki said, "Sir, there's some activity at the forward lifeboat."

"Yes, I see it," Grudziński acknowledged, "looks like they are beginning to comply."

In the distance, they could see sailors beginning to work with one of the lifeboats.

Piasecki kept watching through his binoculars. "What the hell are they doing? They're taking a long time to lower that boat."

"I don't think they're doing anything other than wasting time. They haven't even touched the davits," Grudziński scoffed. He quickly scanned the sky for aircraft.

"Sir, the lookouts will keep watch, you don't need to look at the sky."

"It's a habit of using the periscope, we always have to look around and keep one eye over our shoulder." Standing on the bridge podium, Grudziński breathed heavily as he looked around the late morning sky. "I'm tired of these delaying tactics, they are making fools of us." He then shouted into the voice pipe, "Prepare tubes one and two!" He then ordered the signalman, "Send this message to the Rio: Abandon ship, we will torpedo you in fifteen minutes." Keep repeating that message until I tell you to stop."

"Aye, sir!"

"Take it steady, Captain," Piasecki said. "Let's give them a chance. They have stopped, and there's no immediate threat."

"Don't worry Lieutenant, I'm just making sure we are ready."

"Vessels approaching, three, three, five degrees!" a lookout shouted.

Grudziński and Piasecki aimed their binoculars in that direction.

"Those are gunboats coming at us fast, can you make out the flag?"

"Sir, I see red flags, it could be a Nazi flag," Piasecki said.

"I can't tell at this distance either," Grudziński said. "Since it's coming from the coast, it's probably Norwegian, but let's not assume anything, we have to stay alert." Grudziński turned his attention back to the Rio de Janeiro, "Now what's that damned Rio doing?"

"They finally lowered the lifeboat," Piasecki said, "but they are not in a hurry to go anywhere."

"He seems to be drifting towards the stern," Grudziński said, as he held his binoculars on the Rio. "They should be lowering all the lifeboats. They are making no attempt to comply with our demand. They are wasting time, hoping for a response from their distress signal."

A belch of smoke wafted from Rio's funnel, followed by churning water at her stern.

Grudziński looked back at the Rio. "Those idiots have started their engines and they're moving off!"

"Sir, it looks like they're heading for the gunboats!"

"Well, their time is up, and I'm not taking any chances with them. Helm stay parallel with the Rio, and maintain this distance."

"Aye, sir."

Orzeł's engines revved up and she moved ahead to keep pace with the German ship.

Grudziński yelled into the voice pipe to the control room, "Stand by to fire one!"

"But, sir, we don't have a firing solution," Piasecki warned.

"We don't need one being this close, she's still moving slowly, and we'll close our distance before we fire."

"Gunners!" Grudziński yelled, "Stow all weapons!"

"Aye, sir!" The AA gun was quickly returned to its well while the Bofors 105mm was pulled back into its cover.

"Helm, increase speed to ten knots, run parallel to the Rio's port side."

"Aye, sir, ten knots."

"Piasecki, keep an eye on those gunboats, I need identification. Whoever they are, we have to avoid them. Looks like the Rio is heading towards them for protection."

The Orzeł easily outpaced the sluggish Rio de Janeiro and began to pull slightly ahead of her.

"Helm, I want you to turn to starboard, towards the Rio."

"Turning, sir."

"Line up our bow about five degrees ahead of her."

"Aye, sir, five degrees. I see what you're trying to do," Bosun Dabrowski replied.

"That's good," Grudziński said. "Now increase to fifteen knots."

"Aye, sir, fifteen knots."

As the Orzeł's engines revved up, Grudziński said, "Excellent, now keep us steady on that line."

After some moments, Bosun Dabrowski announced, "Sir, she's still moving slowly, but I think she's starting to turn away from us."

"That's OK, we've closed the distance and we have a nice clear shot at close range. Pull our bow a few degrees to starboard."

"Pulling to starboard, sir."

"Perfect!" Grudziński nodded, "Now hold her steady on course." He then shouted down the voice pipe to the control room, "Fire one!"

A moment later, a belch of compressed air joined the froth of waves on the bow as the torpedo launched from its tube. A faint streak of fine, turbulent bubbles marked the wake of the torpedo as it sped towards its target.

"Now, turn hard to starboard! Ninety degrees!"

"Aye, sir, turning."

"We'll pass behind her and circle to her other side."

Moments later, there was an explosion, as the torpedo struck the Rio de Janeiro on her port side, slightly aft of amidships.

"Good shot, sir!" Piasecki exclaimed.

The lookouts all cheered at the hit on the Rio.

"Stay focused, men, this isn't over yet!" Grudziński announced.

"Sir," Helmsman Dabrowski said, "The lifeboat they launched is dead ahead."

"OK, turn more to starboard, let's pull around him."

"Aye, sir. I'm turning another five degrees to starboard."

As the Orzeł passed Rio's launch, the officer began gesticulating wildly and hurling insults at the Orzeł.

"Sir," Piasecki said, "I don't think that the German officer is too happy with us for torpedoing his ship."

"Well, he should have complied with my orders when he had the chance," Grudziński said. "OK, Dabrowski, now that we passed that boat, turn to port and circle us back to the other side of the Rio." Grudziński indicated towards the crippled Rio behind.

"Aye, sir."

"Sir, fires are starting on board the Rio, and she's beginning to list slightly," Piasecki reported.

Attention returned to the Rio, where panic seems to have broken out on the deck.

"Sir, have you seen what's happening on the Rio?" Piasecki asked, "Everyone is jumping overboard!"

Grudziński turned to look behind with his binoculars, "What the hell are they doing? Why don't they lower the lifeboats?"

"Those aren't sailors or passengers," Piasecki said, "They look like German soldiers to me."

"Helm, slow our speed to three knots."

"Aye, Captain, three knots."

"And bring us about slowly, and point our bow at the Rio."

'Aye, sir, completing our turn now."

"Piasecki, what do you think German soldiers would be doing this close to Norway?"

"I have no idea. Where could they be going? Maybe they're returning from somewhere." Grudziński examined the Rio again through his binoculars, "I see sailors on deck now, lowering the lifeboats, but most of the black uniforms are in the water."

"Sir, I fear that it's too late for them to survive in these freezing waters, the lifeboats won't be ready in time, and we can't get close enough to pull anyone out." Piasecki then looked towards the approaching gunboats with his binoculars, "I can see the flags on the gunboats now, they are Norwegian."

"Good, they're not an immediate threat. They won't fire at that distance while we are close to the lifeboats. Keep your eye on them, we can't be sure what they'll do when they get here. We have to leave before they get close. In the meantime, let's see if we can pick up any survivors. Helm, move slowly towards the Rio at three knots. Keep our bow pointed at the Rio." Grudziński then shouted down the voice pipe to the control room, ordering deckhands to be ready to look for survivors.

As the Orzeł moved in slowly to the Rio de Janeiro, they were greeted with a grim sight. Many bodies were floating in the cold water, some floated face down, others with life jackets bobbed upright like corks, stiff and lifeless.

"Men!" Grudziński shouted down to the deckhands, "Are there any survivors?"

Two deckhands were using a boat hook to reach for a body in the cold dark water, "No, sir," one said, "we can't find anyone alive!" He released the body to drift away.

"Can you identify their uniforms?"

"Oh, yes sir," the other replied, "they are all German soldiers!"

Grudziński looked puzzled. *Why would these soldiers be out here?* he asked himself. Looking at Piasecki, he was about to ask the same question, but Piasecki spoke first. "Sir, I'm worried about those Norwegian gunboats, they're closing in fast. What are we going to do?"

"Deckhand!" Grudziński shouted, "Grab a couple of tunics, from the dead soldiers, I want evidence of what we have found."

"Aye, sir."

Turning towards Piasecki, Grudziński said, "You're right, we have to get out of here. As soon as they have those tunics, we'll pull back."

Once the deckhands had gathered some tunics, Grudziński shouted down to his men, "Deckhands, get below!" He then turned towards Bosun Dabrowski and said, "Helm, put our engines in reverse, slow one quarter. Keep our bow pointing at the Rio."

"Aye, sir, reverse one quarter."

As the engines on the Orzeł churned the waves in reverse, Piasecki said, "The lifeboats seem so be trying to follow us, on the other side they are heading towards the approaching gunboats."

Grudziński watched the scene with a grim expression. "Yes, when we are clear, I'm going to sink that crippled hulk." He then shouted to the control room through the voice pipe, "Prepare to fire two."

Grudziński then waited until the Orzeł had moved back a full 1000 meters. "Helm, full stop!" He ordered.

"Aye, sir, all stopped."

"I think the lifeboats are now clear of the Rio, sir," Piasecki said, "but those Norwegian gunboats are getting awfully close!"

"It's now or never." Grudziński shouted into the voice pipe, "Fire two!"

A moment later, a belch of compressed air joined the froth of waves on the bow as the torpedo launched. There was another telltale streak of turbulent bubbles.

"OK, helm, now I want full ahead, and turn ninety degrees to port."

"Aye, sir, full ahead, ninety degrees to port."

As the torpedo sped towards the Rio, Grudziński and Piasecki watched its progress through their binoculars. It passed underneath the floating bodies and confused lifeboats before hitting the Rio's starboard hull, directly amidships. The explosion sent a spout of water high above the vessel, fatally wounding the ship, and breaking its back. The blast seemed to push the already listing ship onto its port side. When it landed on its side, the forward section broke off almost immediately and sank quickly. The stern rolled back and forth, wallowing as if not knowing how to sink. Debris ejected from its interior, with a noisy inrush of water into its open hull, forcing it to slip under the waves.

Piasecki stood and watched as the broken ship disappeared. He saluted weakly, more like a wave goodbye than a salute to his captain, before saying, "Well sir, that's our first kill."

As the Orzeł turned away from the scene, Grudziński looked back with a blank expression, and quietly said, "I always thought I would feel a rush of pride if I sank a ship. I'm not sure what I feel right now, but it's not pride."

Piasecki said, "Sir, I think…" but Grudziński interrupted, "Let us say no more, we will have to do this again, maybe many times. So let us just get on with our duty."

When the turn was complete, Grudziński said, "Helm, full speed ahead. The Norwegian gunboats will stop to assist the lifeboats, but we need to make some distance as fast as possible."

"Sir, if one of them chases us, we can dive for cover," Piasecki said.

"That's not my main worry, Piasecki, I'm more concerned about why German soldiers are out here. I'm going below to see what uniforms we gathered. If the gunboats chase us, dive and take evasive maneuvers. Otherwise make speed away from here."

———

Grudziński jumped down into the control room, and immediately asked, "Where are those German uniforms?"

"They took them into the mess room, sir," the midshipman answered.

Striding into the mess room, Grudziński saw that three wet tunics were laid out on separate tables. Crewmen were carefully checking the tunics like doctors tending to patients.

"What have you found?" Grudziński asked.

"They are German Wehrmacht soldiers, sir," Lieutenant Mokrski answered. "We have wallets, papers, and have identified their names and ranks."

"Did you find any orders in their papers?"

"Not sure, sir. All we have are these." Mokrski showed some wet papers to Grudziński. "Twenty-first army corps, something about group four," pointing to a smudged line, Mokrski continued, "I think this says 196th Infantry Division."

"Quartermaster Piegza."

"Aye, sir!" Freckles poked his head through the serving hatch.

"Take these papers and dry them out carefully, this is useful intelligence for the British. Mokrski, dry out and stow those uniforms, if you find anything else notify me immediately. I'll be in the radio room. The British must be informed about what we have found."

23 Defending Norway

Ship's Log entered by: Lieutenant Commander Jan Grudziński
Date: April 9, 1940
Location: 35 miles southwest of Farsund, Norway.
Entry: The British Admiralty has alerted us that Germany has invaded both Denmark and Norway. Our orders are to remain on station and to intercept all German vessels.

"Up periscope," Grudziński ordered.

Piasecki first scanned the sky. "Sir, it is cloudy, but I do not see the airplane anymore." He then turned his attention to the horizon. "I do see the three trawlers, bearing zero, nine, seven, degrees." Increasing the magnification, he then used the stadimeter to calculate their distance. "Range, three, six, five, zero meters. Looking at their bow angle they are not heading towards us."

"They are not heading towards us yet," Grudziński said. "I think that spotter plane has informed them of our position, and they're coming to look for us. Down periscope."

"Aye, sir, down periscope," Piasecki confirmed. "You think there are trawlers hunting for us?"

"Any fisherman running in formation is suspicious," Grudziński said. "Let's just avoid them before they call in the real sub hunters. Helm, new heading, one, four, five degrees."

"Aye, sir, one, four, five degrees."

"Maintain speed, five knots."

"Aye, sir, five knots."

"Mokrski, what's our position?"

Without hesitation, Lieutenant Mokrski answered, "Five, seven degrees, four, two minutes, north by zero, eight degrees, one, three minutes east."

Grudziński looked at Piasecki. "Let's give them a few minutes before we have another look. There is a German supply route heading from Hamburg to the west side of Norway, the port of Stavanger will be important to the Germans. We can also circle past those trawlers to the east of Skagerrak. There is a German supply route heading towards Oslo. There will be plenty of targets there, also."

"I like your thinking." Piasecki smiled. "Let's give them five minutes."

Grudziński and Lieutenant Mokrski checked their position on the chart, looking at possible routes they could take. Lieutenant Piasecki checked with all operators and their instruments in the control room before finally getting to the sonar operator. "Can you hear any new targets?"

"No, sir, only distant background noise." He pressed his earphones tighter. Bosun Kozowy then said, "I do hear the trawlers are spreading out." He fiddled with his direction finder. "They also seem to be changing direction."

Piasecki turned towards Lieutenant Mokrski's chart table where Grudziński stood. "Captain, sonar reports changes in course and heading of the trawlers."

"Well, let's have a look, up periscope."

Lieutenant Piasecki completed his scan for threats before reporting the positions of the fishing boats. "The three boats have spread out. One is heading directly south, bearing zero, two, five, range three, one, zero, zero meters. Speed is about eight knots."

Grudziński slapped the chart table with surprise. "Damn, he's getting close! What about the other two?"

"They've turned to different angles, heading southwest. Do you want their heading and range?" Piasecki asked.

"No, they are spreading out in a search pattern, down periscope," Grudziński said, looking thoughtful. He then turned towards Bosun Dabrowski and said, "Helm, new heading: steer zero, nine, zero degrees."

"Aye, sir, steering zero, nine, zero degrees."

"Should we increase speed to avoid them?" Piasecki asked.

"No, we'll maintain our speed to conserve batteries. We can outrun fishing boats on the surface, but we'll stay hidden at periscope depth until we figure out what they are up to."

"So another five minutes, sir?" Piasecki asked.

The Orzeł continued its way eastwards underwater, but only a couple of minutes passed before Bosun Kozowy, clutching his earphones said, "Sir, all three vessels are changing course again."

"What the hell?" Grudziński looked surprised. "What are their headings?"

"The one to our north is now heading east, sounds like he's running parallel to us." As Kozowy adjusted his dials, he then reported, "The two vessels to the west are now heading directly towards us."

"They seem to be trying to encircle us. But how do they know where we are?" Grudziński asked. "Could they be using sonar?"

Piasecki shook his head. "I doubt it, sir, sonar equipment is too big and bulky to install on a fishing boat."

"Maybe they have hydrophones," Kozowy suggested. "They could be listening, just like I do. If they can detect the bearing or direction, then the three of them can find our position."

"Simple mathematics," Lieutenant Mokrski added. "They can triangulate our position."

"This is crazy!" Piasecki exclaimed.

Grudziński laughed. "Do you see the irony? We are now being hunted by fishing boats!"

A muffled explosion was heard, followed a moment later by two other explosions.

"Sir," Kozowy reported, "those sounded like depth charges! They are very distant and behind the vessels, sounds like they're dropping them over their stern."

"Those fools!" Piasecki said. "What do they think they're doing? They aren't nearly close enough. If we had a deck gun we could easily blow them out of the water."

"Wait a minute, that's it!" Grudziński froze. "They're not stupid, and they know they have no chance against us."

"So what are they doing?" Piasecki asked.

"They're herding us!"

"Oh, crap!" Piasecki realized.

"Aircraft will be on their way!" Grudziński announced. "We've no time to lose! Midshipman, sound general quarters! Piasecki, get the Is-Was, and prepare to plot a firing solution! Helm, change course, three, six, zero! Let's put the fear of God into that devil to the north!"

———————

I was having breakfast in the mess room with Petty Officer Henry Rebizant. Other crewmen were collecting their breakfast from the serving hatch. Freckles had made sausage and scrambled eggs, with fried tomatoes. The noise of jokes and laughter filled the mess room.

"Hey Blackie, how are the prisoners this morning?" Alex shouted across the room.

The German tunics that were recovered were stored in the engine room to dry. We all referred to them as prisoners.

"Foterek has tied them up in a sack and stuffed them under the floor," I said.

"You know how he likes to keep the engine room clean," Remi added.

Just then general quarters sounded. "Oh, crap!" Remi cursed, as he stuffed a handful of scrambled eggs into his mouth. "I haven't finished my breakfast."

We both grabbed the sausages from our plates before running back to the engine room.

"Come on," I urged. "I don't want to miss the excitement, we could be getting ready to sink another German ship."

"Yeah," Remi said, "maybe we can stop the invasion of Norway single-handed."

———————

"Helm, slow to three knots. Lieutenant Piasecki, you're approach officer," Grudziński ordered. Piasecki was ready at the periscope. He knew the slower speed would make the periscope less visible when he raised it. At high speeds, the feathered spray it threw up could be seen for miles.

"Lieutenant Mokrski, assist the approach officer."

The lieutenant then grabbed the circular Is-Was from a shelf above the chart table and hung it from his neck on a lanyard.

"Ready, Captain," Piasecki reported.

"Ready, Captain," Mokrski repeated.

Grudziński then called through the voice pipe to the forward torpedo room. "Prepare tubes one and two." As he waited for the confirmation he ordered, "Up periscope." This was the signal for Piasecki to begin his approach observations.

As the periscope slipped up into place, Piasecki immediately began searching for the target,

"Proceed, let's go get him!" Grudziński said.

"Bearing, zero, two, five," Piasecki announced.

"Zero, two, five," Mokrski repeated, adjusting the ring settings on the Is-Was.

"Range…" Piasecki paused as he measured the height of the target vessel using the stadimeter, to calculate distance, "…three, one, zero, zero."

"Three, one, zero, zero," Mokrski repeated.

"Down periscope!" Piasecki ordered as he clicked his stopwatch. "I'll give it two minutes for the next observation," Piasecki said, keeping his eyes fixed on his watch.

That short space of time seemed to drag on in the confined space of the control room. Lieutenant Mokrski stood by his chart desk, holding the Is-Was in one hand while scribbling notes and calculations with his other. Beads of sweat dripped from the temples of Midshipman Brocki. Grudziński wiped the sweat from his brow and eventually broke the silence. "Helm, confirm our course and speed."

"Speed is three knots. Heading, three, six, zero."

"Sonar, anything to report?"

"Nothing, Captain."

Piasecki clicked his stopwatch. "Up periscope!" as it rose, he grabbed the handles and quickly looked towards the target. "Bearing, zero, three, two degrees."

"Three, two degrees," Mokrski repeated.

"Range…" Piasecki paused while setting the stadimeter, "…two, four, zero, zero."

"Two, four, zero, zero," Mokrski repeated.

"Down periscope," Piasecki ordered. "We're in range for torpedo speed of forty-one knots, sir!" he announced with a grin.

"Their speed is eight knots," Mokrski announced, looking up from his calculations.

"Mokrski set gyros, we'll launch a timed separation."

"Aye, sir, setting gyros!" Lieutenant Mokrski didn't look up as he fed the numbers to the torpedo room.

A moment later the torpedo room responded, "Torpedoes ready!"

"Fire one," Grudziński said, almost too calmly.

"Fire one!" Mokrski shouted through the voice pipe to the torpedo room.

They felt the feint judder as a belch of compressed air fired the first torpedo.

"One away!" came the confirmation.

Grudziński counted his time separation, then ordered, "Fire two," this time emphasizing the order with a thrust of his head.

"Fire two!" Mokrski shouted again through the voice pipe to the torpedo room.

They felt the second judder as the second torpedo launched.

"Two away!" came the confirmation.

Everyone in the control room seemed to sigh at the same time.

"Now, we wait," Piasecki said quietly.

Some moments passed as everyone waited silently.

"Jeez!" Bosun Kozowy shouted as he pulled his sonar headphones from his ears. An explosion echoed through the Orzeł, shaking her slightly.

Grudziński whirled around as if searching for the source, "What the hell was that?"

Another explosion echoed through the Orzeł, this time a little louder.

"That's too soon for impact," Mokrski said. "Did the torpedoes explode prematurely?"

"No, I think that came from behind us!" Piasecki said.

Kozowy was shaking but managed to put his headphones back on. Adjusting the volume he then shouted, "Bombs!"

An explosion followed his warning, this time shaking the Orzeł violently. The noise was tremendous as it echoed through the length of the boat.

"Dive! Dive!" Grudziński shouted, "Dive planes down thirty degrees!"

Men shouted and swore, as they struggled to stay on their feet.

"Dive planes, thirty degrees," Dabrowski repeated over the din.

Another explosion, this time the Orzeł shuddered from side to side, throwing men against bulkheads.

"Flood all tanks!" Grudziński shouted above the noise.

Midshipman Edmund Brocki found himself on the floor, blood oozing from his scalp, "What? Aye, sir." Rolling onto all fours, he half-crawled and half-limped back to his station. "Flooding tanks, sir."

The deck was tilting forward by thirty degrees, an indication that the Orzeł was diving downwards. Grudziński asked, "Sonar, where was that one?"

"I think it was right over our heads, sir."

"Helm, what's our heading?"

Dabrowski pulled himself back to his station, grabbing the wheel firmly. "It's still three, six, zero."

"Good, hard to starboard, heading zero, nine, zero."

As the Orzeł turned, Grudziński looked at the depth gauge, "Sixty-eight meters," he muttered, "Slow our descent, dive planes to ten degrees! Level out at eighty meters!"

Dabrowski adjusted the dive plane levers and replied, "Dive planes ten degrees."

Lieutenant Mokrski scrambled around on the floor, picking up papers and charts.

"Watch that depth gauge, Dabrowski."

"We're slowing, sir. Seventy-three meters now."

"Good, level the planes now, we'll still drift a little downwards. Keep our speed at three knots."

"Aye, sir."

"Let's get out of here slowly and quietly."

Another explosion sounded above our heads, quickly followed by a second.

"Those were to our port side and slightly behind us," Kozowy said, as he held his headphones to his ears. "They seem to be following our original track."

"Sir."

"What is it, Piasecki?"

"I'm sorry."

"What?"

"I'm sorry, sir, I nearly killed us all!"

Despite the background noise of engines and machinery, it felt as if the control room went silent. Everyone turned towards Lieutenant Piasecki.

At that moment, Grudziński realized what he was trying to say, "Oh, Jeez!"

"I'm sorry, sir, I wasn't thinking."

A single distant explosion went off, far to their port side.

"I should have looked." Piasecki was leaning against the bulkhead with his eyes fixed on the ceiling, "I should have been more careful. Sir, you should relieve me."

Grudziński moved towards Piasecki and placed his hand on his shoulder, "If I relieve you then we all have to be relieved, we all made the same mistake!"

"But I didn't look for aircraft, I should have seen them coming!"

"You were fixed on the kill, we were all fixed on the kill, including me. That's why I always say to do things by the book. Yes, you must always scan the horizon, and then scan the sky. I should have noticed your mistake, so I am also guilty. What happens on this boat is ultimately my responsibility." Grudziński whirled around to address his crew in the control room. "We all have to be vigilant. We are at war and we have to assume the enemy is hiding behind every wave. If anyone sees something missing, then say something, make sure we cover each other. Is that clear?"

"Aye, sir," everyone confirmed.

24 The Last Patrol

Ship's Log entered by: Lieutenant Jan Grudziński, captain of the ORP Orzeł
Date: May 22, 1940
Location: Rosyth Navy Yard, Scotland.
Entry: Preparing to leave for our sixth solo patrol in the morning. New breeches have arrived from Sweden and are installed on both AA and deck gun. We are fully operational! Officers and crew are in high spirits. I have granted shore leave with strict instructions to return to the Orzeł by 21:00, to be ready for early departure.

On a submarine, we didn't have much space to store things. For instance, Freckles stored a lot of his canned food behind the racks of torpedoes. Crewmen like me had only a small locker in which to put things. These were so small that we didn't have many personal items. We didn't have civilian clothes, only two uniforms. One uniform was kept clean, folded away in our locker. The second uniform was our everyday work clothes, which we wore while we were at sea.

These work uniforms became very dirty, greasy, and of course sweaty. We could wash them in the sink, but only if we had permission. There was an ironing board if we wanted to use it, but this was the least used tool we carried on the Orzeł.

The irony is, when we got our back pay, we didn't spend it all on beer. Whenever we got shore leave, we all went into town, shopping for clothes.

I always wanted a Fedora hat, so one afternoon, Alex and I went on shore leave to Inverkeithing, a few bus stops from the Navy Yard. We were dressed in our clean uniforms and walked along what they called the 'High Street'; this was where all the shops were. I made Alex visit a hat shop with me.

I was amazed at the array of hats for sale. I ambled past the shelves, trying on a few different Fedora hats. I would ask Alex, "How does this one look?" His answers were impatient because he wanted to go to the pub. "Listen Blackie, where are you going to put that when you get back to the sub?"

"I don't know, I'll figure something out."

"We don't have a hat stand on the Orzeł, it'll get squashed."

The storekeeper was very helpful, complimenting me on every hat I tried on in a thick Scottish accent. "Och, yes, sir, that does make you look quite regal."

I thought about the Fedora, and what Alex said about it getting squashed. I could afford one, but I knew it would get ruined in the submarine storage. I looked around at the racks of hats, scarves, and neckties, wondering what to buy. That's when I saw a white flat cap. A simple worker's cap, but brilliant white, clean and elegant. Nearby was a rack of scarfs, cotton, wool, and silk, all different colors. A red silk scarf held my gaze. I tried on the white cap and red silk scarf, without waiting for any compliment I said, "I'll buy these!"

"Very good choice, sir," the shopkeeper said.

I look like a Polish country gentleman, I thought to myself.

"At last Blackie, now pay the man and let's go," Alex insisted. "I told the guys that we would meet across town at a pub. If you want, you can wear your new cap and scarf."

I only had one pint in the pub, because I had a bus to catch. Aila had sent me a letter with instructions on how to meet her. Aila's letter told me which bus to catch and what time to catch it. She told me where she would be waiting and what time she would be there. The letter told me to meet her at seven o'clock, so we could watch the sunset together.

Wednesday was the day we liked to go walking together in the park, but she wrote:

In case you can't get leave on Wednesday, I will wait for you there every evening.

While we were in the pub, I wasn't interested in the jovial banter of my shipmates. Instead, I kept looking at the clock. I hadn't seen Aila for nearly two weeks, and I was excited by her letter. The way she wrote her instructions made this feel like an adventure. She said she would be waiting there every day in case I couldn't get shore leave on Wednesday.

I was anxious to see her again, to touch her, and to kiss her soft lips.

"Come on Blackie, snap out of it," Alex said. "You look half asleep!"

"Maybe the diesel fumes have gone to his head," Rebi said.

"I think something else has happened to him, but it's not his head," Stanley added.

"Oh? What could it be?" Alex asked, "it's only Tuesday. He usually meets with her on Wednesday!"

"Yes, girls, sunsets, and romance!" Stanley said, "and I think the color red has something to do with his mood, that's why he's blushing so much. We're leaving on patrol tomorrow, so I think they're meeting tonight."

"Is that why you bought a red scarf?" Alex asked, "is that a present for your girlfriend?"

I finished my pint and stood up. The red scarf was already around my neck, so I flicked it over my left shoulder. "Gentlemen, my hat and scarf represent the colors of the Polish flag." I then picked up my white flat cap and ceremoniously set it on my head. "I must now leave you all because I have some important business to attend to."

"We all know what that could be," Alex winked.

"I would like to say I will miss you gentlemen, but the color red beckons me on. A red sunset, red hair, and ruby red lips. I hope you all enjoy your beer."

I then turned and walked out of the pub like a suave, sophisticated man about town. As soon as the pub door closed behind me, I ran as fast as I could to the bus stop.

I sat on the bottom deck of the bus. Normally I liked to sit on the top deck to see the view, but everyone smoked up there. Aila didn't smoke, so I tried to avoid the smell of cigarettes. The conductor who collected fares on the bus was an older woman. It seemed all the men were off to war, leaving women to fill the empty jobs. When I paid her for my ticket, she looked at me with a soft smile, as if she seemed to know where I was going.

When I got off the bus, I started to run towards the park. *I know where I'm going!* I thought to myself, but as I got to the end of the high street, I thought to myself, *slow down, I'm not late, so why am I running?* I stopped in front of the last shop to catch my breath. Looking at my reflection in the window, I straightened my hair and brushed off the front of my shirt and sleeves. Besides my cap and scarf, I was wearing my new shirt, trousers and a set of tartan suspenders. These were expensive ones with metal clips to hold up my trousers. I flicked my scarf over my shoulder and resumed my suave walk, this time into the park. I walked off to the ornamental pond, where I knew she would be waiting.

When I got there, I recognized Aila in the distance. Her back was to me, and I could see her red hair catching the fading sunlight. I was startled to see that she was chatting with two girlfriends. Was she planning something for all of us?

As I approached, her two friends folded their arms, making me wonder if they were disapproving of me. When I got close, Aila turned around, pretending to be surprised, and said, "Oh, Leo! How wonderful to meet you here!" She started towards me, and I thought I was going to get a hug or even a kiss, but she stopped and turned to introduce me.

Oh, crap, I thought, *I want to be alone with my Aila, but it looks like we have a pair of chaperones.*

"Leo, these are my two friends, Grace and Christine," Aila said, indicating them both with a wave of her arm. "Grace, Christine, this is my very good friend, Leo." Aila then moved close to me and held my arm. As she did so, I felt a rush of warmth flow through the nape of my neck.

"My pleasure, I'm sure," Christine said.

"He does look a handsome sight," Grace admitted.

They both held out their hands, and I gently shook them, politely, as they curtseyed.

"They're just on their way home." Aila smiled gently.

"Oh, yes, we're just leaving," they both said together, as they started to walk away slowly.

"We'll leave you two love birds together," Grace said over her shoulder.

"Don't do anything we wouldn't do!" Christine laughed.

They both walked off trying to conceal giggles. Aila watched them go with a naughty smirk on her lips. "Those two girls are incorrigible," she said.

"What does that mean?" I asked.

"Oh, never mind that," Aila said, "I'm just so glad you made it this evening. Come on, let's go and sit on our bench." Taking my hand, she led me away around the pond, to our regular sitting place.

Our bench was in a small rose garden, surrounded by tiny box hedges. This reminded me so much of my mother's garden back home. Snowdrops, daffodils, and primroses were flowering around the feet of the leafy rose bushes. While we sat there, we had a perfect view of the setting sun, as it settled behind the distant trees, casting its shadows on the pond.

We sat quietly in each other's arms. I eventually tried to make small talk, "I used to love fishing in ponds like this in Poland."

Aila was resting her head on my shoulder. I cuddled her with my arm. Our hands were clasped in my lap. She looked up at me and said, "Yes, you told me this before. Don't you want to tell me something else?" She squeezed my hand as if to tease me.

Oh, my God, she can read my mind, I thought. *What other powers does she have?*

"There is something I want to say." I moved forward to sit at the edge of the bench and turned towards her.

"Oh, Leo, what is it?" She smiled gently into my eyes.

"I, um, I don't know how to tell you."

Aila began to look concerned, but held her smile, "What is it my darling?"

"I, um, I…" *I wish I had drunk more beer at the pub, maybe I would have the courage to tell her. Such a simple thing to say, yet I can't bring myself to say it.*

"I have never said this to anyone, and I don't know how to tell you."

"What is it? You must tell me."

I took a deep breath.

"I love you!" I finally said.

Aila gasped, and I thought she would slap me. Instead, she threw her arms around me and embraced me tightly. Between her kisses on my neck and cheek, she said my name, "Leo!" She then breathed the words into my ear, "I love you too."

Her breath and words triggered a tingling feeling that shot from my ear down my side into my hip. I never knew words would have that effect. I couldn't tell if it was pain or ecstasy, all I knew was, I wanted her to say it again. Instead, we kissed as we had never kissed before. We held each other and caressed in a way that only lovers know. I have no idea how long we kissed, but as the evening became dark, our passion began to grow. It wasn't until another couple walked by on the path around the pond that we stopped. The woman quietly giggled, while he politely cleared his throat.

Aila gently pressed her hand on mine. "Leo, it's getting late, I would love to stay here forever, but I think we should go."

"Yes, you're right," I agreed. "Can I take you home?"

Walking to the bus stop was like floating on air. When we got on the bus, she led me to the top deck. I said, "Should we sit in the front to see the view?"

"No," she said, "Follow me." She took me by the hand and we sat on the back seat, cuddling together all the way to her village.

We got to her house at the end of the lane, a large terraced house made of stone. We kissed goodnight by the front door. "I can't wait to see you again," Aila said.

"Don't worry," I said, "our patrols don't last forever! While I'm gone, I want you to keep this for me." I took my red scarf from my neck and gently wrapped it around her neck.

She clasped one end of the scarf, holding it to her lips. "I'll keep this safe for you if you promise to stay safe for me."

"I promise," I said.

"However long it takes, I'll be waiting right here for you," she said.

Her father kept peeking out through the curtains in the front room.

"You better get inside," I said, "I have to get back to the Orzeł."

After one last brief kiss, I turned and walked back to the bus stop. Aila watched me go until I rounded the corner. That's when I started to run for the last bus back to the docks.

"Rise and shine!" Foterek was shouting as he passed the bunks. I was on a lower bunk, already dressed. I stood up and saluted. "Good morning, sir!"

"Jeez, Blackie! Are you still drunk?" Foterek asked.

Alex answered for me, laid on the bunk above me he said, "No, sir, he isn't. He left us in the pub and ran off with his girlfriend."

Stanley's voice echoed from a bunk across the passage. "Yeah, rumor has it, they got married last night."

I stood there and smiled. I could see that Foterek wanted to smile too. Instead, he said, "You're all on dress duty this morning as we leave port. Get up on deck, on the double, in your best uniforms."

There were two dress units on deck, one lined forward of the conning tower, and a smaller unit aft of the tower. I was standing in the forward dress line, with Alex, Stanley, and

Rebi. Deckhands also waited on the bow and stern to cast off dock lines.

The turret protecting our 105mm deck gun was withdrawn, leaving it on display. Lieutenant Sosnowski stood proudly alongside it, with his gunnery crew, as if ready to fire. Even the AA gun was pulled up from its well on the cigarette deck and pointed skyward. Both of these guns had new breeches, making them fully working. We proved their effectiveness during a sea trial a few days before, where Lieutenant Sosnowski and his men destroyed every target in record time.

We were now a fully operational fighting force.

Captain Grudziński stood on the bridge podium, looking resplendent in full uniform. Lieutenant Piasecki stood with the captain, his megaphone ready to relay the captain's orders to the deck crew.

While we waited, Alex asked Stanley quietly, "How's your head this morning? Mine is throbbing."

Stanley sighed. "My head? I thought we were doing depth charge training."

"So where are we going on this patrol?" Rebi asked.

"No one knows, until the captain tells us," Stanley said. "We'll find out later when we're at sea."

"It'll be Norway again, where else can we go?" Alex said. "I do know where we're going when we get back."

"Where's that?" Stanley asked.

"Blackie's wedding!"

I just smiled as everyone laughed.

"No talking in line," Piasecki called through his megaphone.

Officials on the dockside gave clearance to depart. A small dockside crane lifted the gangway clear of the Orzeł. Lieutenant Piasecki waited for the order from Captain Grudziński, before calling down to the waiting deck crew. Dock lines were released and hauled in by the waiting linesmen and stowed away. They stood ready in their positions, forward and aft, waiting for further orders.

I could imagine Foterek in the engine room as he responded to the order on the engine telegraph to power up. We could hear the wash of the propellers, as the helm had been ordered to angle the rudder outwards, pushing the stern against the dock. This motion forced the bow away, into open water. The engines then throttled down and we moved gracefully away from the dock.

"Aila loves me," I said quietly to Alex.

"Of course she does," he replied, "do you love her?"

"I'm going to ask her when we get back."

"Ask her what?"

"I'm going to ask her to marry me."

Alex just smirked and nodded. "I knew it, I was right! I could see it in you. Didn't I say you'd be the first of us to get married?"

We moved slowly at first, leaving the dock, Captain Grudziński and Lieutenant Piasecki both saluting the personnel on the dockside. As the engines pushed us away from the Navy Yard, we sailed past a place where civilians could wave as the ships departed. There was a small group of people, mostly women, waiting to wave off a British destroyer, which was behind us. I spotted my redhead dream girl, dressed in white, waving with her arm above her head. In her hand was a red silk scarf, flowing like a banner above her head. I broke my stance and waved back.

Alex stood next to me, and said, "Put your arm down, you fool! The captain will have you on report!"

"I don't care," I replied. "I can see my love, she is waving at me. She has my scarf! I want her to see me as I wave back." I pulled my navy cap from my head and waved that above my head. I even blew a kiss. I could see that she held both her hands to her face, blowing a kiss with both hands, while the red scarf flowed in the breeze. With that, I became ecstatic.

"POLSKA!" I shouted, waving harder.

"Now you've done it," Alex commented.

Someone at the end of our line echoed my shout, "POLSKA!"

"Oh, the hell with it, POLSKA!" Alex shouted.

Then everyone in line joined us in our chant. "POLSKA! POLSKA! POLSKA!"

The whole of Scotland must have heard us as we sailed towards the Forth Bridge, out into the North Sea.

The End

25 Epilogue

On 23 May 1940, the ORP Orzeł departed Rosyth in Scotland on its last patrol in the North Sea. The vessel and her crew were never heard from again. It has not even been confirmed if the Orzeł reached her patrol area in the Skagerrak, between Norway and Denmark, since no radio signals had been received from her since she sailed.

On 11 June 1940 the Orzeł was three days overdue returning from patrol and had not reported her position. The British Admiralty announced that the Orzeł was presumed lost, along with her crew - 60 Poles and 3 British liaison officers. No wreckage of the Orzeł has ever been found and questions remain as to her fate.

The Navy Administration of The Republic of Poland (the Polish government in exile) issued the following message:

Due to lack of information and not returning from patrol within the deadline, the submarine ORP Orzeł of the Republic of Poland should be considered lost.

On 12 June, Admiral Sir Max Horton said that Orzeł's loss was a big one. She was irreplaceable, and her role was very important.

So, what happened to the Orzeł?

Two messages were sent by the British Admiralty on 1 June and then on 2 June, each one instructing the Orzeł to change its operating location. On 5 June, another message was sent, instructing the Orzeł to end her patrol on 6 June and return to base. The Orzeł did not respond to any messages.

The Orzeł was expected to arrive at Rosyth on the morning of 8 June but did not show up. Another message was sent at midday on 8 June, requesting the Orzeł to report her position. Once again, no response was received.

There were no official reports of enemy ships or aircraft sinking a submarine during that time. There was a German broadcast on 25 May 1940 that claimed a British submarine had been sunk by a direct hit from a German aircraft. This is possible, but the broadcast did not report a position, as is usually the case. Since no German aircraft recorded such an incident, it is more likely that this was propaganda.

There were no reported incidents of friendly fire during this time which may account for the sinking.

Technical difficulty cannot be ruled out. Some new British technology was introduced to the vessel during refit. Since the Orzeł succeeded in several missions, with this new equipment, this is generally considered unlikely.

The most likely theory suggests the boat may have encountered a British or German minefield that was unknown to them.

There are two given scenarios.

In 1962, the British Admiralty released a document that is available in public archives that the Orzeł had been lost in a British minefield at approximately 57 degrees north, by 4 degrees east. This is nearly 400 miles east of Aberdeen. That minefield had only recently been laid, and it was admitted that it had not been possible to inform all Allied ships. British acoustic stations also detected a loud noise on that date, which was assumed to have been something hitting a mine.

Another possibility is that while returning to Rosyth on 8 June, the Orzeł might have been caught in a German minefield, designated 16B. It was considered likely that the Dutch Submarine O-13 was lost in that minefield five days later.

Expeditions are being organized to this day by experts in Poland to locate the wreckage of the Orzeł. One day it may be found, but regardless of the circumstance of her loss, the officers and the crew of the ORP Orzeł were regarded as brave and determined. They have also been recognized for their adherence to rules of engagement and the rules of maritime law.

In memory of the officers and crew of the ORP Orzeł, as
they continue their eternal patrol.